A

■ ■ ■

B O O K

The Philip E. Lilienthal imprint
honors special books
in commemoration of a man whose work
at the University of California Press
from 1954 to 1979
was marked by dedication to young authors
and to high standards in the field of Asian Studies.
Friends, family, authors, and foundations have together
endowed the Lilienthal Fund, which enables the Press
to publish under this imprint selected books
in a way that reflects the taste and judgment
of a great and beloved editor.

The publisher gratefully acknowledges the generous support of the
Philip E. Lilienthal Asian Studies Endowment Fund of the
University of California Press Foundation,
which was established by a major grant from Sally Lilienthal.

Passion, Betrayal, and Revolution
in Colonial Saigon

Passion, Betrayal, and Revolution in Colonial Saigon

The Memoirs of Bao Luong

———

Hue-Tam Ho Tai

UNIVERSITY OF CALIFORNIA PRESS

Berkeley   Los Angeles   London

University of California Press, one of the most distinguished university presses in the United States, enriches lives around the world by advancing scholarship in the humanities, social sciences, and natural sciences. Its activities are supported by the UC Press Foundation and by philanthropic contributions from individuals and institutions. For more information, visit www.ucpress.edu.

University of California Press
Berkeley and Los Angeles, California

University of California Press, Ltd.
London, England

Library of Congress Cataloging-in-Publication Data

Tai, Hue-Tam Ho
    Passion, betrayal, and revolution in colonial Saigon : the memoirs of Bao Luong / Hue-Tam Ho Tai.
        p. cm.
    Includes bibliographical references and index.
    ISBN 978-0-520-26225-6 (cloth : alk. paper)—ISBN 978-0-520-26226-3 (pbk. : alk. paper)
        1. Nguyễn, Trung Nguyệt.   2. Women revolutionaries—Vietnam—Ho Chi Minh City—Biography.   3. Women political prisoners—Vietnam—Ho Chi Minh City—Biography.   4. Ho Chi Minh City (Vietnam)—Social conditions—20th century.   5. Ho Chi Minh City (Vietnam)—Biography. I. Nguyễn, Trung Nguyệt. II. Title.
    DS559.93.S2T34   2010
    959.7'03092—dc22
    [B]   2010004555

Manufactured in the United States of America

19 18 17 16 15 14 13 12 11 10
10 9 8 7 6 5 4 3 2 1

This book is printed on Cascades Enviro 100, a 100% post consumer waste, recycled, de-inked fiber. FSC recycled certified and processed chlorine free. It is acid free, Ecologo certified, and manufactured by BioGas energy.

CONTENTS

ILLUSTRATIONS

FIGURES

MAP

ACKNOWLEDGMENTS

The early life of Nguyen Trung Nguyet, the subject of this book, illustrates how important family and friends were to the spread of revolution in Vietnam. To bring her story to print, I have relied on family ties and networks of friends and colleagues. I could not have done it without their assistance and support.

Her children, Nguyen Minh Tri and Nguyen Ngoc Lan; her sisters Van Trang and Han Xuan (now deceased); and her nieces, nephew, and grandnephew—Tran Hong Thuan, Ho Dao, Ho Huu Triet, and Ho Huu Luc—shared memoirs, articles, photographs, and, above all, reminiscences that brought a much-loved relative back to life.

I am grateful to Haydon Cherry, who scanned the entire Barbier Street case file; David Biggs, who researched the various locations mentioned in the text and drew the map; and Eric Jennings, who located a photograph of Nguyen Bao Toan. I also owe a debt of thanks to Lorraine Paterson, who sent a photograph of a ceremony held in front of Pham Hong Thai's tomb that was very similar to the one in which Nguyen Trung Nguyet participated. Sophie Quinn-Judge supplied information about the Revolutionary Youth League in Guangzhou, and Peter Zinoman about prison life and terminology in colonial Vietnam.

I extend heartfelt thanks as well to Tran Bich Ngoc, Dao The Duc, and Dao Hung for supplying visual and written materials, to the staff of the General Sciences Library in Ho Chi Minh City, and to the staff of the Centre d'archives d'Outre-mer, Aix-en-Provence, France.

The lively discussions during the workshop "Telling Lives in Vietnam" in May 2009 gave me much to think about as I wrote the life of Bao Luong (Nguyen Trung Nguyet). The comments of an anonymous reader for the University of California

Press spurred me to reconsider some statements I had made in an earlier draft, and this greatly improved it.

I thank Reed Malcolm for providing valuable feedback and encouragement at various stages of the writing. I would also like to express my deep appreciation of the efforts of Elizabeth Berg and Polly Kummel to make the narrative that follows as seamless, clear, and readable as possible.

May Patrick, Andrew, and Matthew enjoy reading the story of an aunt they never met, a woman who was deeply conservative yet fearless, idealistic, stoic, and, above all, loving.

PRINCIPAL CHARACTERS

IMMEDIATE FAMILY

Nguyễn Trung Nguyệt, aka Bảo Lương, 1909–1976, author of the memoir
Nguyễn văn Nhẫm, father of Bảo Lương
Đào thị Châu, mother of Bảo Lương
Nguyễn văn Đại, aka Viên Đại, 1910–1994, brother of Bảo Lương

THE BARBIER STREET AFFAIR

Lang, aka Lê văn Phát, aka Lê văn Dâu, representative of the Revolutionary
    Youth League, murdered December 8, 1928
Lệ Oanh, real name Trần Thu Thủy, aka Nhứt, object of Lang's attentions
Tôn Đức Thắng, distant relative by marriage of Bảo Lương, head of the
    Southern Regional Committee, member of Bảo Lương's cell
Trần Trương, cousin of Bảo Lương's and of Tôn Đức Thắng's wife, member
    of Bảo Lương's cell
Ngô Thiêm, aka Huệ
Nguyễn văn Thinh, aka Trần văn Công, aka Quế
Bùi văn Thêm, aka Châu aka Mười Thêm, member of Bảo Lương's cell
Đặng văn Sâm, aka Nhuận aka Hai Sâm, member of Bảo Lương's cell
Đỗ Đình Thọ, member of Bảo Lương's cell

OTHERS

Nguyễn Bảo Toàn, aka Bằng Thống, aka Trần Sư Chính, aka Lê aka Năm, suitor of Bảo Lương's, suspected of betraying the Revolutionary Youth League to the French

Hoài Nghĩa, real name Nguyễn văn Ngọc, friend of Bảo Lương's in Guangzhou, arrested 1929

Ngọc Anh and Ngọc Thơ, sisters, friends of Bảo Lương's

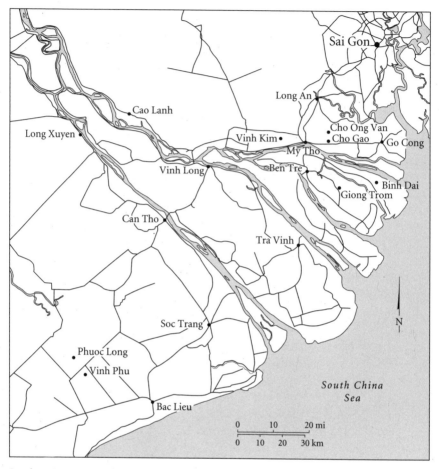

Southern Vietnam in the 1920s.

Introduction

In a seldom-visited museum in Ho Chi Minh City hangs a picture of a woman named Nguyen Trung Nguyet. The museum is dedicated to Ton Duc Thang (1888–1980), the man who succeeded Ho Chi Minh as president of the Democratic Republic of Vietnam in 1969 and later, after the reunification of the country in 1975, of the Socialist Republic of Vietnam. The caption reads, "Nguyen Trung Nguyet, Vietnam's first female political prisoner."

To me Nguyen Trung Nguyet was Second Aunt, my mother's older sister. When I was a child, she left her house in Vinh Long for Saigon only once or twice a year to take part in the annual commemoration of her father's death or to visit her son, who lived with us while attending school. She would arrive with a smile on her face and a large bag of food she had picked up on the way. In her forties, she already seemed old to my childish eyes. Perhaps it was her countrified appearance and weather-beaten face that deceived me into thinking she was at least a decade older. She usually wore a shapeless *ao dai* in some drab and unflattering color. Her hair was pulled back into a chignon that emphasized her receding hairline; her face was utterly devoid of makeup. Only once did she seem to pay attention to her looks: when she learned that a woman who remembered that my aunt had been the belle of their area was coming especially to visit her. Flustered by this reminder of her youthful beauty, she put on some of my mother's lipstick, but it did not feel right and she immediately wiped it off.

In the late 1950s we spent a few weeks of summer at Second Aunt's house "to learn about life in the countryside." Her home, like all others in her village, had neither running water nor electricity. At the close of the day, her chores over, she would lie in a hammock, doing meticulous embroidery by the light of an oil lamp while softly humming snatches of poetry, some of which she wrote under the name Bao Luong. She watched our childish antics indulgently, ready to intercede in our squabbles or applaud our "performances." She never raised her voice.

Her husband made a modest living as the village nurse. His earnings were seriously diminished by his regular provision of free services to the villagers who could not afford to pay him. But while she would occasionally sigh at his generosity, she clearly would not have had him do otherwise. Second Aunt seemed utterly at peace living out her life in straitened circumstances and complete obscurity.

Her appearance matched her old-fashioned ideas, especially regarding the proper conduct of "young ladies." She considered that we were "too French." She gently but firmly deplored our modern ways. Well brought-up young ladies did not throw back their heads and laugh with abandon, "showing all their teeth," she decreed; they were supposed to smile or laugh discreetly behind their hands. They did not walk "as if marching off to war or to fight with the fishmonger's wife, but sedately and never in a hurry." And they did not engage in heated discussions with members of the opposite sex. "Remember, harmonious speech is one of the Four Virtues." Most important, they were expected to preserve their good name. "Chastity is the most precious possession a woman can have," she would remind us. When I was an adolescent, she seemed to me the embodiment of the outmoded values that had kept Vietnamese women subordinate, timid, and ignorant; her unflappable serenity made her appear bloodless.

It was thus with some astonishment that, when I was about fifteen, I heard Second Aunt described as a "heroine who has worked for the cause of women's emancipation and Vietnamese independence." This came from the widow of a journalist who had written for progressive newspapers in the 1920s. While she was waiting for my mother to return from an errand, she explained that Bao Luong had been involved in a sensational trial stemming from an incident that had taken place on Barbier Street (now Nguyen Phi Khanh Street); at the trial the prosecution had portrayed Bao Luong as a kind of Vietnamese Jezebel who had lured a man to his death. In fact, the visitor repeated, Bao Luong had allowed her good name to be tarnished in the cause of revolution. What she meant by "revolution" was not exactly clear. Which group, which movement had Bao Luong joined? Alas, my mother's return put a stop to the visitor's whispered gossip. When I sought further details from my mother, she told me to let the matter drop: "Second Aunt suffered for her actions. The past is ineffably painful; do not try to revive the pain." My mother was wrong, however; her sister was willing to relive her past.

According to Bao Luong's daughter, around that time Bao Luong began filling a notebook with her reminiscences; she kept it by the hammock where she did her embroidery. She also disclosed bits and pieces of her past to my cousin, who was a teenager and listened with only half an ear to her mother's stories; I never got to hear them. While Bao Luong and her sisters loved to relive their childhoods when they got together, they always kept quiet about her involvement in the Revolutionary Youth League and her subsequent incarceration.

Bao Luong went to live permanently in Saigon in 1967, after I left home. Some time before her move, she agreed to let a newspaper publish her story. She had kept in contact with other former prisoners who were now active in the Communist underground. According to her children, these associates urged her to publish her memoir. My parents, who were not given to sharing much information in writing after a lifetime of clandestine anticolonial activism, did not tell me that my aunt's memoir had been published, even when it was serialized a second time by another newspaper, *Dan Chu Moi* (New Democracy), from November 1971 to May 1972.

Years later, while I was doing research in the French colonial archives, I stumbled across a thick file regarding the "crime on Barbier Street." The whispers about Second Aunt's lurid past had stayed in my mind; although my research was on another topic altogether, I put it aside to delve into that file. The picture that emerged of Bao Luong was not of a middle-aged woman doing intricate embroidery by lamplight but of one who had cold-bloodedly participated in murder when not yet twenty. Bao Luong died the very year I was rooting around in the colonial archives and reading the decades-old accusations against her. I did not have an opportunity to ask her for details or to tell her of the sorrow I felt when I read that her family's petition for her early release had been denied on the ground that she was a dangerous revolutionary.

For a long time I resisted replacing the picture I retained of my aunt, old-fashioned and always placid, with that of the firebrand who stood trial in 1930. But I came to realize that Bao Luong's story did not belong to her family alone and that it shed light on the history of the South and the early stages of the Vietnamese Revolution. And so I set out to discover the young woman she had been long before she became Second Aunt.

. . .

How does one reconstitute the life of a woman who disappeared from history at the age of twenty-one and did not write her memoir until more than thirty years later? How much can one rely on the available sources? And, supposing the discrepancies can be accounted for, the different perspectives reconciled, how does one go about telling that story? Many sources recount pieces of the story of Bao Luong, from different perspectives over a span of decades and often at odds with one another. These sources are both written and oral, encompassing official documents, newspaper articles, family memoirs, gossip, poems, and even an entry in a biographical dictionary. Each is rich in possibilities, and each has its limitations.

The earliest source is the most hostile: the thick file compiled by the Sûreté (French police detectives) about the crime that took place on Barbier Street on December 8, 1928. It is comprised of the text of interrogations and confessions, including those of Bao Luong, as well as lists of individuals who were arrested or were in flight and narratives of the murder as pieced together by investigators. Gathering the information that went into the bill of indictment took the police several months. Prisoners were interrogated repeatedly, made to confront one another, urged to confess and to implicate others. Although the questions were not recorded, it is not difficult to guess what they were from the answers, but neither questions nor answers are reproduced verbatim, and the accuracy and completeness of the recorded confessions are questionable. As time went on, the accused changed their stories; however, we have no way of knowing whether what they said at the end was any more truthful or complete than any of the earlier versions they offered.

The tidy appearance of the Sûreté reports belies the chaotic violence that produced them. The police interrogated suspects and extracted confessions, then sent the reports to be typed up by Vietnamese clerks. Some of the clerks assigned to this task tried to give as much comfort as they dared to Bao Luong between interrogation sessions and even shared information with her. What is missing from the neatly organized records, the highly sanitized and formal bureaucratic language, the sedate words about the presence or absence of a lawyer, about prisoners' reading over the transcript and insisting on the accuracy of whatever was stated, is the threatening context in which interrogations were held and the torture that yielded confessions. For such details one must read Bao Luong's memoir. Yet, despite the skepticism that police records engender, the Sûreté file on the Barbier Street murder provides much useful information about various individuals that Bao Luong, trained not to ask too many questions about her fellow revolutionaries-in-training, did not know or chose not to divulge. It also gives accurate dates, which Bao Luong often omitted from her narrative. For example, I learned from her Sûreté file, not her memoir, when she went to Guangzhou and returned.

The Barbier Street murder was well covered in the press at the time. I have chosen to use the coverage by *Than Chung* (Morning Bell) because that newspaper exhibited an interesting journalistic dilemma. Its publisher and editor-in-chief were progressive, and thus it was more sympathetic to reformers, radicals, and revolutionaries than the majority of other contemporary newspapers. A complicating dimension was that Nguyen van Ba, the editor-in-chief, was an uncle by marriage to Bao Luong and to three others who were implicated in the affair. Bao Luong herself had occasionally contributed to a column, "Ladies' Sayings" (Loi Ban Gai), in the newspaper. This relationship was a source of information that no other newspaper possessed, but it also posed a potential danger. Nguyen van Ba was eager to counter the impression the pro-French newspapers gave of Bao Luong as a siren and poisoner and to shore up her reputation as a young woman of good family and good character. But he could do little to rebut the claims that she was a dangerous revolutionary; indeed, he ran the risk that his part in helping her and others go to

Guangzhou would be revealed. He was lucky that the Sûreté did not probe deeply into the technical aspects of clandestine travel to China.

Both the police files and the newspaper articles have the virtue of being contemporaneous to the events they record, but they have their limitations. For the Sûreté, establishing culpability and motives was important yet subsidiary to the aim of uncovering anticolonial networks. It was not interested in personal feelings and individual life stories. *Than Chung* might have been, but it was stymied by colonial censorship as well as considerations of personal safety. Personal experiences and emotions, however, are the main themes of Bao Luong's memoir. It appears that she had decided to focus on what had inspired her to become "Vietnam's first female political prisoner," beginning with her early childhood. She ends her account with her conviction, frustrating readers who would like to know more about her life after prison.

The title she gave her memoir, *The Road to Revolution (Duong vao Cach Mang)*, echoes the title of the pamphlet that Ho Chi Minh, then going under a variety of aliases, had put together—*The Revolutionary Road (Duong Kach Menh)*—to train the young men and women who, like Bao Luong, went to Guangzhou to learn how to organize the anticolonial underground.[1] Bao Luong was also aware of the model provided by the prison memoir of Phan van Hum, an anticolonial activist whom she admired. His *Ngoi Tu Kham Lon* (A Stay in the Central Prison) was serialized in *Than Chung* from January 23 to February 26, 1929, when the French authorities halted its publication. This was shortly after the Barbier Street murder but before her arrest. His memoir was reprinted in Saigon as a book in 1957, ten years before Bao Luong's own memoir was serialized. Phan van Hum likely provided not only some of the topics that Bao Luong explored but also some of the vocabulary she used to describe her prison experience.

Bao Luong's memoir offers a vivid contrast to the neatly typed documents in the Sûreté file. She wrote in longhand on the kind of lined paper used by students. Unfamiliar with editorial conventions, she did not use footnotes or even parentheses, instead putting quotation marks around explanatory words or phrases. She was also as thrifty with paper as she was with everything else. She did not erase, blot, or cross out a passage; nor did she do a cut-and-paste job. She just wrote as she remembered, more or less chronologically. She did backtrack occasionally to insert some information she had neglected to include earlier. Her manuscript thus bears the look of a first draft from memory rather than a polished product ready for the eyes of others. It is choppy in places, especially when Bao Luong describes her life in prison, where time had little meaning.

Different versions of the memoir survive, and each raises different issues. The two newspapers decided not to publish the long poems that she had interspersed throughout her narrative and cut short accounts of endless debates about Confucianism or Vietnamese history. The papers also rearranged some sections. Despite these editorial decisions, the newspapers presented the memoir almost in its entirety. The newspapers, however, are no longer available. In 1990 Van Trang, Bao Luong's younger sister, expressed an interest in having the memoir republished. Van Trang and her husband had been part of a front organization of the National Liberation Front, which was formed in 1960 to overthrow the government of South Vietnam and reunify North and South, and had to flee Saigon after the Tet Offensive of 1968. After their return to Saigon in 1975, Van Trang painstakingly collected back issues of the newspaper that had serialized the memoir in 1971, not an easy task in the immediate postwar period. The collection of back issues that she briefly lent me in 1995 has since disintegrated. Van Trang also borrowed from Bao Luong's son his mother's manuscript of the memoir.

Van Trang then spent several years mulling how to edit her sister's memoir, which admittedly was somewhat disjointed. What resulted was, in the opinion of Van Trang's daughter, "sixty percent the words of Second Aunt and forty percent my mother's."[2] In 1995 Van Trang sent this version to the Women's Publishing House, where her membership in the National Liberation Front gave her entrée, but she was unsure whether it would be published in its entirety as it dealt with a number of topics still considered sensitive seventy years later. Indeed, the book she gave me the following year was missing several important passages, which, Van Trang insisted in the face of my evident skepticism, owed to a paper shortage. This, however, did not account for the new title. From *The Road to Revolution* Bao Luong's memoir had become, innocuously, *The Girl from the South (Nguoi con Gai Nam Bo)*. More important, the published version omitted the entire section describing the murder and the events immediately preceding it. It also included a number of additions, some the result of Van Trang's wish to clarify certain cryptic statements made by Bao Luong, others purely writerly embellishments by Van Trang.

Overall, I have relied on the manuscript version that Bao Luong's son lent to her sister rather than its published versions. I also have used the snatches of stories that my mother and her sisters used to tell about their girlhoods, my cousins' recollections, as well as the unpublished memoirs of two of Bao Luong's sisters, Han Xuan and Van Trang.

. . .

What led to the murder at 5 Barbier Street on the night of December 8, 1928? And what was Bao Luong's part in it? These are the underlying questions of Bao Luong's memoir and of the police investigation. The account she gives of the murder and the events that led to it is problematic. In particular, she describes a foiled rape attempt for which there is no corroboration. The alleged perpetrator was the murder victim, the alleged rape victim disappeared, and the woman who helped fight off the would-be rapist is not mentioned in any other account. The relationship of the would-be rapist and his victim as described by Bao Luong differs markedly from the information provided to the Sûreté by several men who were arrested after the murder. It is possible that the victim confided the full details only to Bao Luong because she was a woman and that the men did not know this aspect of the story or revealed as little as they could about events leading to the murder. One man she told of the attempted rape did not take part in the decision to murder the alleged assailant; although he was arrested for belonging to the Vietnam Revolutionary Youth League, he was not interrogated about the murder. For her part Bao Luong was constantly on the move before the murder, so she may not have been told everything that happened while she was absent. Members of the Revolutionary Youth League operated on a need-to-know basis.

Another issue is the larger context in which the murder took place. The French Sûreté wanted it to be about both anticolonial activism and a sordid affair that would reveal the depravity of those who opposed colonial rule. Bao Luong saw the murder as the unavoidable punishment of a wrongdoer who was threatening to expose all his colleagues in the anticolonial underground. Initially, the conspirators had wanted to pass off the murder as suicide. When things did not go as planned, they tried to make it look like a crime of passion. But at their trial some rebelled against that description and declared for all to hear that the murder had been a political act. Bao Luong's interpretation vacillates between the personal and the political but doesn't go very far in either direction. Yet the rapidly changing political scene of the late 1920s is crucially important to understanding the murder and its aftermath.

By the time Bao Luong and others implicated in the Barbier Street affair had their day in court, the Revolutionary Youth League had ceased to exist and the Indochinese Communist Party had come into being. Only by reading Bao Luong's memoir in the wider context of anticolonial politics in the 1920s can one understand how a murder that involved only a few men and one woman led to the arrest of sixty-one individuals, including a future president and a prime minister of the Democratic Republic of Vietnam. Conversely, her memoir offers a glimpse into the difficult transition from the Revolutionary Youth League to the Indochinese Communist Party in southern Vietnam.

Bao Luong's memoir is a rich mine of information about life in the Vietnamese South in the first decades of the twentieth century, from the opening up of new land in the Mekong Delta to the commercial bustle of Saigon and various market towns. Her account also gives us a window through which we can view shifting ideas about gender. It is easy to forget how young the men and women who joined the Vietnam Revolutionary Youth League were. Some were only fourteen or fifteen; few were older than twenty-five. For them, waging revolution meant, in part, jettisoning what they called "feudal ideas," including those pertaining to love and marriage. Young women who remained unmarried at twenty occupied a precarious position in society. Within the Youth League advocacy of female emancipation coexisted with contempt for "loose women." Although most of the young women who became Bao Luong's comrades-in-arms came from "good" families that taught their daughters the importance of the Four Virtues and the Three Submissions, these young women displayed a remarkable ability to move from place to place on their own or in the company of young men. While male pundits debated appropriate roles for women, and old-fashioned scholars reminded their readers that "the destiny of women is not to fight in the East and clear out the North," many of Bao Luong's friends were fighting for women's rights as well as for national independence. Yet none seems to have been striving to escape a domineering father or husband. Indeed, they came to revolutionary activism through male relatives: fathers, husbands, siblings, cousins. Nonetheless, what comes across most vividly in Bao Luong's recollection is the importance of female friendship.

Bao Luong also provides an insider's account of the recruitment of young Vietnamese into the anticolonial underground, their training in China, and the internal structure and workings of the Youth League in the South. Her description of Saigon's Central Prison, which was razed in the 1950s, forcibly reminds the reader of Jeremy Bentham's panopticon and Michel Foucault's description of it in his *Discipline and Punish.* Her detailed rendering of day-to-day life among female inmates is a valuable supplement to the stories of men's prison experiences under colonial rule.

Because the memoir covers so many different topics, it presents a number of narrative challenges. Should I offer the memoir as an interesting historical document unadorned by my own commentary or should I seek to provide the larger historical and social context in which these events occurred? Should I ignore the details I found in the Sûreté file? If not, what is the best way to integrate them into Bao Luong's narrative? What about press coverage or the memoirs of her sisters? The more I thought about these issues, the more convinced I became that Bao Luong's story would not be accessible to anyone who was not already familiar with the history of colonial Vietnam in the 1920s and that I would have to supply a significant amount of background. I had to combine the roles of niece, translator, and historian. But how should I present Bao Luong's memoir? As an example of the lives of ordinary Vietnamese in the early twentieth century or as a source of information about some still little-explored episodes or second-rank figures in the history of the Vietnamese Revolution? Should the focus be on gender? On what happened at Barbier Street and why?

More than thirty years after these events Bao Luong was able to describe in vivid detail the horrific torture to which she and others were subjected and the hellish prison life she endured. She must have thought long and hard about what she wanted to tell and how she would tell it. It was not just physical pain and degradation that she recollected. She was well aware of how she and her friends were portrayed in the press at the time of her trial. "Patriots?" scoffed the government-supported newspaper *L'Indochine* on October 5, 1930. "Pleasure-seekers, narcissists, ruffians, more like!" Bao Luong's memoir is not just an attempt to recapture the past but an effort to set the record straight about herself, about the character of the dead man, the reasons for his murder and her own role in it, and even the responsibility of the Central Committee of the Revolutionary Youth League for precipitating the debacle.

Whether she is trying to recapture the sense of urgency, the emotions and feelings she experienced, as well as the decisions and the actions in which she was involved or whether she succumbed to advice about how to present her early life, Bao Luong writes in the present tense, as events unfold and as if she has no knowledge of what the future will bring. Time and again, she focuses on her immediate concerns and circumstances and the need to live in and through the present. It is as if she has been transported back to Central Prison in Saigon and is scribbling in her precious booklet of stitched-together pieces of toilet paper with the bit of pencil that her sympathetic lawyer smuggled to her in a loaf of bread. She is exhausted, filthy, and hungry and has to be constantly alert for attacks from other prisoners. She cannot or does not want to dwell on the events that led her to jail, reflect on the rightness of her actions, or explore her feelings about the person who betrayed her and so many other comrades.

But the inescapable fact was that more than thirty years had elapsed. The independence she had fought for had become a reality, albeit a highly imperfect one. The Communist Party, nascent at the time of her arrest, controlled half the country and was extending its reach to the other half. She had changed, society had changed, and the players moving across the political field had changed. And she had had three decades to reflect on what had happened. I could only wonder how much all this affected her memories of her youthful self and of her friends, collaborators, and betrayers. Thus, just as I questioned the accuracy of the information gathered by the Sûreté, extracted under duress from prisoners and presented through the prism of anticolonial conspiracies, I became concerned about the reliability of Bao Luong's own version of the past, even though it was freely produced.

The artless tone running through the memoir gives it an air of utter authenticity and stands in sharp contrast with the formal tone of the Sûreté records. Yet reading her account side by side with other accounts makes one aware of her numerous elisions and evasions as well as opportunities for fabrication. It is doubtful that Bao Luong could remember every word of every conversation that filled her memoir; it is evident as well that she reconstructed scenes in which she was not present, basing her dialog-filled account on what participants told her after the fact. She was also reticent about certain important information, such as the name of the informer who betrayed the whole southern network of the Revolutionary Youth League. She never named him, even to her children. Bao Luong was able to recall the exact time of day when a particular event took place and to quote, supposedly verbatim, entire conversations (although she can be vague about who said what), but she is stingy with dates, supplying few and thereby infuriating the historian, for whom precise dates are all important.

. . .

This book is an experiment in hybridization. The different versions of what Bao Luong wrote and what I have produced here are addressed to different audiences, separated by time, geography, knowledge, and interests. I have decided not to turn her memoir into a work of historical analysis but to retain as much of Bao Luong's narrative as possible. Yet, derived as it is from multiple sources, this book differs from her manuscript, its serialized versions, and the version published in book form in 1996. I have attempted to hew closely to Bao Luong's manuscript and to honor as much as possible its structure and tone, as well as the rhythm with which Bao Luong chose to disclose her information. However, I have excised all the poems. I am doing her a great disservice as poetry writing was a constant in her life from childhood to her final years, something she was rightly proud of and that gave her solace. But I felt unequal to the task of rendering her poems in translation. I have also emulated the serialized versions of her memoir by omitting long discussions of philosophy and history.

But I have augmented Bao Luong's narrative with extracts from confessions and police accounts, adding here and there excerpts from the unpublished memoirs of her sisters Han Xuan and Van Trang. To make the account more readable I have tried to reduce the plethora of aliases used by each of Bao Luong's colleagues. I have also provided some background information that does not appear in the memoir. In certain cases I have tried to reconcile what Bao Luong wrote, what others claimed, and what historians have learned of the events of the late 1920s.

To make the story approachable for the modern reader who is not an expert in Vietnamese history, I have written Bao Luong's story in the third person, interjecting information from other sources, either to clarify what is happening or to provide a historical context for what Bao Luong wrote. These interjections appear in italics. In chapters 5 and 6, which deal with the murder and its prelude, I have combined in a single narrative information taken from Bao Luong's memoir, police confessions, and my own research into the wider political context in which the murder took place. Although different voices, including mine, now tell Bao Luong's story, hers remains dominant.

Although I cannot place total confidence in any of the sources I have used to reconstruct the life of Bao Luong, I have done my best to rescue her from canonization as Vietnam's first female political prisoner, despite the pictures of her that hang in two museums, the street sign that bears her name, and the romantic imaginings that her story engenders. Bao Luong never saw herself as a victim of forces outside her control. Instead, she sought to convey the blend of naïveté and thirst for knowledge that led her to embark on her quest for freedom for herself and her country; to preserve her good name while living in an overwhelmingly male environment; and to uphold her belief in honor and commitment.

As I did background research for this book, I came across an article that was published in *Than Chung* on July 27, 1929, less than two weeks after Bao Luong's arrest. The following description surely came from her aunt Thu Cuu, the wife of the editor-in-chief: "Older people who know her all say that Miss Nguyen Trung Nguyet is a person of strong feelings. Although female, she does not like to sew and embroider. Instead, she prefers to think and to read. Instead of the normal feminine preference for beautifying oneself, she actually donned men's clothes on a few occasions. When she came of age, she refused several offers of marriage."

Reading this, I was glad to have made the acquaintance of the young Bao Luong, not the placid smiling aunt of my childhood who did embroidery and was preoccupied with decorum but the idealistic and passionate girl who, for a brief and tragic moment, sought to play her part in the drama of the Vietnamese Revolution.

1

The Girl from the South

Nguyen Trung Nguyet's parents had named their firstborn child "faithful moon." In Vietnamese culture, whose rhythms follow the lunar calendar, the moon is the symbol of constancy. As the oldest child of Nguyen van Nham and his wife, Dao thi Chau, Trung Nguyet was known as Second Sister by her siblings and, much later, as Second Aunt by their children. This southern custom was said to derive from the belief that the first child should always be known as "second" to fool the devil, who loved to take firstborn children back to the netherworld; others claimed the custom honored the first lord of the South, the ancestor of the Nguyen emperors.

Nguyen Trung Nguyet's father had been one of ten children. When Trung Nguyet was growing up, she knew only three of her father's siblings: Fourth Uncle, Ninth Aunt, and Uncle Ut, the youngest. Only Uncle Ut seems to have been close to Nham in age, political ideals, and love of learning. It appears from Trung Nguyet's memoir that the French had killed one brother and a cousin. Nguyen van Nham was born around 1890 in the province of Ben Tre, one of three ceded to the French in the Treaty of Saigon of 1862. The remaining three provinces of the South were brought under French control in 1867 to form, together with those ceded earlier, the colony of French Cochinchina, but sporadic opposition to colonial rule continued throughout the 1870s. It is thus likely that Nham's brother and cousin died in some futile attempt at overthrowing the French. Whatever the exact circumstances, Nham nurtured a hatred of the French that he passed on to his children. Nham also seems to have blamed the French for abuses perpetrated by Vietnamese officials or landlords, which his daughter witnessed far more frequently than actual displays of French power.

Like many young men of his time, Nguyen van Nham went away to study; literate men were fairly scarce in rural southern Vietnam and good teachers even more so. His teacher was Dao Duy Chung, a man whose granddaughters remembered him as speaking with a "Quang" accent. To Southerners "Quang" was a catchall reference to the center of the country, where many provinces bore names beginning with *Quang*. His family claimed to be descended from the famous scholar Dao Duy Tu, who had left Hanoi because his birth as the son of an entertainer made him ineligible to sit for the civil service exams in 1592. Dao Duy Tu had offered his services to the lord of the South in Hue and had suggested building the walls at Dong Hoi in 1630 that divided the country for nearly two centuries. Dao Duy Chung's descent from this scholar and statesman could not be confirmed, but his progeny took great pride in it. Dao Duy Chung arrived in the South from "Quang" in the early 1880s, in response to the call of Emperor Tu Duc for scholars to mobilize peasants against the French. Enthusiasm for empire, which had diminished in the wake of France's defeat in the Franco-Prussian war of 1871, had revived in France. Apparently, Emperor Tu Duc thought that anticolonial activism in the South might undermine French expansionist efforts in the rest of the country. Dao Duy Chung's efforts proved futile, but he decided to remain in the South and settled in Tra Vinh. Of his wife, we know little except that she came from a large family surnamed Tran in My Tho and that she died in childbirth. Of her four children, only one, Dao thi Chau, survived to adulthood.

For a time Dao Duy Chung served on the Judicial Council of Tra Vinh, but he resigned in disgust at the abuses of power committed by those in authority, in particular their interference in the judicial process. His resignation earned him fame as a man "loyal to Vietnam" *(Nam trung)*. He then opened an academy to teach Chinese classics, even though a new Franco-Annamite system of education had rendered the old curriculum obsolete. He was a stern taskmaster, holding himself responsible not only for inculcating knowledge in his students but also for their moral growth. He maintained this sense of responsibility long after his students had left his care and assumed positions of authority in society. According to a family story, he upbraided a prefect who had once been his student when the man came to extend New Year's greetings to him: "Peasants from your district passing through here recently complained of bad administration. The duty of every mandarin is to care for the welfare of the people. What have you to say for yourself?"[1] Stories such as these enhanced Dao Duy Chung's reputation for both probity and patriotism.

Nguyen van Nham was Dao Duy Chung's favorite student, and to him Chung decided to give his surviving daughter, Chau, in marriage. The young people had not met before the wedding ceremony, which probably took place in 1908. Chau would say later that she was relieved to see that her bridegroom wore his hair in the traditional topknot. In the rest of the country young reformers were advocating the adoption of Western clothing and hairstyles as a sign of patriotic progressivism, but many in the South, the only region under direct French rule, clung to the old ways as an expression of love for their country.

The wedding rituals over, Nham brought his bride back to Binh Dai, where Trung Nguyet was born in 1909. Two more children were born to Nham and Chau in Binh Dai: their only son, Vien Dai, in 1910 and another daughter, Hue Minh, in 1913.

Ben Tre was one of the South's oldest provinces, but a lot of land remained uncultivated. The village of Binh Dai itself was located near the estuary of one of the Mekong's many branches. The house where Trung Nguyet grew up was one of four straw huts erected on land that her grandfather had cleared. By one side was a banana grove, by the other a field of sugarcane. In front was a large rice field. At the back was a jungle full of tigers, boars, monkeys, and foxes. Trung Nguyet recalled that her father and uncles often went hunting. She remembered being terrified one day when she realized that she was still in the jungle as the sun was setting. Luckily, her grandmother's brother, on his way to visit his sister's family, heard Trung Nguyet's cries of distress and brought her safely home.

Trung Nguyet was a carefree child, though she was expected to help out by spreading fertilizer made of dried fish around the banana trees and tending to the family's buffaloes. But her father also insisted that she get an education at the nighttime "school" run by Uncle Ut for the village boys who herded buffaloes by day. Of all his pupils, Trung Nguyet was the most diligent, for the boys were not entirely persuaded of the value of literacy. Some fell asleep as soon as they arrived. Others talked throughout the class at a volume more suited to the rice fields than a hut in the quiet of night. Uncle Ut taught them by lamplight, using banana leaves for paper and purple fruit juice for ink. He also taught them the rudiments of hygiene with the help of a cane. Students who forgot to wipe their noses or whose feet were caked with mud found the cane crashing on their legs before they had a chance to dance away.

One night a notable (a member of the village council) named Ngo came to visit Uncle Ut, ostensibly to remind him that the school he was running was illegal. But after whispering in Uncle Ut's ear, Ngo straightened up and said: "I have great respect for your father; when he was alive, we were good friends. This is why I've come to warn you. The French government has earned our gratitude; we must keep that in mind. So I won't report that you are teaching children in your house. A few kids won't matter, I'll protect you. But you need to prepare for the reception right away." This was the real reason behind his visit: the coming visit of the salt and alcohol inspector. In the imagination of the village children, the French inspector was a fearsome figure. He was tall, gaunt, and pale, with deep-set blue eyes and a sharp, prominent nose. And he carried a shotgun.

Salt was a state monopoly that was expected to bring in revenue to the colonial state, but the price set by the monopoly for this basic commodity made it unaffordable for most peasants and fishermen. For the inhabitants of Binh Dai, which was close to the sea, producing salt was easy, but the punishment for violating a state monopoly was severe. The previous year the inspector had taken away more than ten men for having illegal stores of salt. They had been marched out of the village, hands tied behind their back and roped together in a long file, followed by their sobbing wives and children.

When the estuary had flooded a few months earlier, Trung Nguyet and her mother had painstakingly carried the salty mud home and carefully sifted it until they had a sizable amount of pure white salt crystals that they stored in containers hidden in the orchard under a pile of dried banana leaves. As soon as the notable left, every member of the household, including the buffalo boys, was mobilized to move the salt containers to a better hiding place and covered the hole with grass. For good measure Fourth Uncle covered the lot with buffalo dung mixed with water. Barely had they completed the camouflage when they got word that the salt inspector had arrived. Nham was then away in Rach Gia, seeking out sites where he might move his family to start a new life. His mother and older brother decided that, in case the salt's hiding place was discovered, his wife would take responsibility for it: "A woman will receive a shorter prison term," they said.

At four in the morning, the men convened in the communal house to await the inspector. When the inspector and his large entourage finally arrived, a steady drumbeat alerted everyone to his presence. After the preliminaries were over, the inspector visited each house. He soon uncovered the cache of salt on Nham's property. Just as Chau was about to confess, Uncle Ut arrived. He was unaware of the earlier discussions and took responsibility for it. He was immediately taken away. But to the great relief of his family he returned home a free man a few hours later. He had claimed that the salt belonged to his absent brother, and Notable Ngo confirmed that Nham had been in Rach Gia for some time. Trung Nguyet, who had absorbed her father's tales of French rapacity, was deeply influenced by this first encounter with colonial oppression. When the inspector left, Trung Nguyet and her mother set out to dig up more estuary mud to make another illegal store of salt.

After the inspector had taken away Uncle Ut, Trung Nguyet's grandmother rained invectives and blows on her daughter-in-law—as she often did—blaming her for Uncle Ut's arrest. His sister, whose own illegal store had gone undetected, joined her mother in hitting Chau and yelling at her. Only when Uncle Ut returned unharmed did the insults and blows stop. This was only one of many times when Chau's mother- and sister-in-law treated her badly. Throughout the first ten years of marriage, Chau was at the beck and call of all her in-laws. Trung Nguyet regarded the old woman as an indulgent grandmother and blamed "feudal" tradition for the mistreatment of her mother because it produced oppressed daughters-in-law who later became oppressive mothers-in-law. In the early decades of the twentieth century, progressive young Vietnamese were beginning to use the word *feudal (phong kien)* as a term of opprobrium for any practice or belief they disliked. Feudalism and colonialism would be the twin targets of Trung Nguyet's revolutionary zeal.

Nham was aware of the difficult relations between his mother and his wife, which was why he was exploring a move to Rach Gia. Several times during their marriage, Chau had lamented her husband's refusal to accept help from her father. Dao Duy Chung was famous not only for his patriotism and his erudition but also for his knowledge of herbs, and he had proposed to set his son-in-law up in an herb shop, but Nham had refused. When his wife, smarting from her mother-in-law's abuse, wept at his refusal to go into the herb business, Nham would retort, "Do you think it is fitting that a man should live off his wife?" Moving to Rach Gia would solve both problems.

As he was preparing to move his family from Binh Dai, his mother urged Nham to sell a few acres *(mau)* in order to have some capital with which to begin his new life. After his father's death, Nham had continued to clear the jungle and opened up more land for rice cultivation. But he refused. He was a proud and unbending man, confident that he could provide for his wife and children without the help of either his or his wife's relatives. When Nham and Chau left Binh Dai with their three children, they took only some mosquito nets, three large trays, and a few earthenware bowls. They loaded their meager possessions onto a sampan and set off for Vinh Phu in Rach Gia. Trung Nguyet, then nine, never returned to Binh Dai and never again saw the friends of her childhood.

Much of Rach Gia (now Kien Giang) was marshy land only recently reclaimed from the sea. Land was still plentiful and only beginning to be brought into cultivation. The province had been incorporated only at the turn of the twentieth century. By the mid-1920s it would rank first among the Vietnamese provinces in rice production. Nham bought some land by a river at auction, having decided to earn his living from fishing. He proposed to stretch fishing nets across the river, leaving enough of an opening for sampans to pass through. No one in Vinh Phu had ever used that technique, and his proposal was easily accepted. But his success excited the envy of neighbors. One day a notable brought along a dozen of his Cambodian employees to destroy the dam and the nets. But Trung Nguyet and her siblings had made friends with the daughters of the wealthy widow of a magistrate. When Mrs. Magistrate, as she was known, heard the commotion, she walked out of her house and silently looked from the group of Cambodian laborers to Trung Nguyet's parents and back again. It was enough to unnerve the notable and his laborers, who feared that she would bear witness to the destruction of the nets. They left but continued to harass Nham throughout the rest of the fishing season so that he eventually decided to give up fishing and return to growing rice.

While Nham looked for suitable land, Chau supported the family by making pastries for Trung Nguyet to sell. Few rural women were literate in those days, and Trung Nguyet was much in demand for reasons other than her mother's pastries. Among her steady customers was an old Cantonese lady who loved to be read to from *The Chronicles of the Eastern Zhou,* one of several Chinese historical novels that were beginning to appear in Vietnamese translation. Mrs. Magistrate also often bought up all of Chau's pastries in return for Trung Nguyet's reading from a Chinese historical novel or reciting poetry.

One day Nham followed his daughter into Mrs. Magistrate's house just as two of her servants brought in a man of about fifty whose hands were tied. He was a tenant who had fallen behind in his rent, and she was sending him to the communal house for sentencing. It was a foregone conclusion that he would have to remain in jail until his family could pay up. Some men in his straits languished in prison for years; others left their bones on Con Son penal island. When Nham learned of the man's debt, he immediately said he would provide the thirty measures of rice the tenant owed. Mrs. Magistrate knew very well that Nham did not have the means to pay her; otherwise his daughter would not be selling pastries door to door. But after staring at him in silence for a while, she agreed to release her tenant without demanding payment. The following day the grateful man brought his teenage son and daughter to live with Nham as his assistants. Nham insisted that he would accept their help only if he could teach them to read and write. (The task actually fell to Trung Nguyet.) A few years later Nham heard that the tenant was again behind in his rent and once again faced prison. Nham sent the man's two children home so that they could help their father, and Nham gave them some money to pay off the man's debts.

Shortly after this incident a relative of Chau's came to live in the village. Chau no longer had living siblings, but she had many cousins on her mother's side of the family. One cousin was married to a man named Quoi, a canton chief and thus the most powerful figure in their area. Quoi and his wife built a substantial house of brick and tiled floor near the mud hut where Nham and his family lived. Trung Nguyet became fast friends with Quoi's daughters, but Chau and Nham kept their distance because they did not approve of Quoi. As canton chief he was in charge of interrogating prisoners, and Trung Nguyet, on her visits to his home, witnessed many scenes of interrogation. Prisoners would be kneeling in a row on the floor, their arms tied behind their backs and a metal rod inserted between their wrists. Every time Quoi asked a question, he would strike the man who answered with a rattan stick that had a spiny, rock-hard fruit on one end.

Quoi's brutality and Nham's sense of justice were bound to lead to a showdown. Quoi did not like an answer supplied by Nham's helper and tried to beat the boy up; Nham intervened. Seeing the two men about to come to blows, their wives tried to restrain them. Quoi hit his own wife so hard that she fell down in a dead faint. This created enough of a distraction that the two combatants retreated. When Quoi returned to resume hostilities, he found Nham sitting in his usual chair in front of his hut, a cigarette in his mouth and an axe by his side.

Trung Nguyet, who was then about ten or eleven years old, was deeply disturbed by what had happened. Her greatest concern was that her friendship with her girl cousins would have to end, as the two families were no longer on speaking terms. She did not appreciate the rights and wrongs of the matter. It seemed to her that her father was just as ready as Quoi to commit violence. Nham realized that he had neglected his daughter's moral education. After the scene at Mrs. Magistrate's house, Trung Nguyet had exclaimed to her father enthusiastically about the woman's soft skin. Trung Nguyet, who walked barefoot like all village children, especially admired Mrs. Magistrate's pink heels. Nham had retorted that there was beauty of the body and beauty of character and that the latter was more important; Trung Nguyet had not appeared convinced. When she seemed to equate her father's behavior with that of Canton Chief Quoi, Nham decided to become more involved in guiding Trung Nguyet's moral development. Under her father's supervision Trung Nguyet began learning in earnest a mixture of history, literature, and moral precepts. She learned how to write Tang-style poetry and to distinguish between literal and figurative meanings, about images, metaphors, and allusions. Her father also taught her about justice, using his father-in-law as an example of honor and loyalty.

Just as Nham decided that he did not want to go on living next to Quoi, an old friend of Nham's began to visit him. This was another relative of Chau's. He was named Nguyen van Duong, but everyone called him Bo Tong. In 1905 Bo Tong had gone to Japan, following the reformist scholar Phan Boi Chau and Prince Cuong De, whom Bo Tong and Nham called "our king" in disregard of the puppet rulers installed by the French.[2] Bo Tong had later returned to Vietnam to raise funds to support Phan Boi Chau's anticolonial activities (Nham had sold a piece of land to help out) but had been arrested and thrown in jail. Bo Tong was now out of prison, still eager to oppose the French. When he visited, Nham and he would challenge each other to poetry-writing contests. They asked Trung Nguyet to copy their poems down but to burn them right away, much to her dismay. The poems, however, were too dangerous to leave out, containing as they did new words such as *nation, invasion,* and *revolution.*

Bo Tong urged Nham to move from Vinh Phu to Phuoc Long. He introduced Nham to a Frenchman who had failed to get rich from the salt marshes of Rach Gia and was willing to sell his house and all his lands.[3] Once again, Trung Nguyet, who still dreamed of the friends she had left behind in Binh Dai, was being uprooted. She was twelve years old and disconsolate.

Phuoc Long today is part of Bac Lieu Province, which was incorporated even later than Rach Gia. When Nham bought property there, the area was still underdeveloped and offered plenty of opportunity for a hard-working couple. For Nham and Chau life became easier and more prosperous. They had three more daughters—Han Xuan, Mong Trung, and Van Trang—in Phuoc Long between 1921 and 1927, the year Trung Nguyet left home. As in most Vietnamese households of the time, the older children were given responsibility for minding their younger siblings. Vien Dai, the only boy in the family, was seldom at home, so Trung Nguyet and Hue Minh had to mind their younger siblings and were punished when they failed in their duty. Nham, like his contemporaries, believed in collective responsibility. If one child did wrong, all her older sisters were punished as well. At the yearly reunions to commemorate Nham's death, his daughters would reminisce ruefully about his method of punishment. He would tell the children to find a twig with which he would cane them. They were then to arrange themselves in a row face down on the floor while he lectured them about their misdeed. He invariably ended his peroration by asking, "How many strokes do you think you deserve?" One was the predictable answer. And, just as invariably, the twig would break at the first stroke. What his daughters remembered most keenly was the sense of having failed to live up to their father's expectations as he droned on in his sorrowful voice about their dereliction of duty. It was clear too that, notwithstanding the traditional preference for sons, Trung Nguyet was his favorite child. They recalled the many times he returned from his trips with special presents for her. They giggled as they remembered the time he returned from a trip with sanitary napkins for Trung Nguyet, who was entering puberty. When he showed these newfangled items to his wife, she was overcome with embarrassment. "But nothing was too good for Trung Nguyet," her sisters would say without rancor.

In their daughters' recounting, Nham and Chau embodied traditional virtues. Chau was the skilled, thrifty housewife who had tried her best to please a demanding mother-in-law, had ably managed the household finances, and contributed to the general well-being of her family. She shunned confrontation, cultivated good relations with neighbors, and always put her family's interests first. Nham, by contrast, fulfilled the stereotype of a good man: learned, generous, not afraid of danger, quick to anger when he saw injustice being done, interested in the affairs of the world beyond his family and his village. Trung Nguyet and her sisters might lament his unbending sense of right and wrong, but they idolized him.

In Phuoc Long, Nham stepped up his anticolonial activities. Over games of chess or poetry contests he would ask Trung Nguyet, "Did you know that the French stole our country?" Many of his visitors shared his ideas. Besides Bo Tong, another frequent visitor was Tran Ngoc Vien, a cousin of his wife's. Widowed at twenty-one, Ngoc Vien had never remarried. She headed a theatrical troupe, Dong Nu Ban, which was involved in launching a new kind of opera called *cai luong*, or reformed theater. From its headquarters in Tran Ngoc Vien's native Vinh Kim near My Tho, the whole troupe traveled throughout the Mekong Delta by barge. On her frequent visits Aunt Ngoc Vien taught Trung Nguyet to do intricate embroidery, all the while keeping up a flow of anti-French rhetoric.

During visits to her maternal grandfather in Tra Vinh, Trung Nguyet also heard stories of anticolonial resistance: "There have been many heroes who fought the French. But Hoang Hoa Tham was able to resist for ten years because he had his headquarters in a remote and inaccessible location, because he had the complete support of local people, because he had enough supplies, a good strategy, and weapons. Whether or not a struggle is successful does not depend entirely on weapons, but eventually, they must be used. . . . The reason why Hoang Hoa Tham was assassinated [in 1913] was that an informant had insinuated himself in the ranks of his followers."[4] To the youthful Trung Nguyet these stories of patriotic derring-do were more exciting than the Chinese historical novels that were so popular. Nham continued her education by bringing home the writings of Sun Yat-sen, from which she absorbed her commitment to the people's welfare, democracy and people's rights.[5]

Nham got together with other landowners to establish a branch of the Society for the Promotion of Education (Hoi Khai Tri Tien Duc) in Phuoc Long and rented a small house near the market for the purpose. They set up a library with books and newspapers and opened it to the public.[6] Nham organized many meetings at the society. One visitor was Nguyen An Ninh, a young radical who in 1923 had launched a French-language newspaper, *La Cloche Fêlée*, which was enormously popular among idealistic young Vietnamese.

Not all Nham's dealings with his fellow landowners were harmonious. When he disclosed that the local magistrate had taken bribes from a landlord to drop a charge of exploiting his tenants, Nham became known as a champion of the poor, who flocked to work on his land. This got him involved in another, even more serious, case when the village police officer came to ask for his advice. The police officer had discovered a body hanging from a tree behind the rice store that belonged to Mr. T, an important member of the village and, like Nham, a patron of the Society for the Promotion of Education. When the corpse was cut down, the officer saw that it was covered with bruises and lacerations. The police officer was too frightened of Mr. T to write a report to the prefecture, so Nham made one out for him. The next day Mr. T came to ask Nham to retract his accusations, calling on their friendship, their collaboration in the Society for the Promotion of Education, and their past joint venture in a line of boats plying the river between Rach Gia and My Tho. Nham refused to take back his report unless Mr. T. gave a large tract to the widow of the dead man so that she could support herself and her five children. It turned out that Mr. T had once raped her. Her husband had at first not dared to protest for fear of being driven from the land he rented from Mr. T, but one day rage had gotten the better of him, and he had gone to shout insults at Mr. T. The landlord had gotten members of his family to tie the husband up, and they had hung him upside down and whipped him with thorny twigs till he died. Despite Nham's report, Mr. T was not prosecuted. Bao Luong does not record whether he gave the man's widow any land.

Despite his frequent conflicts with the rich and powerful, Nham continued to prosper. He no longer tilled his own land but left its management in the hands of a tenant Nham had saved from the magistrate. Nham went by horse from place to place where land was being auctioned in Rach Gia.[7] Meanwhile, Trung Nguyet was growing up, pretty and accomplished. She was the epitome of the young lady of good family. Her forays outside her home brought gawkers outside theirs. Her ankle-length hair was set in three chignons covered by a scarf; she wore three gauze tunics, the inside ones in pale yellow and pink, the outer one in green silk embroidered with small bunches of flowers. She wore a necklace of gold beads, three gold chains, rings on both fingers, and bracelets on both wrists. Chau would take her to their relatives in Vinh Kim to boast of her pretty daughter but also to look for suitable marriage partners. Her father had already turned down an inquiry from Mr. T, whose son was about to graduate from medical school. "Who would want to give a tiger to a dog?" he had asked rhetorically, using a classical allusion to express his contempt for Mr. T and his family.[8] Other families were also pressing their sons' cases. But Trung Nguyet refused all inquiries, and her father did not press her.

On March 26, 1926, Nguyen An Ninh was arrested for distributing inflammatory flyers to protest the deportation of a worker to North Vietnam. Nguyen An Ninh's arrest followed by one day the death of Phan Chu Trinh, a leader in the Reform Movement of 1907. Nguyen An Ninh symbolized the new generation of patriotic Vietnamese educated in French or in the hybrid Franco-Annamite schools. Both Phan Chu Trinh and Phan Boi Chau were anticolonial activists who were scholars steeped in the Chinese classics. Phan Chu Trinh had returned to Vietnam only in late 1925 after many years of exile in France. To honor him the Vietnamese wanted to mount a national funeral on the model of Sun Yat-sen's two years earlier. Colonial authorities put a stop to it and expelled from school students who wore black armbands as a sign of mourning. The national student strikes that followed became the catalyst for Trung Nguyet's decision to engage in revolutionary politics.[9]

For a while Trung Nguyet tried to persuade her parents to let her leave home to engage in anticolonial activities. They resisted, fearing that she would lose her reputation if she ventured forth on her own. But Trung Nguyet felt imprisoned by the fortress of traditional expectations. One day in 1927, as her father was at the Society for the Promotion of Education proudly sharing with his cronies the eulogy she had written for Phan Chu Trinh, and while her mother was away on an errand, Trung Nguyet walked to the river with a small valise and caught a barge to My Tho. Within a few days the neighborhood was awash in rumors that Trung Nguyet had "gone off with a man [theo trai]." Her father declared to anyone who would listen that she had gone to study, but her mother cried for days of the shame that Trung Nguyet was bringing on her family.[10]

Trung Nguyet, however, was not interested in romance. During the long trip she reflected on the stories she had heard about heroes of the resistance against the French. She thought about her mother's words: "Virginity is the outward sign of a woman's virtue. Beauty without virtue is worth nothing." To which her father would add: "I hope that engaging in revolution does not mean abandoning all the virtues of an Oriental woman." As she sailed away, she vowed, "I will do my duty. Do not worry, Father and Mother."

2

From Faithful Moon to Precious Honesty

A year or so before Nguyen Trung Nguyet left home, Nguyen van Nham had taken his two older daughters to a studio in town to have their photograph taken. In the photo the two girls stand stiffly on either side of a bentwood chair, a piece of furniture that appears in many other photographs of the period. Trung Nguyet, who was then sixteen or seventeen, wears her hair up in several elaborate chignons, a sign of her status as a grown-up young lady. She is wearing two *ao dai*. Her sister Hue Minh would have been twelve or thirteen at the time, too young to put her hair up, as the dividing line between "child" and "young lady" was fifteen. She is dressed more simply in a single *ao dai*. Like Trung Nguyet, she is wearing embroidered slippers and holds a parasol. The picture on display in the Ton Duc Thang Museum has been cropped so that Hue Minh does not appear in it. This is the only visual record of Nguyen Trung Nguyet, "Faithful Moon," before she began her revolutionary activities. Her expression is resolute: she had already started making plans to become involved in the exciting yet nebulous adventure she knew as "revolution." Around the time she left home, Trung Nguyet decided to use the pen name Bao Luong—"Precious Honesty"—under which she had begun writing poetry.

Trung Nguyet / Bao Luong decided that it would be too easy for her parents to deduce that she had gone to stay with her aunt Ngoc Vien, since the boat sailed only between Rach Gia and My Tho. So she caught the train straight to Saigon, where Ngoc Vien's younger sister, Ngoc Anh, resided. Bao Luong spent only one night at Ngoc Anh's home; the next day another aunt, Thu Cuu, came to take Bao Luong to the home of their niece Kim Oanh. Because Bao Luong was related to Kim Oanh through Thu Cuu and Ngoc Anh, they were confident that Kim Oanh's husband, Ton Duc Thang, would treat her with all due courtesy.

FIGURE 1. Nguyen Trung Nguyet (right) and Nguyen Hue Minh,
ca. 1926. Author's collection.

At the time Ton Duc Thang, who was then about forty, worked as a mechanic
for Kropff and Company at the Ba Son shipyard by the Saigon docks. He seemed
to spend all his free time reading and studying. Bao Luong gathered that he was
reading up on various ideologies and pondering what it would take to wage revolution. On the whole she kept her distance from him, as befitted a young woman
who was not related to him by blood, but she became fast friends with his wife. Kim
Oanh told Bao Luong about Ton Duc Thang's difficult childhood and the fierce determination that had turned him into the man he had become. Ton Duc Thang was
born in 1888 in My Phuoc in Long Xuyen Province. His parents made him study

Chinese, but on the way to his teacher's house, he passed the Franco-Annamite school, where other children were learning the romanized script introduced by the French as a replacement for Chinese characters. The schoolchildren were far more numerous than the pupils of his teacher, and when they were not in class, they were outside playing soccer. Thang asked his father to enroll him in the new school, but his father hated the French and everything connected with them: the school, the use of romanized script, the rowdy soccer games. Repeated entreaties proved unsuccessful. Even a hunger strike did not sway his father. Thang was determined, however, and enrolled in the school on his own. When his father learned what he had done, he threw him out of the house.

When the first day of school was over, Ton Duc Thang remained behind while other children went home, unsure what to do next. After his teacher found out that Thang was now homeless, he brought him home and convinced his wife to take the boy in. There Ton Duc Thang remained until he received his school certificate *(thanh chung)*. In 1913 he entered the school of Asian Mechanics of Saigon and remained there until September 1915. Upon graduation he was sent to France to take part in the Great War. He was at the Toulon Arsenal until January 1919, when he was repatriated to Vietnam.[1] Later on, rumor would have it that he had taken part in the Black Sea Mutiny by French sailors sent to Sebastopol by the Allies in response to the Russian Revolution, but that story does not figure in his police confession or in Bao Luong's memoir.[2]

Kim Oanh told Bao Luong that when Ton Duc Thang returned from France, he went straight home to Long Xuyen. When he entered his father's house, his parents exclaimed, "Is that you, Thang? Are you really alive or is it your ghost? Don't scare us so!" Having disowned him, they had lost touch with him and had thought him dead. Thang embraced his father; when he turned, he saw that his mother had run away, terrified. In fact, Thang had little feeling toward his own family; his love went to the teacher and his wife who had taken Thang in so many years before.

As Kim Oanh shared with Bao Luong a photograph of her husband taken in France, Kim Oanh laughed: "Even though he is not good looking, he had plenty of girlfriends." While in France, Ton Duc Thang had taken care of a young man who had fallen gravely ill. When the young man died, Thang organized his funeral and sent photographs of the ceremony to his family. Kim Oanh was filled with gratitude toward this stranger who had been so kind to her brother, vowed to marry Ton Duc Thang, and refused all proposals of marriage. One day Ton Duc Thang emerged from a photographic studio in My Tho just as Kim Oanh's uncle was passing by. He recognized Thang from the photograph of the funeral and told Thang of Kim Oanh's vow. Thang thought it over and agreed to the marriage. He immediately went to see her family in Vinh Kim and began to organize a wedding ceremony. When Kim Oanh, who had been away, returned home, the festivities were being prepared. A pig had been slaughtered, several chickens had been killed. Things had proceeded

FIGURE 2. Ton Duc Thang, 1929.
GGI 65535.

so fast that the groom had not brought the requisite trays of areca nut, betel leaves, and lime pot, and the bride had no wedding clothes. But Kim Oanh was happy. As she explained to Bao Luong, she considered that her task was to make a comfortable life for her husband, by taking on all the household chores and other worries herself so that he could devote all his time to his studies and to "great affairs." By the time Bao Luong came into their lives, Kim Oanh and her husband had two daughters, five and three, who often tried to distract their father from his studies. But he kept on reading, intent on learning as much as he could.

As Kim Oanh was finishing the story of her marriage, Nguyen An Ninh, the young editor of *La Cloche Fêlée*, walked in. In December 1926 he had been released from jail, where he had been held since his arrest in March for distributing inflammatory flyers. Bao Luong gathered that Ton Duc Thang, like her own father, greatly admired the newspaperman. From the little she could hear from behind the wall, the two men talked about "revolution" and some meeting. The next day Nguyen An Ninh and Ton Duc Thang set off for Hoc Mon. This district, which happened to be Nguyen An Ninh's birthplace, was famous for its tradition of rebellion and thus a favorite recruiting ground for anticolonial activists. When he returned from Hoc Mon, Ton Duc Thang unexpectedly paid attention to his lodger: "Bao Luong, what did Aunt Thu Cuu say about me?" "That you are progressive," she replied, "that you value learning; that you want to participate in revolution." Over dinner Thang suddenly said, "Nguyen An Ninh is a great speaker. He can really reach out to rural people and rouse them to action. This is really hard to do: you can't afford to speak for long."

"Is he a good revolutionary?" Bao Luong asked.

"What do you mean by 'good'?" Thang demanded.

"How is he at organizing?"

"I haven't really asked him."

"Oh, you have not joined him, then?"

"No," said Thang, "I don't quite agree with him, so I have not joined. I'm not sure I can follow his theory."

"And what is his theory?" Bao Luong asked.

"It is to rouse people, to create a really strong movement, and then to improvise according to circumstances. But he does not believe in political parties," Thang explained. "He thinks that the national cause belongs to all, and that everybody can join in."

"And you?" Bao Luong probed.

"I can't tell you yet."

Bao Luong had never before engaged in serious discussion with Ton Duc Thang. She was staying with his family while she waited for her cousin Tran Truong to return from abroad so that he could advise her on her next move. But she was getting impatient to acquire knowledge. One day she decided go to My Tho to study with the scholar Mai Bach Ngoc, a well-known figure who was poor but highly respected in patriotic circles.

"What do you want to study with Mai Bach Ngoc?" asked Ton Duc Thang.

"Chinese."

"That's fine," he said. "But if you want to study what your aunt Thu Cuu said, you should go to Russia."

Aware that Kim Oanh took care of all household chores without help from her husband, Bao Luong had privately thought that Ton Duc Thang was like all other men, interested only in keeping women tied to their home. Now she looked at Thang with new eyes. "Why should I be going to Russia? I only want to learn—"

"If you want to learn about revolution," he interrupted, "you should see for yourself the whole revolutionary process, from the destruction of the old to the establishment of the new. Since you've embarked on the path, you need to go to the end. Why are you still hesitating?"

Yet Ton Duc Thang was a cautious man. Aunt Thu Cuu wanted Bao Luong to write articles for *Than Chung,* her husband's newspaper. The journalist Tran Huy Lieu urged her to give speeches, just like Nguyen An Ninh. But Ton Duc Thang counseled her to think carefully. Bao Luong refused all advice and entreaties and set off for My Tho in search of Mai Bach Ngoc. At his house Bao Luong found only his fifteen-year-old daughter. A lonely child, Huynh Hoa was aware of the comings and goings of adults and eager for another young person's company. "I've heard from Aunt Ngoc Vien that you want to study with my father," she said.[3] "But what do you want to study? Uncle [Phan van] Hum and Uncle [Nguyen An] Ninh come here all the time; you can ask them questions directly." Bao Luong wanted to ask Mai Bach Ngoc for advice, but before she could do so, she got word that Ton Duc Thang wanted her to return immediately to Saigon. A disconsolate Huynh Hoa rowed her off on a sampan.

Bao Luong learned later that she had been carefully monitored for quite a while by an organization of which she then knew nothing: the Vietnamese Revolutionary Youth League (Viet Nam Thanh Nien Cach Mang Dong Chi Hoi). Ho Chi Minh, then operating under different aliases, created the organization in 1925 in Guangzhou. Ho posed as a Chinese interpreter for Borodin, Stalin's man in China, but Ho's actual mission was to promote anticolonial movements, not only in French Indochina but in all of Southeast Asia, and to advance the cause of communism. The Revolutionary Youth League built on a previous organization called the Like Hearts Society (Tam Tam Xa), which was made up of long-time Vietnamese residents of South China. It also received assistance from the Chinese Communist Party, which was then allied with the Guomindang under the United Front. The Revolutionary Youth League had representatives in the three regions of Vietnam; they were charged with expanding its membership and sending recruits to Guangzhou for training.

Bao Luong did not know that she was living in the home of the new head of the Southern Regional Committee *(ky bo)* of the Youth League. All she knew was that Ton Duc Thang was the husband of Kim Oanh, a distant relative by marriage on her mother's side. In fact, Ton Duc Thang was somewhat surprised to find himself in this position. As he later declared to the police, "I was initiated into politics while I was still at the Toulon Arsenal by some French workers and through reading newspapers such as *L'Humanité.* When I was back in Cochinchina, I gave up my ideas; but, through friends such as Ngo Thiem, who never ceased telling me that only in politics could one find prestige, nobility, and an atmosphere of freedom, I joined their organization, the Vietnam Revolutionary Youth League, whose Central Committee is in Guangzhou. I started out as a member of a cell. Two or three months later a delegation comprised of Lang and Ngo Thiem went to Guangzhou to propose my promotion to representative of the Central Committee on the Southern Regional Committee.[4] I was instantly promoted, somewhat to my surprise, for in the two or three months since I had joined the cell, I had not accomplished anything that deserved the promotion, which was requested without my knowledge."[5]

Indeed, it remains unclear why Ton Duc Thang, who had never gone to Guangzhou and had never personally met the leaders of the Revolutionary Youth League, was selected to head the Southern Regional Committee. "I thought it might have been done to flatter my ego," he said, "and incite me to carry out propaganda among workers of whom I was one."

In 1927 recruitment into the Revolutionary Youth League was at its peak, thanks to an influx of young Vietnamese who had been radicalized by confrontations with the French authorities after the death of Phan Chu Trinh and the arrest of Nguyen An Ninh in March 1926. Most students expelled from schools in the South went to France; but a few went to Guangzhou, where they met up with Vietnamese from the North and from central Vietnam at the league's headquarters.

While Bao Luong was still living at home, two members of the league had spent time in Phuoc Long with her father's support. One, Do Dinh Tho, had stayed at the Society for the Promotion of Education and had eaten meals at her house for a whole month without her encountering him—that's how strict the sex segregation was in many households at that time. While men ate in the front room of the family's house, the womenfolk huddled in the kitchen. Thus Do Dinh Tho was able to share many meals with Nham without actually meeting Bao Luong. The second person dispatched by the Youth League to Phuoc Long was Nguyen Bao Toan, a northerner. Like other activists, he operated under a variety of aliases for security reasons.[6] Nguyen Bao Toan was young and good-looking. Since Bao Luong had left home so abruptly, her parents feared that if Nguyen Bao Toan left soon afterward, it would be said that he had seduced her. To protect her reputation he had remained in Phuoc Long for a while after her sudden departure. Even so, Chau had had to endure nasty gossip about her daughter.

When Bao Luong returned from My Tho, Ton Duc Thang reproached her for going there so impulsively: "Why did you go? It looked as if I had urged you to do so." "I wanted to study with Mai Bach Ngoc," she replied. Bao Luong paid little attention to Nguyen Bao Toan, who was visiting Ton Duc Thang that day; she was focused on her cousin Tran Truong, whose return from China she had been awaiting impatiently. He had left home before she did in late March 1927, and she wanted to ask his advice about how to advance her revolutionary career.[7]

Tran Truong was astonished to learn that Bao Luong had left home on her own: "What about Nguyen Bao Toan and Do Dinh Tho?"

"I don't know them," she said. "I left to seek the path I told you about."

Suddenly, Tran Truong lowered his voice: "Bao Luong, please accompany two men to the Botanical Garden tomorrow. They're good friends of mine, but I'm busy and I can't go with them. Go with my sister Ban and treat them as if they were just like Ban."

"But Ban is my cousin and they are total strangers!" she said.

"Don't worry," he told her. "They are very courteous toward women."

Bao Luong wanted to ask who the two men were, but she had learned not to ask awkward questions.

The next day two men, one middle-aged and one tall and slim, arrived in a horse-drawn carriage; Tran Truong introduced his sister Ban and Bao Luong to the two men and helped them get into the carriage. In the Botanical Garden the four kept up a conversation. Ban and Bao Luong were reserved, leading the middle-aged man to exclaim, "We need to cure you of your prudery!" After lunch he proposed that they should rest in upstairs rooms in the pavilion. Bao Luong was furious. It was unthinkable for a young woman to "go upstairs to rest" in the company of men. She wanted to leave, but Ban had followed the men. Bao Luong spent the afternoon sitting on the balcony outside a bedroom, listening to her cousin talk about the oppression of women in Vietnamese society. Ban had joined Aunt Ngoc Vien's theatrical troupe and had met the two men they were accompanying while performing in the Saigon suburb of Dakao. Time passed; it was getting dark when they finally left the Botanical Garden. As they parted ways, the younger man suddenly whispered to Bao Luong: "You don't know me, but I've just returned from visiting your father. He's told me about your aspirations. We will meet again in a very distant place."

Bao Luong and Ban did not know that the little excursion in the Botanical Garden had been a means of vetting their suitability for being sent abroad. The younger man, none other than Nguyen Bao Toan, was the liaison with the Central Committee of the Revolutionary Youth League and had just returned from Guangzhou. The older man was the treasurer of the Southern Regional Committee. But that was something Bao Luong learned much later.

A short while later Tran Truong met up with Bao Luong and took her back to the Botanical Garden, where he told her, "You're leaving tonight."

"Where? Is Ban going also?"

"I don't know—just that you're going where you wanted, to China. Tell Kim Oanh that you're going to visit your family. From now on, you'll be on your own. You need to get rid of your prudish ways. You must be firm. Timidity will lead to failure. Prudence and determination are the two important factors for success in this enterprise. If you give in to girlish qualms, you will be thrown overboard immediately. You understand me?"

"Are you trying to scare me?"

"You're not going to a dinner party," Tran Truong responded. "You're entering a life of danger, looking for a path of survival amid bloodshed. Are you ready to accept all risks and not regret whatever happens?"

"Why should I regret anything or blame anyone? There's one thing that I will never sacrifice, however: my chastity."

Truong retorted, "You have to be willing to sacrifice everything for the cause."

"No, to lose my chastity is to lose my virtue. I won't let anyone take advantage of me. I will risk everything to protect myself. I'll go to My Tho [to study with Mai Bach Ngoc] after all."

During this exchange Nguyen Bao Toan had been nearby. When Tran Truong was finished, Toan asked Bao Luong to get into the carriage to return to Ton Duc Thang's house. This was the first time that Bao Luong had been alone in an enclosed space with a man, and she was tense. Toan gazed steadily outside, waiting until they were close to their destination before he began speaking: "You know, you don't have to be guilty of anything to be arrested. There have always been evil men. Beauty is a kind of crime. Suppose you were stopped at a checkpoint. The men stopping you might not know that you were carrying precious documents with names, meeting places, locations of caches of weapons. But if they asked you for your favors, what would you do?" Bao Luong did not answer. She thought bitterly about the hard choices facing women. Yet even though she knew that what Nguyen Bao Toan had described might very well happen, she was still set on going. That very night she said her good-byes to Kim Oanh. Ton Duc Thang joked, "If you go to Russia, remember to describe it in detail when you return!"

· · ·

September 1, 1927.[8] It was easy to be anonymous in the crowds when offices and factories let out and workers went home. Kieu Bridge would then be full of pedestrians, carts, and carriages. As they waited for Bao Luong to be picked up, Tran Truong confided, "I can now tell you that I joined the Revolutionary Party a long time ago. We humbly call it Revolutionary Youth League because as yet we do not have many members, and it would be an exaggeration to call it a party. Our rules are that each new recruit must be introduced by two current members. But we did not want to let women go abroad."

"So why am I allowed to go?"

"It's your own doing. Nguyen Bao Toan and Do Dinh Tho were known to your parents. That's why they could visit them. Your background and your character have been thoroughly investigated. Your sudden departure from home and your behavior on the balcony were factors in the decision. The two men, Nguyen Bao Toan and Cong, whom you met in the Botanical Garden, both agreed with us that you could go to Guangzhou for training. Although authorization has not yet come in, Nguyen Bao Toan said that at the Central Committee there are women with whom you can stay. So we've had to guarantee the Central Committee that you will not create difficulties."

"What kind of difficulties?" she asked.

"Let me tell you so that you can take precautions. Before, women went but none came back. They stayed . . . in the bellies of sharks. There were too few women and too many men, and the men vied for the women's favors. So, for the sake of equity, the women would be thrown overboard. That was the quickest way to restore peace among the men. So we stopped allowing women to go. But you are different. You've proved you can take care of yourself. The organization has made careful preparations."

When it was dark, Tran Truong brought Bao Luong to the house of their aunt Thu Cuu and her husband, Nguyen van Ba. The couple invited them in and immediately left. Tran Truong locked the door behind them: "You're going to disguise yourself as a boy. Let me cut off your hair." "How will I cope with short hair when I get back?" It was not an idle question. Young Vietnamese women did not wear their hair short. Bao Luong was very proud of her long hair. When she cut it so that it fell to her hips instead of to her ankles, her mother had cried for days. Bao Luong tried to overcome her feeling of loss at the prospect of cutting it even shorter. But Tran Truong only undid her several chignons and braided her hair. He carefully shaved off the wispy strands over her forehead, nape, and ears. He then pinned her hair up very tightly on her head and covered the whole with a beret. She took off her earrings. Then off came her clothes. Blushing furiously, Bao Luong removed her *ao dai* but not before looking at herself as a girl for one last time. In those days girls of good family flattened their breasts by wrapping them tightly with fabric. Bao Luong sheepishly put on the undershirt and open-neck shirt that belonged to Nguyen van Ba and the socks and shoes that Tran Truong had procured. Her transformation was complete. Her aunt and uncle came home just as Bao Luong finished putting on her disguise. Nguyen van Ba looked at her from tip to toe and smiled in approval.

Tran Truong and Bao Luong left the house, making their way among the swarms of prostitutes looking for French clients. Bao Luong had the impression that her cousin was making her walk so that she could get used to her new shoes and clothes. Along the way they greeted acquaintances, and Truong made her shake hands with them, something that women did not do. "Don't be shy," he warned. "According to feudal tradition, men and women should not touch; but my friends must know you only as a boy." Nguyen Bao Toan was waiting for them at the train station. He gently teased her: "Hey, young master, have a good trip. We two are going down to the provinces on business."

Bao Luong was left on her own. She was frightened by the enormous step she was taking, but her man's disguise reminded her that it was a man's destiny to be adventurous. A Chinese man appeared from nowhere and seized her hand, saying by way of greeting: "Have you eaten?" They joined a group of five or six men walking toward the Khanh Hoi Bridge. Suddenly, a whistle went off and everybody started running. As Bao Luong was trying to keep up with the men, she thought she heard familiar laughter from below the bridge. She reflected that the Revolutionary Youth League had made careful preparations and was reassured that she would find other friends on the way. All of a sudden, she and the men were crossing the ramp to the lower deck of a boat leaving for Hong Kong. Bao Luong never bothered to learn what kind of boat she was on or its name.[9] She was too busy trying to cope with a new emergency: how to relieve herself. Putting her hands in the pockets of her trousers for the first time, she found them full of handkerchiefs. Her immediate need taken care of, she spread black powder over her face to mask the pallor that betrayed a life spent indoors. In the middle of the night a Chinese man came by with a stack of blue uniforms. While the men put them on quickly and handed their clothes to the Chinese man whom Bao Luong thought of as "Fatso," she hesitated. "Come on, hurry up. It's just us!" someone said. In the light of the moon, Bao Luong could make out a tall man of perhaps forty with a long face who seemed to be looking for someone. "What did he mean by 'us'?" she wondered. The man moved away and Bao Luong found a dark spot, where she put on her blue coolie's uniform. After she gave her French suit to Fatso, he guided the group toward a big boiler.

They were among stowaways, and they were all tense. A voice rose to complain: "Do you want us all to roast?" Before they could crack a smile, Fatso opened an iron hatch and signaled for them to go into the boiler room. As they were hesitating, a voice said softly but firmly, "Whether we roast or are buried alive, we can only die once." The hideaway filled up, the cover closed. The stowaways were packed tightly. Human breath and the odor of sweat mixed with the heat of the fire from the boiler, creating an oppressive atmosphere that was made worse by the smell of bilge from the bottom of the boat. In her corner Bao Luong felt sweat run down her body in rivulets, as if she had taken a dose of medicine to bring down a fever. Her clothing was soaked; she found some relief from her thirst by passing the corner of her damp top over her lips. Even worse were the mosquitoes. Fearing that the sound would carry to the outside, the stowaways did not dare slap at them and could only wave them away ineffectively.

The sudden sound of footsteps and shouted orders galvanized the stowaways. They immediately moved to the sides of the hideaway to avoid being hit by the sticks and iron bars they had been told would be thrown down; the stronger ones lifted some in the group to hold tight to the iron rings overhead. Then arms and feet knit together to serve as seats for the weaker ones. The whole thing took place in complete silence in less than two minutes. Immediately, a volley of sharp sticks followed by iron bars fell into the bilge below. The stench of bilge mixed with urine rose from the bottom of the boat, but the stowaways could not cover their noses. Their nerves stretched thin, arms and legs aching, they continued to press themselves against the sides of their hideaway in complete silence. After a while the boat's motor kicked on and its horn blew, signaling that it was leaving the quay. The stowaways dropped down weakly on the mass of iron bars now lying horizontal. Some called out: "I'm dying of thirst." Bao Luong had learned that there were spies on each trip; when someone forgot and spoke up, she would tap him on the shoulder to remind him of the need to maintain silence. She did not dare say a word for fear of revealing her gender.

When the boat stopped at Vung Tau, Bao Luong contented herself with imagining the wonderful scenery she had heard about, too afraid that if she moved into the light, someone would recognize her as a woman. Another inspection took place, and the stowaways silently resumed their place by the sides of the hatch. This time Bao Luong stood up, allowing someone to stand on her shoulders. She was beginning to fear she might fall down and become food for sharks when the horn blew and the boat resumed its voyage. Fatso opened the hatch and the stowaways rushed out into the fresh air. All were streaked with dirt and sweat, and many began washing perfunctorily. For Bao Luong the ability to stretch after being cooped up under the hatch was heavenly. Suddenly, nostalgia mixed with fear of the unknown overcame her. What awaited her at the end? Now Bao Luong tried to identify her fellow trainees. She thought she had found five. She began to wonder about them. What were their names? Where did they come from? How had they gotten onto the boat? For whom was the tall man with the long face looking? Did he and the others realize that she was the sixth member of their group? How would they react if they knew she was a girl? Might they even throw her overboard?

Rooting in her pocket, she found she had only a couple of handkerchiefs left. She had plenty of money, however, enough to buy some bread. She was about to set off in search of food when she heard her name: "Bao Luong, Bao Luong!" It was Van Thong, the brother of a notable in her village. His family was very close to hers. But after she had turned twelve, she had not seen him because of the enforced segregation of the sexes. Van Thong, whose real name was Nguyen Hanh Thong, had gotten married only two months earlier. He happily explained that Tran Truong had asked him to look after her. Van Thong and the tall man took her to a more secluded spot on deck and gave her a sandwich. As they ate, they were joined by the three others, who hugged her and began teasing her gently, still not realizing they were dealing with a woman.

Van Thong made the introductions: the tall older man was Hoai Nghia; the short one was Kim Huong; the tough-looking fellow was Truong Phong; the young one was Thanh Huyen; he was Van Thong; and this was Bao Luong.[10] Fearing the men were embarrassing her, Van Thong hastily proposed a poetry-writing session, a popular pastime in Vietnam. Amid much joking, the men began to compose limericks aloud. Van Thong was from Bao Luong's village and knew her reputation as a wordsmith and urged her to compose a poem. When she finished, the men crowded around her to read the poem. One tapped her on the head, thereby dislodging her beret and revealing her braided hair. Truong Phong's jaw dropped; Kim Huong and Thanh Huyen quickly scooted away from her. Van Thong, who had known her gender all along, looked at Hoai Nghia and laughed: "Why be embarrassed? We've just sworn to regard one another as blood kin. If we treat each other as relatives, we can all live in harmony." Hoai Nghia held Bao Luong's hand and said, "Don't be shy, little sister. We are united in a common purpose. Don't hold us in suspicion; it could lead to failure." During the voyage Bao Luong learned that Hoai Nghia had a daughter; at various points he was reminded of her as he sought to make the passage to China more comfortable for Bao Luong.

Through Fatso Van Thong rented a cabin for her. She demurred at first, wanting to follow the rest on deck, but Hoai Nghia reminded her that it was too dangerous for her to stay with them. If her gender was discovered, the Revolutionary Youth League would no longer be able to bring out new recruits as stowaways. When she learned that Thanh Huyen had taken part in student demonstrations, Bao Luong spent the next two days pestering him for information about history. After two days someone told Bao Luong that she could stop pretending to be a man and gave her a set of Chinese women's clothes. Once she had assumed her new disguise, the real Chinese women on the boat began to visit her in her cabin, chatting away. Bao Luong had been practicing saying as little as possible and kept largely silent. That night Fatso, who had made arrangements for the group to travel clandestinely, returned, upset at having been duped about Bao Luong's gender. He directed a stream of angry words at Van Thong. Truong Phong whipped out pen and paper so that he could communicate with the Chinese man in writing and soothe him. Little sister, he claimed, was married to a Chinese man who had gone back to his country and had not returned for a long time. She was worried about her husband and had been literally crying her eyes out, shedding tears mixed with blood. So the group had agreed to take her to China so she could look for her husband, but she did not have money, and her friends had decided to let her disguise herself as a man so that she could stow away. Fatso seemed to swallow this tale of marital woe and was so mollified that he treated them all, and especially Bao Luong, to a sumptuous feast.

After four days the boat arrived in Hong Kong. A flotilla of small boats, sampans, sailboats, and even round boats put out to bring the passengers ashore. Bao Luong was taken aback when she saw women come aboard to unload cargo. Their hair was disheveled, their faces streaked with dirt, and their clothes were soaked with sweat. All the passengers except the six stowaways disembarked. Finally, Fatso came to fetch them and guided them onto a sampan; when they disembarked, he led them on a tour of Hong Kong. Bao Luong was fascinated, not by the fashionable cheongsams on display but by women in military uniforms and short hair. They carried a shotgun on their shoulder; at their hip was a sword. To Bao Luong they seemed ready to fight off anyone who dared try to steal their country. They were the embodiment of her secret aspirations: in a country where only male children were recorded in family genealogies and women had traditionally hobbled about on bound feet, young women were now able to participate in revolution. Whether at the post office, a school, a hospital, a pharmacy, Bao Luong thought she could discern the presence of women. She reflected with sadness that education was still considered unnecessary for women in her own country, where a woman might, at best, aspire to be an elementary school teacher or a secretary. She blamed this state of affairs not on Vietnamese tradition, which forbade women to take the civil service exams, but on colonial rule, which made little provision for general education.

Halfway through the tour, Fatso introduced the group to another man whom he called A Suc, then made his farewells. A Suc took them up on a sightseeing tour to Hong Kong Peak and to the Flagpole. Afterward, they rented rooms and bought food for their meal. While her companions were still resting, Bao Luong decided to explore on her own. On this walk she gained a totally different impression of Hong Kong from the one she had formed when looking at the young women in their snappy uniforms. The sight of dire poverty alongside unfamiliar luxury made her realize that the 1911 revolution led by Sun Yat-sen had not solved all the problems of Chinese society. At street corners child beggars with stick-thin limbs and haggard faces cried pathetically; old people in tattered rags dragged themselves along sidewalks, their voices full of tears. What was the use of revolution if it could not bring peace, enough food, and warm clothes to its people? Lost in these unsettling reflections, Bao Luong was surprised when Hoai Nghia came running after her and scolded her for having gone out on her own. He was soon joined by the rest of the group. "Hurry up, the boat is about to leave."

They left for Guangzhou at four in the afternoon. Along the way the passengers had to produce their papers five times. As she watched men and women carrying water past the bare-branched trees of late autumn, Bao Luong asked Hoai Nghia why there was still so much misery after the triumph of the Chinese revolution. Hoai Nghia explained that the fall of the Manchus had rid China of only one layer of oppression, and it still suffered under the Unequal Treaties with the Western powers. Addressing the people's welfare would be a long and arduous process.

"After five days and five nights we arrived in Guangzhou, where no one was awaiting us," Bao Luong told police in 1929. The six Vietnamese straightened their clothes, checked their appearances, and prepared to enter China's wealthiest city. Upon disembarking, they were unnerved by the spectacle of human beings used as beasts of burden. Cart after cart was pulled by a woman with a rope around her neck while three other women pushed the cart from behind. They walked past hordes of prostitutes who trawled for clients openly, advertising their profession by wearing blue dresses. Everywhere the group saw corpses lying by piles of garbage, only perfunctorily covered by mats from which their heads and feet stuck out. People walked past them without even stopping to look, perhaps all too familiar with this sight. And then there were the beggars, their faces streaked with blood, holding on to one another by the shoulder in endless lines, their cries of agony filling the air.

The Vietnamese lost interest in sightseeing. They found their way to Sun Yat-Sen University where students in white uniforms were enjoying recess and playing soccer. A uniformed female guard gave them directions, but they could not find the address they were looking for. Tiredly, they made their way to a park. The five men left Bao Luong on a bench while they went in search of their destination. Her feet swollen inside her unfamiliar shoes and her legs aching from so much walking, Bao Luong gave in to self-pity and fright. Time passed. Night fell. She tried not to recall stories from her childhood about ghosts' coming from behind bushes and snatching the living away. Suddenly, she heard her name whispered. Her companions had made contact with someone else who was using the alias "A Suc," the sixth such person since the morning.

The latest A Suc took them through a maze of streets until they reached an imposing house surrounded by trees. Several young men spilled out onto the stairs and welcomed the stowaways. A Suc introduced the two groups to one another, then made his farewells.

3

Apprentice Revolutionaries

The men living in the house were Korean revolutionaries. Overjoyed at finally meeting them, Truong Phong and Hoai Nghia immediately engaged in a furious written exchange with the Koreans in Chinese. While someone heated leftover food and prepared beds for the newcomers, Kim Huong and Thanh Huyen inspected the house; Van Thong worked out what he would say when his group reached the headquarters of the Revolutionary Youth League the next day. Exhausted by her long day of walking, Bao Luong lay down and went to sleep. Suddenly, a youth in military uniform yanked her mosquito net open and pulled her upright. Her protests died when she saw the dimpled smile on the youth's face and the pierced ears. The youth spoke Vietnamese: "When did you arrive? A Suc told me you had come, and a Korean also came to let me know. He thought that where I live is the headquarters of the Youth League. I know all the places where the Vietnamese revolutionaries live here. I'll take you there tomorrow morning."

The young woman took off her hat, shoes, and uniform and got under the mosquito net with Bao Luong. Overcoming her discomfort at sharing a bed with a stranger, Bao Luong asked her new friend about herself. She went by the name A Tac, the young woman said. Her parents had taken part in the Aid-the-King Movement of 1885–95.[1] After its defeat many of its participants had fled to Siam, which had become a second motherland. They were all determined to fulfill their anticolonial mission, and those who could afford it sent their offspring to the Huangpu Academy in China or to some other country where they could learn how to become revolutionaries and throw off the yoke of colonial rule. A Tac said that she did not belong to the Youth League, but she did not disclose her affiliation to Bao Luong.

A Tac asked whether Bao Luong had thought about the issue of sex. Bao Luong, understanding sex to mean marriage, rebelled at the idea that she had joined the revolution in order to find a husband. But A Tac explained that activists, who were mostly men, were divided in their opinions regarding the presence in their ranks of unmarried women like themselves. Some considered that revolutionaries were ordinary people who ate and loved like everyone else; like other men, they wanted to dominate and possess, and this would lead to trouble. Women should get married as soon as possible to resolve their status, putting themselves out of reach. Others countered that women had joined the revolution precisely because they detested oppression. If they were forced into marriage, what meaning would emancipation have for them? Revolution involved the transformation of individuals' mentality as well as the mentality of society at large. Men must stop harassing women, behaving discourteously, or exploiting them emotionally. Women, for their part, must not engage in flirtatious behavior or get involved in promiscuous affairs. If men and women of goodwill could not exercise self-control, how could they hope to achieve great things? A Tac, who revealed that she was twenty, had benefited from this second argument and had so far managed to avoid marriage and children.

When morning came, A Tac accompanied the group to the headquarters of the Revolutionary Youth League. As they walked through an iron gate into a lane, she said: "You're getting to the headquarters of the Youth League. A man named Tran is in charge there. All the names are false, by the way. Don't give in to curiosity; don't ask for real names. Bao Luong, you will probably forget me after you meet Duc and Thuan, the two beautiful and kind female members of the Youth League. Remember: ideal and reality are two different things. You men: when you play soccer, it will be in the yard next to the headquarters of the Guomindang. If you get lost, it will be easy to ask for directions." A Tac introduced the group to Tran; then, after more explanations and words of welcome had been exchanged, she left.[2]

The man named Tran took down the name, profession, and family status of each newcomer and filled out a "file" for each.[3] Then he led the men away, leaving Bao Luong alone to look at her surroundings. The headquarters had two stories. The first floor included the room where Bao Luong stood; it contained a blackboard, chairs, and benches. Beyond were two rooms, and in the back was a kitchen. Bao Luong looked up and saw two women gazing down at her from the landing. One was short and round; the other was of medium height. They looked to be about twenty-one or twenty-two. The short one was named Duc and the taller one was named Thuan. Duc and Thuan inquired about her trip. Bao Luong was about to tell them in detail, when she remembered that she needed to be cautious and said merely that she had arrived the previous evening and had had an uneventful trip. More people arrived and were introduced: "This is Little Thong and this is Trong; he's ten and he still wets his bed."

[*Duc was Ly Phuong Duc, and Little Thong was Ly Tri Thong, her brother. They*

FIGURE 3. Head-
quarters of the
Revolutionary
Youth League, 13
Wenming Street,
Guangzhou.
Museum of the
Revolution, Hanoi.

*and their adopted sister, Ly Ung Thuan, had been brought to Guangzhou in 1920
from Siam, where their father had fled after the failure of the Aid-the-King Movement in 1895. Hong Son (1899–1932) and Ho Tung Mau (1896–1951), two of the
founders of the Revolutionary Youth League, had brought the children to Guangzhou.[4]
Bao Luong noticed that Duc and Thuan not only wore Chinese clothing, they spoke
with a Chinese accent. This was not surprising since they had been in Guangzhou since
1920. A fourth child, Ly Tu Trong, who also was adopted, had arrived later, either in
1923 or 1925. Ly Tu Trong was thirteen in 1927, not ten as Bao Luong records in her
memoir, though she makes him sound like a precocious child.]*

Another group of recruits was expected soon, so the training program was de-

layed. In the meantime the residents of the house were expected to take turns doing household chores in teams of two. Unused to the cold, Bao Luong shivered every
time she had to use the ice-cold water, and Hoai Nghia would admonish her: "If
you want to oppose the French, you must be able to deal with cold." Bao Luong eventually acquired clothes that made her look like a Chinese woman; it was a great im-
provement over her previous disguise featuring cut-off trousers, sleeves that were
too long, and shoes whose soles flapped about. Hoai Nghia even secured a jacket
for her. Thus equipped, Bao Luong was ready for some sightseeing.

Thuan proposed to go to hear Wang Jingwei, a prominent political figure and a
rival of Chiang Kai-shek's for the leadership of the Guomindang, and He Xiangning, whose late husband, Liao Zhongkai, had been the architect of the United Front
formed by the Guomindang and the Chinese Communist Party. Bao Luong's father
had told her something about the two speakers, and she was eager to see them in
action. Before they set off on their exploration, Hoai Nghia reminded Bao Luong
to always stick by Duc and Thuan. The three women joined a huge crowd waiting
to hear these two famous figures but could not see or hear much amid the sea of
people and banners and the noise of applause. Bao Luong was determined to take
a look at He Xiangning, whose courage when her husband was assassinated in 1925
had made a great impression on Bao Luong. She moved toward the stage, abandoning Duc and Thuan by the gate. Bao Luong could not understand a word of what
He Xiangning said, as the little Chinese Bao Luong had learned at home was the
vocabulary for food and domestic affairs. She decided not to wait for Wang Jingwei and made her way toward the exit behind the stage, opposite the gate where
she had left her two friends.

After a long walk Bao Luong reached a hill where a crowd had gathered. As she
moved closer, she understood why Duc and Thuan had warned her not to go off on
her own. At the foot of the hill was a row of spikes. A covered truck arrived and
disgorged fifteen prisoners who were led to the spikes, to which each was firmly
tied. Some men stood impassively, others sported a defiant smirk and even whis-
tled. After the prisoners were blindfolded, a firing squad loosed a volley of bullets.
When the condemned men stopped twitching, other prisoners untied them, piled
the corpses onto a cart, and took them away.

Since she arrived in Guangzhou, Bao Luong's dream of postcolonial prosperity
had been colliding with the realities of life in postrevolutionary China. She had seen
children of five or six stick their hands into dishwashing water to get a drink; she
had seen them rummage for bones in piles of garbage, then chew whatever meat
was left. She understood then that independence would be meaningless if it was
not also accompanied by social revolution. Haunted by the scene she had just witnessed, Bao Luong wondered how it applied to her own country's situation. She wondered whether killing political opponents was acceptable and whether it was right
for a new government to eliminate the remnants of the party that had preceded it

in power. She concluded that it was necessary to destroy those who would undermine revolutionaries' efforts to transform society. She should be willing to mete out violence and also endure it.

By now she had walked to the edge of another crowd. Standing on a chair was a man younger than twenty who directed a stream of impassioned words at his audience. His listeners were street hawkers in rags who seemed fearful and furtive. A smile occasionally broke their impassive mien, but they did not applaud. Bao Luong had just managed to insert herself among them when a shot rang out, and the speaker toppled from the chair, dead. The crowd dispersed in panic, but Bao Luong, fearing more shots might be fired at the fleeing hawkers, decided to stay where she was. Shaken, she sat down on a bench a short distance away, reflecting that if such a murder had been committed in Vietnam, a swarm of police would have been on the spot immediately. They would have detained bystanders, cordoned off the street, taken away the corpse, and covertly observed those who came to see what had happened. Here in Guangzhou the corpse was left where it fell, undisturbed and neglected.

The sun was going down. Bao Luong made her way back to the gate she had entered. The once-packed arena was now empty; only chairs remained. Bao Luong sat beneath a tree and continued her musings about revolutionary violence. Suddenly, Hoai Nghia and Truong Phong arrived, scolding her soundly for going off on her own.

· · ·

More people now resided in the house, so they took their meals in two separate groups. Bao Luong ate with Tran and the Ly family: Duc, Thuan, little Thong, and Trong. They also went out together on walks or just stayed indoors and gossiped. The training session could not start because Ho Tung Mau, who went by the nickname of "Old Luong," had not returned from his travels. One of the newly arrived men predicted that the training they were about to receive was not going to be very good "because the person who is a good teacher is gone."

[*"The person who is a good teacher" was Ho Chi Minh, who had fled to Hong Kong in April 1927 to avoid being arrested by the Guomindang when the United Front broke down.*][5]

Bao Luong, who admitted to not knowing much about Ho Chi Minh, was not convinced that his absence was such a blow to the league. Little Thong volunteered to relate the origins of the Revolutionary Youth League in order to explain Ho's importance. The next day Little Thong led the new recruits into a small park that held a temple to Ma Yuan, the general who had defeated the Trung sisters in 43 C.E. in the first recorded Vietnamese uprising against Chinese domination. Thong and the recruits crossed the river to a Tang-era monastery and made their way up the hill. They walked to the bridge and looked across the Pearl River toward Shamian Island, site of the French concession. Then Little Thong launched into his account:

On June 19, 1924, Vietnamese learned that the patriot Pham Hong Thai had thrown himself to his death in the Pearl River. A native of Nghe An in central Vietnam, he had been in Siam for three months before he arrived in Guangzhou. He heard that the governor-general of French Indochina, Martial Merlin, was on his way to Japan. Although Merlin's movements were kept secret, Vietnamese expatriates in Shanghai and Guangzhou learned his itinerary. He was expected to stop in Hong Kong and then Guangzhou. Activists in the expatriate community had long plotted to undermine the aura of invincibility of the colonial government. Pham Hong Thai volunteered to "eliminate the bandit."

Bao Luong was familiar with the story. Hong Son (who would help found the Revolutionary Youth League the following year and was now married to Ly Phuong Duc) had rowed Pham Hong Thai to the Victoria Hotel in Shamian where Merlin was attending a reception. Pham Hong Thai, dressed in formal clothes, penetrated the hotel and threw a grenade at the table where Merlin sat. Merlin escaped, but the director of a hospital and the head of a bank and his wife were killed. Pham Hong Thai ran out. Police immediately surrounded the hotel. Pham Hong Thai could not get back to the sampan without revealing that he had an accomplice and chose to throw himself into the river. Because the Vietnamese were in the good graces of Sun Yat-sen, Hu Han-min, the governor of Guangdong, refused French requests to expel all Vietnamese expatriates and demands for reparations on the grounds that the assassination attempt had occurred in the French concession, not on Chinese soil . He even gave the Vietnamese three thousand yuan to bury Pham Hong Thai and erect a monument to him on Huanghuagang, facing the monument to the martyrs of the 1911 revolution.

Little Thong left for another day the rest of his history of the beginnings of the Revolutionary Youth League. Bao Luong's group had reached Huangpu Academy and stood looking in from the outside. After the assassination attempt, the scholar Phan Boi Chau and other expatriates had contacted Chiang Kai-shek and Li Jishen, the vice president of the Huangpu Military Academy, and had obtained permission to send Vietnamese to the newly opened academy. Ly Tri Thong, who was enrolled there, mentioned that many other Vietnamese were also cadets at the academy. Two cadets who had already graduated, Hoang and (Truong Quang) Ngo, continued to work at Huangpu. Ngo in particular had attained high rank and was free to come and go, while other cadets were subjected to the strict discipline of the academy.

. . .

Thirteen-year-old Ly Tu Trong liked to needle his sisters. He teased Thuan, who was self-conscious about her relationship with the much older Ho Tung Mau: "Bao Luong, I'm going to tell you something really interesting. Thuan's lover is coming back soon. . . . Old Luong is very good at carrying people. He carried Thuan all the way from Siam to make her his wife."

Ho Tung Mau indeed came back, and finally the day arrived when Tran distributed pens and paper as well as a pair of socks to each person and informed the group: "Classes begin tomorrow." The following day was a Sunday. The group got up early and cleaned the house. It was cold even with the doors and windows closed. Dew still clung to the slates on the roof. The mountains in the distance were hardly visible through the mist. The welcome scent of jasmine tea filled the air. Trainees from the Huangpu Academy and representatives from various political parties came to lend their presence to the opening ceremony for this new training session.

Tran took up the role of master of ceremonies and asked that a chairman be elected. Lam Duc Thu, who went by the nickname of Fat Truong (Truong *map*), won the election. He was an imposing man and was always well dressed. He was a great orator; Bao Luong recalled that he had a big voice and spoke "in a loud voice that at times rose shrilly and at others rang out like hammer blows." Bao Luong had been assigned to a table in front, but, fearful of both Thu's physique and voice, she moved to the back of the room. Lam Duc Thu made an impassioned speech in an urgent voice, but Bao Luong was not won over. He was followed by "Old Luong," who was his opposite in both appearance and voice. Ho Tung Mau was gaunt and always wore a black Chinese outfit. He was not eloquent like Lam Duc Thu but spoke calmly. He made Bao Luong see that nothing was more precious than freedom; he also made her believe that only one path was possible for anyone who held dear the virtues of loyalty, filial piety, virtue, and chastity: revolution. The next speaker was a man who wore the uniform of a Huangpu Academy cadet. He pointed to his gun and his sword, declaring himself ready to sacrifice his life for the righteous cause of national freedom. Bao Luong seems to have found his performance rather showy, although she appreciated the ritual opening of the training session.

Classes began in earnest the following day with twenty-seven trainees. Bao Luong thought that some would be sent to Siam or perhaps other countries. Lectures were held in the morning and afternoon every day except Sunday, which was reserved for free discussion. Anyone who wanted to discuss a particular topic would write it on the blackboard. Bao Luong conscientiously read and reviewed materials with some friends in the evening, while other students relaxed by singing and playing the guitar. Although the ranks of the regular instructors were thin because some had been arrested and others had fled, Bao Luong thought the training session, featuring Russian, Indian, Korean, Chinese, and Vietnamese lecturers, was effective.

[Although she does not say so in her memoir, Bao Luong may have been disappointed by the limited curriculum: "During my studies I was taught the history of France and of Vietnam, comparing the two; I was also taught the theory of the Revolutionary Youth League. I asked to learn French and English but was told that I would be learning only Chinese and, anyway, I would not be staying long in Guangzhou."][6]

The "school" produced a newspaper, *Thanh Nien* (Youth). Everyone had to write for the journal. Everything had to serve the cause. Every piece of writing was an act of propaganda. Bao Luong was in charge of the poetry section, but she also tried her hand at other types of articles. Tran used a gelatin-based photographic printing process to make copies of the paper, and Little Thong took away the copies for distribution. Many were sent to Siam, and from there they made their way into Vietnam.

Two days into the training session, Thanh Huyen, one of the men who had come to Guangzhou with Bao Luong, asked Lam Duc Thu, who was presiding, "Is this the headquarters of Phan Boi Chau?" Upon being informed that it was not, Thanh Huyen declared that he wanted to leave. He was told he would have to wait until the next boat. Hoai Nghia took Bao Luong aside and whispered, "I'm so embarrassed by Thanh Huyen! He is so feudal in his worship of personality. Whoever introduced him deserves to be pulverized into little pieces!" That evening Thanh Huyen argued that the character of the leader was the most important factor in revolution. Ly Tu Trong got up to argue that the organization was more important than its leader. To rely on a leader was sheer laziness. Members of an organization should not only support but also monitor one another; anyone who was found to be deficient would be eliminated. Bested by a thirteen-year old, Thanh Huyen agreed to stay on.

During the first month the recruits learned about the origins of various ideologies, their evolution, and their results. After each session the organizers solicited written comments from the recruits to guide adjustments to the curriculum. Nothing was said openly yet, but the recruits understood that all they had been learning led to only one possible conclusion: that socialist revolution was the only way to free humankind from slavery. The day finally came when the organizing committee asked each trainee to select an ideology. Some chose the Three People's Principle of Sun Yat-sen; others, nationalism; still others, revolution. Most raised their hands and declared they were for socialism. Kim Huong selected anarchism: "There's a contradiction between not wanting to be oppressed and accepting a government because, if there is a government, then there are laws. And laws are based on punishment and penalties; they are unjust and biased and reinforce the power of certain groups."

When Thanh Huyen declared his preference for monarchism, the group gasped. Hoai Nghia, who was presiding, looked like he was ready to jump up and down in frustration. Thanh Huyen hastened to explain: "The reason I choose monarchism is that the king is the only person who has the authority to make decisions, so he can decide quickly. He needs only to promulgate an order, and the whole country will implement it. This is how King Tran Nhan Tong and Tran Hung Dao defeated the Mongols [in 1285]; this is how the Ly king, together with Ly Thuong Kiet, repulsed the Chinese [in 1076] and sowed terror among the Chams [in 1069]. It was monarchism without despotism. This is why the Tran king held the Dien Hong conference to ask for the advice of the common people [about whether to surrender to the Mongols]. I studied the classics: I know that in the era of Yao and Shun or of the Duke of Zhou, the people [of China] enjoyed peace. They were better off under their rule than under any system of government since. What is important is the people rather than the specific political system."

Truong Phong slowly got up and advocated democracy, invoking many instances from Vietnamese history in which rulers had abused their power. "Bad rulers are more common than good ones," he argued. "How many are like Yao and Shun, and how many are like Zhouwang [the last of the Shang dynasty rulers] or Qin Shihuang?" One by one trainees rose to defend the ideology they had adopted. Hoai Nghia was irritated that, of the six recruits he had brought to Guangzhou, three were advocating different ideologies, but as presiding chair he was not allowed to take part in the proceedings. He looked meaningfully at Bao Luong, who had remained silent despite Ly Tu Trong's urgings of the previous day: "Practice how to speak in public." He had encouraged her to go to the rooftop in the evening to practice. Finally, she could not avoid speaking up. Bao Luong started with questions. How was the anarchist platform going to be implemented? Why did Thanh Huyen think that monarchism was the best political system when it had been applied to Vietnam for so many centuries with disastrous results? For her part she advocated pursuing democratic nationalism as a first stage. A heated discussion ensued. Ho Tung Mau interrupted to ask, "Could Bao Luong envision a situation in which Vietnam was independent *[doc lap]* but alone in the world, without allies, like a tree in the middle of rice fields?" Bao Luong's negative reply provoked accusations from the other trainees that she did not know what she was saying. *Doc lap* was a neologism created to introduce the concept of independence that literally meant "standing alone." She had to explain that national independence did not mean isolation in the international arena.

Someone finally introduced Marxism-Leninism. What would happen if another ideology emerged that was superior to it? Hoai Nghia believed that nothing could be better than Marxism-Leninism: it was the ideology best suited to weak and poor nations. A member of the second group of recruits believed that the different stages of the revolution should be combined in order to reduce the amount of bloodshed necessary at each. At the end of the session the organizing committee took over. Lam Duc Thu, Le Hong Phong, and Truong Quang Ngo from the Huangpu Academy declared that national conditions dictated that the revolution must be waged in two stages. But the goal was to eradicate social inequalities according to socialist principles.

. . .

Halfway through the training session, Ly Tu Trong fell sick. Although his sisters, Duc and Thuan, and Lam Duc Thu's wife tended to him, Bao Luong thought that their nursing was somewhat perfunctory and that he missed a mother's touch, so she took over much of his care. She would pick him up and bring him downstairs to sit in the courtyard, covered in a blanket. During this time Bao Luong picked up a great deal of information from the boy. Mischievous and demanding but also highly articulate and intelligent, Trong was acutely aware of what went on around him. He shared with Bao Luong what he knew of the Youth League. Bao Luong learned that the boy had been brought from Siam to Guangzhou by Ho Chi Minh, whom the child knew by one of his aliases, Comrade Vuong Son Nhi. Ly Tu Trong missed Ho Chi Minh very much; he spoke of the care the older man used to show to newly arrived recruits and illustrated what he meant by relating the experience of Bao Luong's own cousin. Tran Truong had come to Guangzhou in the company of Dang van Sam and Bui van Them. Trong described how Ho Chi Minh had taken over the household chores, cooking, cleaning, and doing the laundry, so that Truong and his companions would have more time to study. When they found out that Ho was also their instructor, they were so full of admiration that they worked harder for him than for other lecturers. Other leaders scolded them for indulging in the cult of personality and scolded Ho Chi Minh for appearing to want to monopolize leadership.

Bao Luong asked Ly Tu Trong for information about Ho Chi Minh's wife. According to the boy, she was the younger sister of Lam Duc Thu's wife. She had not been able to follow her husband when he fled from the Guomindang to Hong Kong in April, but she still came to the league's headquarters. Nguyen Bao Toan confirmed to Bao Luong that Ho's wife was the younger sister (em ruot) of Lam Duc Thu's wife and added that while the older sister was boastful, Ho's wife was more modest and totally dedicated to supporting the Revolutionary Youth League.

[Ly Tu Trong's and Nguyen Bao Toan's information about Ho Chi Minh's wife conflicts with the report made to the Sûreté by Ly Phuong Duc's second husband after their arrest in 1931. According to Duc's husband, Tang Tuyet Minh was the daughter of a rich merchant and his concubine. Lam Duc Thu's wife introduced Tang Tuyet Minh to Ho, and they married on October 18, 1926.]

Once Ly Tu Trong recovered, he moved to another place; he seemed to move frequently from one set of living quarters to another and to join different cells. But Bao Luong soon fell ill. For five days she had a high fever and was only half-conscious. One day she found herself lying under the bed without any knowledge of how she had gotten there. Once her fever abated, she discovered a lump on her breast. Ly Tu Trong came back to accompany her to the hospital, where she had surgery, which was performed without anesthetic while she was tied down to a chair. She was discharged immediately after the tumor was removed but had to return every day for five days to have her bandages changed. Between the two of them, Bao Luong and Ly Tu Trong had little money, and what they might have used for tram fare they spent on persimmons, of which Trong was inordinately fond. The walks to and from the hospital were long, painful, and halting for Bao Luong. They would stop several times on the way so that she could rest. Each time Trong would get up on a makeshift stage to make a speech while Bao Luong sat on a bench, with her heart in her mouth, fearful that he might be killed by sniper fire.

. . .

Ly Tu Trong had told Bao Luong that Nguyen Bao Toan was in love with her. She had scoffed. But when she fell ill, Nguyen Bao Toan complained to Duc and Thuan that they were not taking proper care of her. Thuan had smirked. Now that Bao Luong was better, Toan suggested that he and she take a walk in the evening. When he heard of the plan, Hoai Nghia laughed: "Are you getting engaged?"

The scene could not have been more romantic. The moon was full, and from the courtyard Bao Luong could hear the plangent tones of a stringed instrument being played by another trainee. Nguyen Bao Toan opened his heart to Bao Luong: "When we met in Saigon, I was already interested in you. At the time I had great respect for you, since both your father and your cousin vouched for your commitment to the revolution. Now that we've been here for some time, I must tell you that I love you." Toan recognized that he had nothing to offer a woman since he was always on the move as the courier of the Youth League. Bao Luong demurred. She told him that she could not enter into any commitment since she would be returning home at the end of the training session. "Revolutionaries do not live long," said Toan. "But if I were to escape death and reach my goal, would you remember this night?" Bao Luong replied: "I promise, so as to give you hope, a hope that will enable you to avoid danger and to survive by whatever means, as long as it does not mean allowing yourself to be bought by the enemy and acting as spy in order to pay for an easy life. I am proud that you love me, but we must put our love in the service of our cause. Although we may not hope to meet again, let's not be afraid of separation. Our generation cannot afford to think of love. The promise we must make is not of marriage but of commitment to the revolution." Nguyen Bao Toan said that he was not discouraged. As long as she was not in love with anyone else, he could nurture the hope that one day she would return his love. Suddenly, he noticed that Duc, Thuan, and many others were gazing down at them. Someone was playing music. He stopped suddenly and laughingly proposed a poetry-writing session.

. . .

On several occasions Bao Luong had been reproached for her excessive prudery. One day Thuan returned to the subject of Bao Luong's unmarried status: "Our male colleagues have commented that you still have very feudal ideas. What do you have to be shy about? When you get back home, you will have to deal with many difficulties. You need to know that in this case, 'dealing with' means pretending. It's quite a skill. If you indulge in misplaced bashfulness, you'll ruin everything." Bao Luong, however, thought that revolution was incompatible with family life. And as long as marriage was out of the question, she needed to be circumspect in her behavior so as to safeguard her reputation and not give rise to unfounded hopes or, worse, harassment.

[Bao Luong was not the only woman who delayed marriage in the cause of revolution. In 1930 the Sûreté reported: "Some [Youth League] cells even include female members. Sometimes, these form special groups which then take up the appearance of 'societies for domestic education' or 'weaving studios.' Abandoning marriage in order to devote all their energies to the Great Cause, young women take up various tasks, open bookshops and little stores which often serve as political offices."][7]

The following evening Duc took her aside and asked Bao Luong to accompany her. Bao Luong happily agreed, thinking she would have a friend on the voyage home. Duc disabused her: "No, I'm going into the hospital." Bao Luong was taken aback. She had thought that Duc, who wore loose Chinese outfits, was merely fat. She had not guessed that Duc was pregnant. Her bewilderment, her sense of disappointment, must have been obvious, for Duc took Bao Luong's hand in hers and confided: "You are so much like me when I was eighteen. When I arrived here [from Siam in 1920], together with Thuan and Little Thong, I was very proud. I was committed to the revolution. I did not want to be married, to be held back by a sick husband and delicate children. But reality made it impossible to live inside my dreams. Think about it. Every man and woman who joins the revolution wants to remain single. This alone is enough to arouse suspicion; it is something that they must deal with if they want to be effective. For example, if an unmarried woman wants to carry out her mission among peasants, can she live on her own in a hut by a rice field without a husband? Not only will she be the target of male villagers' attentions and a cause of trouble among them, but she will not be able to welcome [male] friends into her home. So she will need to pretend to be married. She'll have to choose someone to play the role. And perhaps some day that man will fall in love for real. And then the two may have a falling-out and get into even more trouble as a result. Wouldn't it be better if you chose a spouse and settled your marital situation so that the group would not have to worry about you? Bao Luong, you are inexperienced. But women are the seeds of instant success and also instant failure. This is why Thuan and I got married early, and the group no longer has to be concerned about our situation."[8]

Bao Luong replied, "Everything has its pros and cons. Take your case, Duc: your husband [Hong Son] is in jail, and you are soon going to have a child. Won't you be torn in different directions?"

"When waging revolution," Duc told her, "if you don't die, you end up in prison. But having children is a woman's sacred mission. Having children won't get in the way. Is there anything that would prevent a woman from bringing her child along while engaging in propaganda? In fact, that may help her get past Sûreté agents more easily."

Three days after giving birth Duc moved to the house of Lam Duc Thu, whose wife was good at nursing. As Bao Luong was coping with the bedding for the new baby, Thuan exclaimed, "Sister Vuong [Ho Chi Minh's wife] has come to see Duc!" Bao Luong looked up to see a young woman in her twenties. She was fair-skinned and slim; she wore a striped blouse over a skirt. Smilingly, she approached the bed, stroked Duc's forehead, and caressed the baby's head.

Bao Luong had heard a great deal about Ho Chi Minh, the revolutionary who worked ceaselessly in exile, was in and out of jail, and dreamed of pacifying the world through socialism. She wanted to know more about him, his personality and his character, through observing the woman whom he had married. Alas, although Bao Luong and Ho's wife got to sit next to each other, they were separated by language. Bao Luong asked Thuan to translate for her. Thuan agreed but cautioned her not to ask too many questions. Whatever Thuan asked on Bao Luong's behalf elicited answers that, although produced with a friendly smile, were not revealing.

"Sister Vuong says she is very happy to meet another comrade from her husband's country; she hopes to meet many more. In the international revolution, all will be as brothers and sisters. She hopes that, when that time comes, her husband will take her on a visit to his country."

Through Thuan, Bao Luong asked whether the Chinese woman had plans to follow her husband to Russia, where she thought he had gone.

Ho's wife replied, "There is no such plan. The more I miss him, the more involved I am in revolutionary activities. If I were to follow him, I would only interfere with his mission."

"How many children do you have?"

Ho's wife smiled, stuck her head inside the mosquito net, nodded, and said: "I have a daughter." Then she smiled brightly again.

"Has Comrade Vuong told you when he will return?"

Tang Tuyet Minh sighed and clasped her hands together. Thuan translated: "Sister Vuong wants to tell you that revolutionaries never tell their wives when they will return by their side for good. Such wives would no longer be the wives of revolutionaries."[9]

Just then Lam Duc Thu's wife called everyone in to eat. Bao Luong extended her hand; Sister Vuong patted her affectionately. That was the end of the exchange.

This was the second time that Bao Luong had been invited to eat at Lam Duc Thu's house and the second time that a group picture was taken. As before, Bao Luong thought that Lam Duc Thu was living large. He and his wife had a beautiful house, ate well, and wore nice clothes. He was able to support many revolutionary trainees. Under the cover of absolute secrecy, Thuan had told Bao Luong that Lam Duc Thu was good at diplomacy. He had gained the confidence of the government of Guangzhou and had been given a fairly important position. As a consequence he was able to secure the early release of trainees who happened to get arrested.

[Either from lack of curiosity or because she had been warned not to delve into her colleagues' background, Bao Luong never sought to discover the roots of her dislike for Lam Duc Thu and the sources of his affluence or to assess his reliability as a revolutionary. But the Sûreté used some of the pictures he took to identify enemies of the French colonial regime.]

. . .

Training continued. The recruits were taught the practicalities of clandestine work. Then came the day when some would be initiated into the "group." Huangpu Academy cadets attended the solemn ceremony. The recruits were asked to state in writing whether they agreed to join the group. Then it was time for oaths and speeches. The recruits were overcome with emotion. To Bao Luong it was like a wedding ceremony in which she committed herself to the revolutionary cause. It reinforced her resolve to remain single. The ceremony over, the older recruits, Duc, Thuan, Trong, and a few others, came over and embraced them. The group then walked over to the tomb of Pham Hong Thai and stood in a single row. Lam Duc Thu and Thuan had brought along incense sticks and matches. Thu lit the incense sticks and said aloud: "Pham Hong Thai, be content; be at ease in your tomb. We will emulate you and expel the foreign invaders from our land." Tran said, "We do not believe in superstition. But an oath sworn before a tomb is an oath that cannot be taken back. Today marks the day when we will be as close to one another as limbs of the body. Today is the day when we officially engage ourselves on the same path."

The ceremony over, the group ambled over to the Martyrs' Memorial. Once again Bao Luong was overwhelmed by the solemnity of the occasion and the feeling that she had chosen a path that would demand great sacrifices of her.

[The oath that each had to swear to gain admission to the Youth League read: "This day, this month ____, I, named ____, admitted as member of the Party swear: 1) To sacrifice my family, my life, my property, and my own initiatives to wage revolution; 2) to preserve absolute secrecy about all the business of the party and to work for its prosperity; 3) to conform to orders and regulations of the party and to be liable to the death penalty if I perjure myself; not to join any other party."[10]

This was the usual prelude to returning home, as the French Sûreté discovered: "Tran Ngoc Que, aka Danh, declared on August 6, 1929, that [Nguyen van Thinh] had arranged for his trip to Guangzhou where he had received revolutionary training and that one week before his return to Cochinchina, he had sworn an oath on the Pham Hong Thai marker; afterward, he had returned in the company of Hoai Nghia, Bao Luong, and Phong."][11]

. . .

Bao Luong's time in Guangzhou was coming to an end. Duc and Thuan were heatedly discussing a favorite topic: the emancipation of women. "Let's abolish the feudal system and outmoded customs that have tied down women for thousands of years. The Three Submissions and the Four Virtues promote our exploitation and keep us in inferior positions." Bao Luong was not interested. She was already looking forward to going home. She left in the middle of the animated discussion to walk toward the headquarters of the Guomindang. Thuan hurried after her and tried to shake her out of the melancholy Bao Luong felt at the prospect of leaving her friends. One day Bao Luong learned that she would be leaving that very night. Nguyen Bao Toan, who could not go on the same trip, put her into the hands of Hoai Nghia. Their farewells were bittersweet. Bao Luong was touched by Toan's devotion. She was not in love with him, but she considered him a good friend.

That night Duc, Thuan, Trong, and Bao Luong stayed up and exchanged gifts. Duc gave Bao Luong a top, Thuan a skirt, and Trong a pen; Bao Luong only had a hair comb to give them. Duc and Thuan vowed that they would be going home too, eventually. When Bao Luong pointed out that their short hair and Chinese accents would make them stand out, they joked that they would open Chinese convenience stores. The next day Bao Luong walked around the house a last time. She looked at the pile of notebooks in which were written questions and answers and notes from readings. She flipped through a stack of issues of *Youth*. She took a last look at the messages that had been sent clandestinely from Vietnam, written in code and inserted in newspapers. She absorbed memories and said her good-byes to this place where she had lived for several months, made good friends, and had been shown the path she would be following. She then walked to the end of the street where Lam Duc Thu was hurrying the travelers. Two men had been added to the original group of six. Bao Luong once again disguised herself as a man.

It was still dark when they reached Hong Kong and transferred to the boat that would take them home. This time the group was lodged together with a cargo of ginseng. The new A Suc had given money to the wrong staff person so they were late getting food. The last stage of the voyage was spent at the very bottom of the boat, in a puddle of water. They were tense with anticipation. They had been gone for several months. How would they explain their absence to their families and neighbors? But when they heard Vietnamese being spoken on the quay, they forgot their discomfort in their joy at being back in their own country.

Bao Luong didn't notice when her companions got off the boat, leaving her alone in the middle of water. Eventually, A Suc arrived with a set of Chinese clothing for her to wear. When she went on deck, the sun was shining brightly. A group of women in cheongsams was getting ready to disembark. A woman wearing an outfit in the same color as Bao Luong's took her hand. A Suc gestured for Bao Luong to go with her. The women went into a restaurant and began talking animatedly, seemingly oblivious to Bao Luong. After about half an hour a man in a black Chinese outfit and a felt hat sidled up to her. She looked at him fixedly and then realized how careful the arrangements for her travel had been: it was her cousin Tran Truong. She followed him to a secluded spot where she could change back into the clothing of a young Vietnamese woman.

[*"I fell ill," she would declare to the police, "and did not return to Saigon until November in the company of Hoai Nghia, Nguyen Hanh Thong (Van Thong), and one other man I did not know."[12] Bao Luong missed by a few weeks the Canton Commune, an armed effort by senior Communists to install a Soviet government that failed after two weeks; in the wake of the commune's collapse two key figures in her early life were imprisoned for several months. Nguyen Bao Toan and Lang, the man who would be the victim of the Barbier Street murder.*]

4

Vignettes from the Revolution

Upon her return Bao Luong rejoined her old cell. It included Ton Duc Thang, her cousin Tran Truong, and Do Dinh Tho, the man who had checked her out in Phuoc Long together with Nguyen Bao Toan. After settling back in, she went home to Phuoc Long. Her first task was to persuade her family to support her activities. This proved easy. Her mother assured her that she would deal with their neighbors' curiosity. Her father gave her money and cooperated with Van Thong, who had returned home on the same trip, in organizing local activities.

On the way back to Saigon, Bao Luong wracked her brain to find a way to begin her new revolutionary activities. She settled on joining a women's clothing boutique in Dakao, then a suburb of Saigon. From there she could make new acquaintances and try to recruit them. When Bao Luong returned to Saigon, however, she was met by Ngo Thiem at the train station. Thiem, whom she had met before leaving for Guangzhou, acted as liaison with the Central Committee. He was her age (although she did not know it at the time) and hailed from central Vietnam, as did two-thirds of Youth League activists in the South. Accompanying Thiem were two older men and two girls whom he said she should accompany. Her original plans thus delayed, she traveled with the two girls, Ngoc Anh and Ngoc Tho; their father, Tran van Hoai, who was a village headman (*huong truong*); and their Chinese teacher, Mr. Tu, who hailed from Hoi An in central Vietnam.[1] Their destination was Cho Gao, a town whose name meant Rice Market and that was located on a major canal.

Bao Luong felt lucky that her first assignment was with Headman Hoai, who was already known to her parents as a great admirer of Phan Boi Chau's. A small landowner, Headman Hoai had sold land and raised funds for Phan Boi Chau's Vietnam Restoration League when it was founded in 1913. Penetrating Bao Luong's disguise, he assured her that she could stay with his family to whom he introduced her as a relative of Ngo Thiem's wife. Headman Hoai's wife told everybody that Bao Luong was a relative of theirs who had come to Cho Gao to learn martial arts. In fact, girls in Cho Gao often learned both classical Chinese and martial arts. Headman Hoai himself was a teacher and never failed to remind his guests to go out into the courtyard and practice every day.

The first night she spent under his roof, sharing a bed with his daughters, Bao Luong was overcome by a wave of longing for her friends Duc and Thuan, and suddenly she was struck by the realization that Nguyen Bao Toan had not been on hand to welcome her on her return to Saigon. Had he been reprimanded for showing partiality toward her?

[Bao Luong did not know that Toan had been arrested in the wake of the Canton Commune in early December and remained in jail until February 1928.]

The following day Ngoc Tho and Ngoc Anh, who were fourteen and sixteen, respectively, took her on a tour of the various floating markets along the Cho Gao canal. Farther down the canal Ong Van market had a chapter of the Society for the Promotion of Education to which Ngoc Anh belonged; she also had a large circle of acquaintances in that town as well as in other nearby market towns. Bao Luong had been wondering how to approach two male teachers to persuade them to join the Revolutionary Youth League. How could she, an unattached female, make overtures toward either of them? She would be regarded as sexually promiscuous. It turned out that fourteen-year-old Ngoc Tho was enrolled in the school where one of the teachers was employed; to her, then, would fall the task of recruiting the teacher into the league.

Ngoc Tho and Ngoc Anh had not been told much about Bao Luong except that she was related to Ngo Thiem and that her given name was Nam, an alias that she had used in Guangzhou. But one day, after Ngoc Tho found out a little about Bao Luong's political sympathies, she exclaimed, "Come with me tonight!"

"What's happening tonight?"

"The festival of the Trung sisters."[2]

At the time, commemoration of the Trung sisters, who had led a rebellion against Chinese rule in 39 C.E. and had met their death in 43, was not widespread in the South, where the French authorities considered it potentially subversive. Under cover of darkness Bao Luong, Ngoc Anh, and Ngoc Tho made their way through the reeds to the bank of the Cho Gao canal. A small altar was already set, laden with offerings of bananas and oranges, a vase of flowers, and a packet of incense sticks. Ngoc Tho had brought matches, but, to Bao Luong's surprise, she did not light the incense sticks immediately. She told Bao Luong to wait a bit and advised her to hide under bushes. Eventually, four more women arrived; they turned out to have been practicing martial arts behind Headman Hoai's house that very afternoon. Ngoc Tho lit the incense sticks, and the seven women bowed in front of the altar. Ngoc Tho then asked Bao Luong to write a poem to commemorate the occasion; Hoai Nghia had told his family that she was a poet. Bao Luong felt bitter about having to express her admiration for the two national heroines in secrecy. But by night's end she had won over six new recruits, and a sketchy organizational structure had emerged. Ngoc Tho would be in charge of operations in the Ong Van area; one of the martial arts practitioners would work in her hometown of Giong Trom; and Ngoc Anh would supervise women's recruitment in the whole region. The three friends went on to Go Cong, where they enlisted the daughter of a friend of Headman Hoai's. From there they went to Giong Trom, walking past five villages and crossing a river. Amid much laughter and teasing, Ngoc Anh and Ngoc Tho towed Bao Luong, who could not swim, across the river by tying a rope under her armpits.

The person they had come to meet was another friend of Headman Hoai's. Mr. Tram lived in a hut by his rice field, his garden of betel leaves, and a buffalo barn. After exchanging greetings, he called to have mats spread out in the courtyard and proceeded to grill catfish and mudfish to eat with green mangoes and crackers. Before they began to eat, he climbed up a coconut tree and brought down a yellowed piece of paper that he showed to his three guests. It was a poem by Phan Boi Chau. Ngoc Tho, who had the best voice, was asked to read it aloud so that they could imagine Phan Boi Chau himself reciting the poem. "Do you know what the poem says?" Tram asked. "It says that Vietnamese, and especially the young, were feckless and decadent, and they allowed the Six Provinces [of the South] to be lost to the French."

"So what can be done now?" someone asked.

"Well, since Phan Boi Chau is in prison, it's up to Nguyen An Ninh. We have too little talent to be effective leaders and to make a difference," Tram said.

Ngoc Tho countered: "It's better to depend on more than one person [to assume all the responsibilities for the success of our cause]. Should Nguyen An Ninh be arrested again, what would happen then?"

Mr. Tram became thoughtful. He then raised his head and invited the three women to visit him from time to time to teach his daughter and his son to read and write and "to discuss various things." They needed a cover for their visits, and this seemed the most convincing one.

In Cho Gao one had to practice martial arts; in Giong Trom one had to love music. Farmer Tram organized an impromptu performance of vong co. Although her aunt Tran Ngoc Vien was one of its chief promoters, Bao Luong had little knowledge of this new musical genre. Nonetheless, she improvised lyrics for Ngoc Tho to sing that were appropriately full of revolutionary fervor. After they stopped singing, Mr. Tram asked them to write down the words on a piece of paper, which

FIGURE 4. Tran Ngoc Vien, wearing necklace and seated in armchair at center, with Dong Nu Ban troupe. Museum of Women, Ho Chi Minh City.

he then hid together with the poem by Phan Boi Chau in the coconut tree. Ngoc Anh, Ngoc Tho, and Bao Luong made their farewells the next day, confident that they had three excellent new recruits in Mr. Tram and his children.

Bao Luong next traveled to Vinh Kim in response to a summons from Ngoc Vien. Her aunt's barge, which housed her troupe of nearly thirty female *cai luong* performers aged seventeen to twenty-one, was moored in front of the house. Bao Luong immediately plunged into the circle of women sewing costumes for an opera. But Ngoc Vien was eager to come straight to the point. It concerned the wife of Ngoc Vien's younger brother Trieu, an accomplished artist also active in the promotion of *cai luong*. His wife, who also came from a musical family, had once taught at the School for Native Young Ladies, which everyone called Truong Ao Tim after the purple *ao dai* that served as uniform. She loved to discuss current events with her husband's relatives. Still, no one guessed that she wanted to do more than talk. As the women listened to Trieu play his instrument, his wife confided to Bao Luong that she wanted to follow her into "the group." Bao Luong cautioned prudence, especially since Aunt Trieu had young children.[3] Bao Luong also suggested combining forces with one of the actresses in the troupe. On another trip Bao Luong took the two women to Cho Gao to meet Ngoc Anh so that they could be inducted into her cell. The Youth League thus now included members of the opera troupe, which became a vehicle of patriotic propaganda.

. . .

Buoyed by her success, Bao Luong organized the first women's meeting at Do Dinh Tho's house behind Huynh Khuong Ninh School in Saigon. She was proud of the number of recruits and the geographical spread they represented, with women from Cho Gao, Vinh Kim, Giong Trom, Ong Van, and Go Cong. But once the meeting was over, Do Dinh Tho scolded Bao Luong for her imprudence: "Nine or ten young women in one house, that's sure to attract attention. Why did you not invite a whole village while you were at it? I had to let [Tran] Truong and Bui van Them know so they could watch both ends of the street. You'll have to find another meeting place."

Do Dinh Tho, in fact, was taken aback by the extent of Bao Luong's travels; despite his wooden leg, he had traveled several hundred miles, from Phuoc Long to Vinh Kim, as he tried to catch up with her. He wanted to put a proposition to her: to write a column called "Ladies' Sayings" for the newspaper *Than Chung* in his stead. This was one way that Nguyen van Ba, the editor-in-chief of the newspaper and the husband of Bao Luong's aunt Tran Thu Cuu, proposed to support the anticolonial activists. Bao Luong had already agreed to join a tailoring shop and to help a neighbor make candied fruits. She was also thinking of learning enough French to enable her to get a job in another boutique owned by a Frenchwoman, all so she could pursue her recruiting activities. Despite her many plans, Do Dinh Tho nonetheless extracted from Bao Luong a promise to write a column every other day.

Smarting under Tho's criticism, Bao Luong returned to Ton Duc Thang's house and asked him if she'd been wrong to organize all-women cells. This was not something that he could decide on his own, he said, so he brought it up at the biweekly meeting of the league's cells. He and Bao Luong were told that training for admission into the Youth League took place in three stages. The first involved action among the masses of the people, such as organizing demonstrations or commemorative ceremonies. The second stage consisted of organizing members, people who were enthusiastic about activism and who could adhere to discipline. The third concerned comrades who would be the core of the revolutionary movement. In addition to being utterly loyal to the movement, they would have to have a will of iron, not be blinded by ideology, and be ambitious only about bringing happiness to their people and paradise to humankind. There were two types of comrades: first, those who put ideology above everything and would not tolerate any deviation. The second type considered that circumstances demanded ideological flexibility. Ideology needed to be amended to reflect practical reality. No single ideology could apply equally well to all countries and all people.

[It seems that Bao Luong's desire to create all-women groups was approved. Still, these would be made up only of stage one recruits since none had the two mentors required for full league membership. This meant they would not be in actual cells but only in auxiliary associations and would thus not take part in decisions by the league, of which Bao Luong was the only female member.]

According to plan, Bao Luong got a job in the tailoring shop of Mrs. Bay, an acquaintance of Ngoc Anh's who had moved to Saigon. Mrs. Bay's mother had pleaded with Bao Luong to help her daughter adjust to their move. Bao Luong had agreed, but she did not think Mrs. Bay would make a good recruit. She had two young children but no husband. Bao Luong, who was quite old-fashioned despite her advocacy of women's emancipation, was inclined to look askance at Mrs. Bay's unwed motherhood. But the wages came in handy, and the two hours of rest at midday allowed her to write her columns for *Than Chung*. Her other job, making candied fruits, at first held more promise. Mrs. Nam was related to an acquaintance of a man named Phan Xuan Dinh, who belonged to the Youth League. Bao Luong thought she might be able to recruit supporters among the cooks and chefs Mrs. Nam knew. The two women rented a stall on a street corner, and in the evening Bao Luong helped Mrs. Nam make candied fruits from papayas, oranges, mandarins, ginger, gourds, and pineapples. An acquaintance of theirs then took the jars of candy to sell throughout the delta. But it turned out that Mrs. Nam was a fatalist. She believed that one's destiny is preordained and there is no point seeking to change it; hers was simply to cook. She was no help to Bao Luong in bringing more women into the ranks of the revolution.

Bao Luong was more successful among teachers. Phan Xuan Dinh asked Bao Luong to help him win over two young women who belonged to the Tan Viet Revolutionary Party. This was an organization that had begun in central Vietnam but was spreading to Saigon, appealing to the same individuals as the Revolutionary Youth League. That evening, when Phan Xuan Dinh and Bao Luong arrived at the house of Ngo Thiem, they met two young women who taught in a private school in the Thu Thiem–Khanh Hoi area. The men immediately absented themselves, leaving the three women to talk. Already primed by Phan Xuan Dinh, the two teachers, who were eager to make more friends, jumped at Bao Luong's suggestion that they move in with her. They did not realize that they were being surreptitiously drawn into the Youth League. Phan Xuan Dinh was having similar results among men, so the Revolutionary Youth League was able to draw many new members away from Tan Viet.

After recruiting two seamstresses, Bao Luong resigned from Mrs. Bay's shop and looked for another position. She thought of working at the French establishment but needed to learn some of the language first. Ton Duc Thang's wife, Kim Oanh, tutored Bao Luong for three days; Bao Luong then secured an introduction to the shop and was hired. Her task consisted of embroidering flowers onto women's blouses and knitting children's clothes. The shop owner's cook intimated that Bao Luong's working hours, from eight to eleven in the morning and three to five in the afternoon, were so few because the boss did not want her around when the owner and her husband left for work or returned home. The cook also told Bao Luong that when she rested in the afternoon, she should not open her door to anyone. He invited her to take her meals with him, his twelve-year-old son, and the chauffeur. He came from central Vietnam and was bitter at having gone so far from home without prospering and gaining financial independence. He took out his disappointment on his French bosses by cooking sumptuous meals for the servants instead of making them eat leftovers. He charged Bao Luong one piaster per week. Bao Luong, who earned five piasters, thought she had a good deal but also had some qualms about partaking of food that should have been served to the owners.

After she had been at the shop a week, Bao Luong introduced Tran Truong and Bui van Them to her fellow employees. To meet the cook Truong used the pretext of escorting Bao Luong home, while Them, who worked in a garage, spent his siesta time chatting with the chauffeur. Bao Luong would have liked to stay on at this shop because of the ease of moving among cooks and chauffeurs. But one day, as she walked up the stairs to the workroom, she saw the owners standing on the landing holding each other. They were stark naked. Her face afire, Bao Luong hurried down the stairs, pursued by their laughter. The cook tried to dissuade her from leaving: "Don't you know that the Trung sisters were defeated by Ma Yuan when they rose up against Chinese rule because their army of women could not bear the sight of naked men? That's how Ma Yuan [who had conceived the stratagem] was able to erect a marker [predicting the loss of our country after defeating them in 43 c.e.]." But Bao Luong refused to stay. Her next position was with an unmarried Frenchman who, his servants claimed, treated his female Vietnamese staff with the utmost courtesy. One servant marveled that he never docked her wages if she happened to break some piece of china, and he was always solicitous of her welfare. Bao Luong remained suspicious of her new boss simply because he was French. Oppressed by the luxury in which she found herself and by her mistrust of her employer, she kept the light on at night. During the resulting sleepless nights, she tried to imagine a gloriously independent Vietnam and realized she did not know how what that would look like. Would it be a socialist country? What did this mean? She was no nearer an answer than when she had left for Guangzhou. This uncertainty, however, did not prevent her from recruiting more members and achieving great success.

[By the time of Bao Luong's arrest in mid-1929, the nineteen women's cells in Saigon, My Tho, and Can Tho had about one hundred members; the auxiliary associations had 275 female sympathizers.]⁴

The second meeting of the women's cells took place in Cho Gao at the home of a female recruit named Xuan Dieu. It was the anniversary of the death of Xuan Dieu's great-grandfather, so neighbors came throughout the day to share the food that had been prepared for the occasion. Only in the evening were the Youth League recruits free to eat leftovers and restore some order to the house. As they sat around a tray of betel leaves and areca nuts, the women tidied up stacks of banners on which were inscribed traditional pairs of parallel sentences while discussing strategy. Ngoc Anh complained that the method they used to recruit new members was too slow; it involved making the acquaintance of individual women and gaining their confidence before disclosing their own ideological affiliation and attempting to get the women to join their association. Perhaps some rabble-rousing activity was in order. Uncle Trieu's wife wondered whether rabble-rousing meant making public speeches. Xuan Dieu, the host, suggested staging demonstrations. Farmer Tram's daughter asked: "How about an assassination?" Another suggested distributing pamphlets; still another, opening private schools. A recruit from Giong Trom said: "I saw a woman named Lê Oanh make a speech in Go Den. Sooner or later she and the daughters of Councillor [Vo Cong] Ton in Ben Luc [a man already well-known for support-ing anticolonial activists] will be brought into the league. But when she's a mem-ber, I'm afraid no one will agree to let Lê Oanh continue to make public speeches."

"Why?"

"Because it's not a good idea to draw the attention of the colonial masters before we have had the chance to really sow the seeds of revolution among the people. A person acting on her own is better than one who could reveal the whole chain of membership if she were caught."

The meeting adjourned after the women decided to use poetry to spread the an-ticolonial message. But instead of getting some sleep, the women went on talking. Like Bao Luong, they longed for the opportunity to engage in intellectual conver-sations like their menfolk. Uncle Trieu's wife said, "We need to make the most of this night's meeting. Let's spread out the mats, snack on dried squid jerky, and ar-gue with one another." Forty years later Bao Luong could still recall each person's argument in these exhilarating exchanges.

The women debated what kind of poem to write. Something historical might serve their purpose if it could be interpreted as patriotic and did not make direct reference to French colonial rule. Bao Luong composed two stanzas about a Cham queen who had committed suicide after the Vietnamese had defeated her husband in 1044. The other women objected that such a poem would stir up ethnic ani-mosities. Wouldn't it be better to foster national unity against the French? They spent the rest of the night reviewing Vietnamese history from the time of the Chinese conquest in the third century B.C.E. through the centuries. They decided that the revolutionary message would include stories of exemplary women from history and instructions about how to behave.

This led to a discussion of the proper behavior for female revolutionaries. Ngoc Tho advocated that women rid themselves of feudal ideas such as the need to sub-mit to male authority; they needed to begin the revolution by waging it within them-selves. Her older sister Ngoc Anh cautioned against ill-considered behavior: "Women must behave decorously. They must not sway their hips while walking; they must not laugh with abandon, their mouth wide open, their feet tapping on the floor. They must not speak rudely or look about flirtatiously. That is not being 'a new woman.' If you do, people will mistrust you, and they will hold you in con-tempt. How could you possibly wage revolution? You'd be chased away wherever you went." But Farmer Tram's daughter and another recruit thought that new women should not follow old ways. Women should not walk timidly or hide their mouth while laughing, as if they were denizens of a harem. They should walk with firm steps, purposefully.

The night wore on, and still the women went on talking. In the morning they separated after vowing to write poems on the subject of women's rights and calling on listeners to join in the anticolonial struggle. And indeed, soon thereafter, many poems along these lines began to appear. Some were about taxes, some were in the voice of an older woman urging her son to become active in the revolution, some were in the voice of a wife wondering when her husband would return, with the implication that he might be in prison. They were all written in direct, simple language, without pretension to literary merit, and were meant to appeal to ordinary Vietnamese who might not be literate.

During that night meeting in Cho Gao, the *Tale of Kieu* became the subject of heated debate among the women, just as it was in the male-dominated press. This story in verse, considered a masterpiece of Vietnamese literature, concerned a young woman named Kieu whose father was arrested and thrown into jail. While trying to raise money to secure his release, Kieu had fallen prey to a seducer who had sold her to a brothel. The story went on to describe her adventures and the men she met along the way. In the 1920s controversy surrounded the significance of Kieu. Was she a victim of fate, a young woman whose fall from grace was due solely to her attempt to rescue her father from jail and her family from destitution? Or was she a stand-in for those who were collaborating with the French out of greed and cowardice and were thus traitors to their country? Like the male pundits, the young women could not reach consensus. After tiredness overcame the women and conversation stopped, Bao Luong continued to think about Kieu. She saw Kieu as a young woman who had left home—as Bao Luong herself had done—knowing that she might have to sacrifice her chastity to save her family, as Bao Luong had been cautioned might happen if she were arrested with incriminating documents. But was it not a more heroic decision than that of Kieu's sister, who would have left their father to languish in jail so that she could adhere to traditional notions of female virtue?

[Bao Luong wrote her memoir forty years after this episode took place. I could not decide whether she actually entertained these thoughts then or whether the sullying of her name during the trial colored her recollection of that night's musings.]

5

Prelude to a Murder

In 1967, when she first published her memoir, Bao Luong Nguyen Trung Nguyet was one of only two surviving participants in a murder committed nearly forty years earlier; the other, Ton Duc Thang, who had left for North Vietnam in 1946, never talked about this period of his life. Hers is therefore the principal insider account of what led up to that fateful night of December 8, 1928, when a former peddler-of-herbal-medicine-turned-anticolonial-agitator was slain. Although her memoir does not contain the only extant account, since the police extracted confessions from other participants in the murder and in its plotting, it is the only one that was not produced under the threat of violence. This does not mean it was free of biases, elisions, and misdirection. Long past the time she had paid for her part in the murder, Bao Luong still strived to minimize it and protect long-dead friends. While she wrote as if she were omniscient and omnipresent, pinpointing exactly what she knew and when she knew it is difficult, if not impossible. Before the murder she was often away from Saigon and was not always told what had happened during her absences. She is silent about her movements on the day of the murder. Between the murder and her arrest, she may have learned much that she did not know beforehand. After her arrest she was repeatedly forced to square her story with the equally unreliable accounts provided by her codefendants. Finally, during the thirty-nine years between the events and the writing of her memoir, she may have forgotten a few things, learned new ones, and revised her interpretation of others.

Bao Luong's account does not follow strictly the order in which she learned of developments or participated in certain meetings. The narrative that follows further rearranges the chronology she provided to include information contained in the thick police file on the crime committed at 5 Barbier Street on December 8, 1928.

Murder was far from rare in colonial Vietnam, but the suspicion that there was far more to the story than could be told, that the conspirators were part of a vast network of anticolonial agitators, and, above all, that a woman "of good family" had participated all made for a potboiler that rivaled the Chinese historical novels the young Trung Nguyet had once read to illiterate rural women. She herself was ironic in her assessment of how the murder had been offered up to an avid public: "The Barbier Street murder unfolded just as the newspapers described it, like a romantic novel, both tragic and thrilling, with bloodshed, tears, sighs, and laments and even the image of a beautiful woman who carried out the poisonous stratagem; it had a car that transported the beauty to the place where she eliminated a seducer or perhaps a rival in the world of smuggling or even an obstacle in the path of an illicit romantic affair. The circulation of these rumors reassured the participants [that the true motives for the murder had not been discovered]. But what was the truth?"

Bao Luong implies that presenting the murder as a crime of passion was a deliberate ploy to mask its political character. The murder in fact took place in the context of intensive recruiting into the Revolutionary Youth League, competition between the league and other anticolonial groups, and the disruption caused by league leaders' flight from Guangzhou on the one hand and, on the other, pressure to transform the league into a communist party acceptable to the Comintern in its most radical phase. Without competition between various groups—especially between the old Revolutionary Youth League and the nascent Communist Party—the Sûreté would probably not have been able to solve the murder.

Bao Luong gives little sign that she was aware of the significance of the political upheavals that were taking place in Moscow. Yet the ultraleft program that the Comintern adopted at its Ninth Plenum in 1928 had a significant effect on Vietnamese anticolonial organizations. The Comintern's new policy was based on the belief that the capitalist system was entering the period of final collapse. Moderate left-wing parties were to be replaced by true communist parties that would emphasize class struggle rather than national independence. By late 1928 some adherents of the Revolutionary Youth League were agitating for this transformation faster than the leadership, with its ranks depleted and its operations disrupted, was willing to contemplate. Working with information gleaned from police reports, the anonymous author of a history of the early Vietnamese political parties concluded: "The most characteristic result of the party's efforts during the year 1927–1928 resided in the change in the mentality of its members. In 1926, still, the best among them believed themselves nationalists. In May 1929, they were Communists and impatient to show themselves as such."[1] But this was not true all over Vietnam. The South, with its plentiful undeveloped land and bustling economy, proved to be most resistant to change.

Both Bao Luong's memoir and press reports of the trial provide clues to why many southern activists were unwilling to enlist in the Annam Communist Party, which was being created to conform to the ultraproletarian Comintern line. In its edition of October 5, 1930, the newspaper *L'Indochine* pointed out that a large number of recruits into the Revolutionary Youth League in the South were teachers. The Sûreté made similar observations: "In . . . Cochinchina, the social composition of the [Revolutionary Youth League] was mixed. Workers, teachers, students, and even peasants were recruited. The structure of the party [city, subprefecture, prefecture committees] was made up of teachers or semi-intellectuals who had failed an exam or had abandoned their studies."[2]

Bao Luong only hints at the shifting ideological and operational landscape; she was more exercised by the cautious approach of the Central Committee to the recruitment of women in the South. She wanted to bring women into regular cells instead of shunting them into auxiliary associations but was rebuffed. She complained, "Throughout 1928 the recruitment of women into the Revolutionary Youth League was growing steadily. It seemed that it was about to enter a new phase and could not continue to be restricted to the old organizational framework, but the Central Committee counseled prudence: 'Wait for the right time.'" Meanwhile, "almost all the important functions were held by young people who had been trained in Guangzhou," the Sûreté noted.[3]

Lang, the man who was targeted for murder, had gone to Guangzhou, where he had gained the confidence of the Central Committee, which named him its representative in the South. The Southern Regional Committee *(ky bo)*, which oversaw three provincial sections (Saigon, My Tho, and Ben Tre), was led by Ton Duc Thang, who had never gone to Guangzhou but whose time in France had given him a veneer of cosmopolitanism. The lines of authority between the two men were unclear and probably contributed to the debacle. Bao Luong, who was hardly impartial, was scathing about both Lang and the Central Committee: "He [Lang] had started out well, but gradually, after he had gained the confidence of the Central Committee, he had become arrogant and abusive of his authority. Lang had joined a revolutionary movement that was not meant to work for the benefit of any single individual; instead, it required sacrifices from all. But he had found something of benefit in revolution: power. Power to lead and power to represent the Central Committee. He took advantage of the confidence of the Central Committee, which in turn enjoyed prestige in the Youth League's organizations of the three regions. . . . The Barbier Street incident would not have happened if the Central Committee had been located inside the country and had understood the circumstances and the aspirations of the majority. . . . Even though the Central Committee included people of talent and goodwill, it must not evade responsibility for the tragedy. If it had heeded the majority, which protested against the character and actions of Lang, and if it had transferred him or warned him; if it had put a stop to his abuses of power and thus reassured our comrades and restored the prestige of the Youth League, then the Barbier Street murder would not have happened."

Who was Lang? Bao Luong and her colleagues in the Youth League did not really know much about him. They thought his name was Nguyen van Phat, but that
was not correct. According to what the police investigation uncovered, his real name
was Le van Phat, and he went by several aliases in addition to Lang. He was born
on June 7, 1898, in My Nhon, Ben Tre, one of seven children. In his youth he helped
his father in the rice fields. Between the ages of twelve and seventeen he learned
Chinese characters and romanized script from a neighbor. In 1916 he left his first
wife and married a woman named Do thi Ngu. They had three children, who were
twelve, nine, and five at the time of Lang's death. One year after his second marriage, he became secretary to the council of notables of his village, a position he retained for one year. In 1920 he was put in charge of rituals that were not connected
with the functioning of the council (phuc huong le), but he was discharged from his
position a year later for unknown reasons. He then learned traditional Sino-Viet-
namese medicine from books and began going on tours of three to nine months.
He would not disclose his itinerary to anyone. He was uncommunicative and little
liked by other villagers. Village notables claimed to have last seen him in March
1928, when he was distributing propaganda that advocated the emancipation of children through reading Vietnamese newspapers. It seems that he had severed most
ties with the inhabitants of his native village, including his wife, children, and
mother.[4]

The police were unable to locate a photograph of him. He was described as tall
and stout. The police were particularly interested in his hairstyle. Before 1927 he
had worn his hair in an old-fashioned topknot. But when he was last seen in his
native village, his hair was cut short, "Manila style," according to a neighbor. People
interpreted Lang's new hairstyle as an outward manifestation of his new urban
lifestyle as well as of his embrace of revolution.

Ton Duc Thang first met Lang through Ngo Thiem, who had gone to China with
Lang in 1927 and was in charge of organizing the departure of trainees to Guangzhou. "Lang told me that he was a traditional herbalist. I don't know where he was
from, and I don't know anything about his family. He was thirty-two or thirty-three
years old," Ton Duc Thang told police (Lang was in fact thirty, ten years younger
than Thang).[5] It was Lang who introduced Bao Luong's cousin Tran Truong into
the Revolutionary Youth League.[6] Lang and Ngo Thiem brought Truong to Guangzhou in mid-1927 and "led him to a house where three Vietnamese named Luong,
Truong, and Hoang provided him with revolutionary training," Tran Truong confessed to police.[7] He claimed to have gone on that trip only six or seven months before the murder, which took place in December 1928, maintaining that story even
after he was shown a photograph of himself taken in front of the tomb of Pham
Hong Thai on June 19, 1927.[8] Ngo Thiem, too, clung to his claim that he had known
Lang "only since early 1928," telling police: "I had received orders from Guangzhou
to go to Saigon and wait for someone from the party. That was Lang. He came to

see me at my boarding house at 119 Lagrandiere Street. He eventually told me he was married with children."[9]

Nguyen van Thinh, one of the men who had returned from Guangzhou with Bao Luong in November 1927, met him soon after Lang was released from his Chinese jail in February 1928 and returned to Vietnam: "The first time I met Lang was in a coffee shop in My Tho, in early 1928. He wore Western-style clothing; his hair was cut short, Manila style. I don't know when he had it cut short; I don't know what job he held; in our party, it was not proper to ask for personal details that were not volunteered. However, he had the air of a secretary."[10] As for Bao Luong, she claimed, "I saw Lang for the first time in May 1928 in My Tho. Thiem told me that . . . he was a vendor of herbal medicine."[11]

[In her memoir Bao Luong jettisons chronology and jumps ahead to the day when she shared the story of Lang's murder with her friend Ngoc Anh, sometime after the Revolutionary Youth League had been ordered disbanded in June and before her arrest in mid-July.]

. . .

For months after the murder Bao Luong continued her anticolonial activities as though nothing had happened. One day Ngoc Anh reproached her: "Bao Luong, you're hiding a lot of things from me that you don't need to hide." Bao Luong looked at Ngoc Anh in surprise. She had indeed kept things back from her friend, but Ngoc Anh had obviously discovered her secret: "Like the murder on Barbier Street—it's clear that it's connected to the disappearance of Lang. We're friends for life, and yet you are as close as a clam. I've been really worried about you, Bao Luong, though everything has been quiet so far. I want you to go to Siam with Lê Oanh." Lê Oanh was the young woman who had made the public speech in Go Den and had been brought into the league with Councillor Ton's daughters.

"What's this about going to Siam with Lê Oanh?" exclaimed Bao Luong. Ngoc Anh slapped her shoulder, laughing: "Very good! Lê Oanh told me that Lang was a traitor. What's the point of keeping this secret?"

The loft in Councillor Vo Cong Ton's house was quiet. Councillor Ton and his wife were in Saigon; their daughter Kim Lang was at her grandmother's. Only Ngoc Anh and Bao Luong were there, looking out onto the rice fields below. It was the end of the summer of 1929; the weather was oppressively hot. Soon the monsoon would arrive. Bao Luong decided to unburden herself of her secret, but she did so in a roundabout way, telling Ngoc Anh, "Tran Truong, whom you consider as close as your brother, has given me some secret documents relating to the Barbier Street affair. I've compared them with documents from Comrade Ngo Thiem and verified that the versions are in total agreement. Two of the three people involved have described fully their plans and their feelings; if we can't put our trust in their accuracy, where else can we look for truth?"

"Why are you telling me about all these different versions?"

"The truth is like a novel. Why embellish it? I'm going to tell it in detail so that people in distant places will be able to remember it," Bao Luong replied.

"Remember what?"

"That the advice and the concerns for me [about being the target of men's amorous designs] were really about someone else," Bao Luong said.

"Who?"

"Ngoc Anh, just spread some of that special compound onto the pages of *Luc Van Tien*, especially over the empty lines; you'll learn everything. Keep in mind that I wrote down [in disappearing ink] what my mission was. Although it is the truth, I admit that I wanted to boast to friends across the Southern Sea that I have done all I could for the revolution."[12]

Bao Luong went on: "Lang was a close friend of Nguyen van Thinh's, Ngo Thiem's, and Tran Xuong's. Tran Xuong is now active in Siam. Funny, all those men use aliases that are the names of flowers: cinnamon *[que]* for Thinh, lily *[hue]* for Thiem, peach *[dao]* for Tran Xuong and orchid *[lan]* for Lang. That's especially funny for Lang and Xuong, who could be described only as portly—"

"Let me get the compound and read what you wrote before it gets too late," Ngoc Anh interrupted. She sat down in the hammock in Councillor Ton's loft, watching as the words began to appear on the pages of *Luc Van Tien*.

[The document that Ngoc Anh read that day survives only as a long anecdote within the memoir that Bao Luong wrote thirty-nine years later. It is not clear when Bao Luong wrote the original account; it could have been any time during the seven months between the murder and her arrest. She wrote it in the third person, as if to give it a semblance of detached objectivity.]

. . .

The account began by saying that when Bao Luong returned from Guangzhou, she joined a cell that included Ton Duc Thang, Tran Truong, Do Dinh Tho, and two other men, Bui van Them and Dang van Sam, who had gone to Guangzhou with Tran Truong, Lang, and Ngo Thiem.[13] While she was on mission in Ong Van and Cho Gao, she received word that she was needed back in Saigon. Upon entering Do Dinh Tho's house in Phu Nhuan, she saw Hoai Nghia, her old friend from Guangzhou, who seemed irate: "Where are Lê Oanh and Nhu?" he demanded, referring to the beautiful young recruit and her neighbor, who had accompanied Lê Oanh to Saigon primarily out of friendship.[14]

"Why are you so impatient?" Bao Luong asked. "Since my return I've missed my friends so much. Truong Phong is always asking me to come to Cao Lanh so he can boast that his wife writes poetry as well as I."

Hoai Nghia explained, "Bao Luong, I've waited for you for two days. I wanted to introduce two women [Lê Oanh and Nhu] to you. I am always looking for ways to help you in your mission. But I could not wait; Lang said that he could train them and that when you came he would introduce them to you. But Tran Truong now says he has not seen the two women, so I've gotten worried."

Hoai Nghia had recruited Lê Oanh's brother-in-law, who lived in Mo Cay district in Ben Tre Province and had persuaded Lê Oanh to study with Hoai Nghia. Lê Oanh, who was just eighteen, was very pretty, with a high forehead, well-drawn eyebrows, and shining eyes. She had a pretty mouth with red lips and a wide-open, innocent look. She was fair-skinned and had delicate hands. She was the daughter of a well-off family in Ba Vat village in Mo Cay district, but despite her affluent background she was not spoiled or indolent. She did not care to complete her studies merely to receive a diploma and left her family to join the ranks of the revolution. After hearing Nguyen An Ninh, the young editor, talk during a stop in Go Den, Lê Oanh began to engage in public speaking. Some of the women who gathered in Xuan Dieu's home on the night of the commemoration of her grandfather's death had already heard Le Oanh speak in public against colonial rule. Hoai Nghia wanted Lê Oanh, who was fluent in French, to go abroad for training; he had sought out Bao Luong so she could share her experience with Lê Oanh. When he could not find her, he had put Lang in charge of Lê Oanh and Nhu.

When Hoai Nghia left, Bao Luong followed him worriedly with her eyes. He was a decent, insightful man who treated her like his own daughter. And now he was worried about Lê Oanh. Maybe he was being too cautious; it was not possible that Lang could be so evil as to have harmed Lê Oanh and Nhu. Almost as soon as Hoai Nghia left, Nguyen van Thinh and Ngo Thiem arrived. Thiem said: "Since Thanh Huyen returned from Guangzhou, he has been idle; he has not undertaken a single mission. What do you and Thinh think?"[15]

"Who sponsored him?" Bao Luong asked. "And with whom has he been working since his return?"

"With Lang—and it was Lang who sponsored him," Thiem replied.

"Let's give Lang twenty strokes of the cane!" Thinh declared.

This was no idle threat. By failing to properly supervise Thanh Huyen, Lang had committed an infraction of party discipline that was punishable by caning.

"You've got to find him first," Thiem said. "He's been reprimanded several times for his lackadaisical organizing. Not only has he not corrected his behavior, he is babbling so much that one day we'll all be caught."

"He has collected monthly dues and has used them up. That's created real difficulties," Thinh said. "There are people ready to leave for Guangzhou, but we have no money for them. Tran Truong is giving up his watch; if you contribute all your jewelry, we might just have enough."

"What made Lang change so much?" Bao Luong wanted to know. "Thinh, do you think we need to do some investigating?"

They sent Huynh Nhuan, who had gone abroad with Lang, Tran Truong, and

FIGURE 5. Lê Oanh (Tran Thu Thuy), 1929. GGI 65535.

Ngo Thiem, to check on Lang's movements.[16] Nhuan cased the rooming house in Saigon where Lang was staying. As he reported what he had learned, his face contorted with irritation: "The way Lang is behaving, we'll all get caught. When he stayed at another rooming house, he talked loudly and indiscreetly; we had a really hard time coping with him. And now, he's back at it. I rapped on the door and then hid in the shadows. After a while, the door opened and a couple of young men crept down the stairs. And I thought to myself, 'If I were the Sûreté, I would have caught Lang red-handed several times already.' He's been reprimanded already; why is he still so lax?"

The next day Ngo Thiem, who was the secretary of the Southern Regional Committee, went to warn Lang in the name of their personal friendship: "You need to be more cautious. Everything you said could be heard from the outside."

"I've always behaved like that, and I have never had a problem," Lang retorted. "If you are going to be as fearful as a rabbit, you might as well go to sleep."

"You forget that we've now entered the phase of secrecy," Ngo Thiem said. "Mistakes are going to be costly. As for the monthly dues, even though they don't amount to much, our comrades rely on them. Why did you spend them all in such a wasteful fashion?"

"This is unreasonable! I'll reimburse the group; why make such a fuss? I don't care to be reprimanded," Lang said angrily. "Only the Central Committee can strip me of my position."

Instead of introducing Lê Oanh and Nhu to Bao Luong as he had promised Hoai Nghia he would do, Lang put them in a separate cell with a civil servant named Hoang Don Dzan and a student named Ngoc An. These four people were sitting in a house across from the Lê van Duyet Temple in Ba Chieu, waiting for Lang to arrive so they could begin the meeting as agreed. But Lang was late, and the four began to grumble. Just as they were about to give up, they saw him walking unsteadily at the end of the street without taking the usual precaution of looking around first to see if it was safe. Lang did not explain the reason for his tardiness but immediately plunged into a tirade: "They took turns criticizing me, but I'm not scared of them. Soon, I'm going to meet the she-devil; she's very clever." He burst into unrestrained laughter. Hoang Don Dzan was annoyed: "Let's get this meeting underway; we're late already. Lang, are you drunk?" Dzan threw himself down on a chaise longue, dejected. Lang slapped Lê Oanh's shoulder: "Let me stay at your place tonight; mine has been discovered." "No, you can't," she replied. "Why don't you go to Ngoc An's place?"

It was called a training meeting, but in fact no training took place, no assigning of mission. All Lang did was ask Lê Oanh to let him stay with her, and then he told the two women not to go out in case they were recognized by acquaintances. When Lang had disappeared from view, the four stayed behind and vented their disgust: "What kind of revolutionary training is this? How come such a person was allowed into the party?"

"What does he mean by 'she-devil'?" someone else said.

"He means Bao Luong, Hoai Nghia's friend," another member pointed out.

"What should we do?"

"Let's tell Hoai Nghia."

"Don't let him sleep at your place," someone advised Lê Oanh.

"But he said he's been found out," Lê Oanh said.

"It's just a pretext."

Lê Oanh had met Lang in Ben Tre before she moved to Saigon, though she had been recruited by Hoai Nghia. From the beginning, Lê Oanh had looked up to the revolutionaries as if they were demigods—men of utter integrity, with a will of iron and a pure character. She was full of optimism and did not believe a snake could be living in the garden. But Lang, the representative of the Central Committee, was very different from the herbal doctor she had met earlier and whose love of country had led him across the seas to China. It was as if he were a completely different person. Do Dinh Tho also noted Lang's changed character. Lang, he believed, had developed the "disease of self-satisfaction." He was like "a small man who, after attaining his goal, abuses his authority." Friends had warned Lang several times that he was showing signs of despotism, seeking to exercise power for its own sake, without plan or purpose.

• • •

Lang was sitting in Do Dinh Tho's house, which served as a meeting place, when Bao Luong arrived. He readied himself for a confrontation, but all she did was sweep the floor and tidy the room, ignoring him. His face lost its red hue; he started laughing.

"Bao Luong, let me tell you something," he said. "When Nguyen Bao Toan and I were arrested by Chiang Kai-shek's police [in December 1927], Toan drew your picture on the prison wall. It was such a likeness! He also wrote two lines of verse. If you want to hear them, give me a packet of cigarettes."

"I'm not interested."

"Lots of people say you have a heart of wood from which all life-giving sap has drained," Lang declared. "I'll tell you anyway, so that the love does not rot away like a Guangzhou persimmon: 'Separated by oceans, but not separated in our hearts; / She may not miss me, but I will always be waiting.'"

Bao Luong did not rise to the bait. Instead, she asked, "Have you ever trained females?"

"Two," he replied. "It's very easy work. One of these days I'll introduce them to you; you'll see how talented I am." From his pocket he removed a booklet titled "Essay on Women Defending China" and said, "It's a great book, you'll love it."

Bao Luong ignored his pomposity and asked, "How is your work going?" As soon as she said these words, his face grew red and he said angrily, "They're always criticizing me. I'll tell you, Bao Luong, the people abroad, they really believe in me; they appointed me representative. Others envy me my title and my authority. Isn't that right, Bao Luong? They said that I leaked secrets; that I was power hungry; that I issued threats; that I misused funds; that I did not correct my shortcomings. Oh, they said so many things; it was really hateful."

"What did they mean by 'misused funds'?" prodded Bao Luong, who was well aware of the facts.

Lang changed color again and muttered, "Well, the monthly dues." He waited for the caning that league discipline required her to administer, but Bao Luong only said mildly, "That was pretty bad. Don't do it again, that's all."

But Lang wouldn't give it a rest. "I'm so mad at them! Ngo Thiem is my best friend, but he was the harshest. If I leave the group, they'll know me!"

"He was forthright precisely because he is your best friend; have you forgotten party discipline?" Bao Luong asked.

"I'm afraid only of the Central Committee. They're all putty in my hands," he boasted.

"Abuse of power, nepotism, corruption, nurturing pests—that's a lot."

"The people in Guangzhou said you were naive and it's true," Lang shot back. "You have power, but you don't use it. What have you achieved, little sister?"

Bao Luong couldn't resist asking him, "For the disease of the self-satisfied small man, is there any cure, Oriental herbalist?"

"You're pretty good at veiled insults! But I have not got the disease. I only want to destroy the party, to sate my manly ambition," Lang replied.

"So you're no longer committed to democracy?"

"You believe that real democracy is possible? How naive you are!" he exclaimed.

When Lang left, Do Dinh Tho came out of his hiding place with a somber look on his face: "I've heard everything. The disease is really advanced. The cure has to be a purge, don't you agree, Bao Luong?"

"The patient will go mad and will strike back at those who administer the cure," she warned.

"If we leave things as they are, his bad influence will derail the whole group."

"Lang knows too many comrades; that's why he issued his threat," Bao Luong said. "And we'd need the okay of the Central Committee. I don't think we'll get it. Those who are flattered always protect those who do the flattering."

After Bao Luong left, Do Dinh Tho thought about his life since he joined the party. A nasty worm was about to spoil a whole pot of broth.

· · ·

Lê Oanh wanted to go with Hoang Don Dzan's wife and learn how to do machine embroidery. It would give her a chance to look for Hoai Nghia, but Lang told her not to go out in case someone spotted her. "Making revolution means staying in all the time?" she scoffed. "I might as well live at home! Please go home—it's late. If we can't study during daytime, I'll stop studying."

"It's very bad to close your door during daytime," Lang told her. "But if you don't, what would you do if someone came in unexpectedly?"

"I'm resolved to learn machine embroidery," she said.

"And I'm resolved to sleep here!" he declared.

"Nhu, wake up!" cried Lê Oanh. "Let's stay up all night together." The two women sat by the side of the bed, dozing off and on together, because they did not trust Lang.

For five nights Lang slept on a cot in the living room. During the day Lê Oanh happily went off to learn embroidery. At night she chatted with her friend. Nhu, who was very strong, told herself: "If he wants to get up to some monkey business, he'll have to deal with me. I'll give him a few punches and break his jaw for him. He'd better beware!" After five uneventful days Lê Oanh began to drop her guard around Lang. She stopped thinking of him as a panther ready to pounce; perhaps he was just thoughtless.

One day, while Nhu was making dinner, Lang told Lê Oanh, "I want to marry you. What do you think?"

Lê Oanh replied: "You're forty, and you're married with children, aren't you? I'm your child's age. I only want to learn how to do embroidery; then I'll go home."

"So who will guide your studies?"

"I'm not interested in revolution anymore," she told him.

"Sun Yat-sen's wife was seventeen," Lang said, apparently trying to get her to change her mind. "Liu Bei [a general of the Han dynasty and main character in the *Romance of the Three Kingdoms*] was sixty. A difference of a few decades is of no importance."

"I am determined not to get married soon," Lê Oanh replied. "I'm away from home for only a few months to learn embroidery. That's enough for my mother to cope with."

Lang's face turned dark and violent; he looked like he wanted to strike someone, but Lê Oanh was no longer frightened; now she was filled with contempt. She got up, muttering, "How to get rid of him?"

Nighttime in the suburbs of Ban Co was no different from nighttime in her village of Ba Vat. The sound of crickets was the same; so was the clacking of banana leaves as the wind blew through them. The whole atmosphere made Lê Oanh homesick. She decided to get into bed with Nhu. Suddenly, a large hand seized her smaller one. She tried to shake it off, but Lang had an iron grip. Nhu was already up and slapped Lang hard and yelled, "What do you want?" Lang swayed under the force of her blow. He dropped Lê Oanh's hand and started hitting Nhu. As the two of them faced each other like mortal enemies, Lê Oanh ran toward the door but bumped into Lang's cot and brought down the mosquito net. The cot collapsed with a loud crash. Lang became afraid that the noise would wake the neighborhood. He dropped his fight with Nhu and turned to Lê Oanh. Nhu ran to open the door, but Lang had managed to push Lê Oanh back in. Nhu punched him in the kidneys, and Lang fell to his knees.

The three continued to fight. Lang managed to corner Nhu against a wall. Lê Oanh pulled at his hair until she got the idea of throwing water at him. Lang became worried that the mosquito net, the blankets, and especially his books would be soaked. He tried to end the fight with a blow at Nhu's temple, but she evaded it and taunted him: "Do you want to die?"

"I don't care," he said and took another shot at Nhu, but he decked Lê Oanh instead. Afraid of attracting the attention of neighbors and reprimands from members of their cell, Lê Oanh pulled her friend away. The two women huddled by a wall. Lê Oanh's blouse was torn, and her face was bruised. Nhu had an injured hand, she limped, and her face was swollen. Lang was badly injured, too. He looked at the two women with venomous eyes, then slammed the door behind him. Nhu put her mouth at the keyhole and called out, "Bastard."

The neighbors had been told that Lang and Nhu were married and that Lê Oanh was Nhu's cousin. They had heard the fight through the walls. That would explain the bruised faces: the cousin had sided with the wife and had been hit by mistake. However, Mrs. Hoang Don Dzan was not so easily gulled and kept asking questions. But she was not part of the cell, so Lê Oanh did not want to tell her the truth about Lang. Hoai Nghia, who had looked in vain for Lang at his old house, was still searching when Lê Oanh saw him in the distance. She hastily excused herself to Dzan's wife, then ran over to Hoai Nghia, who pelted her with questions: "Where are you going? Where do you live now? How are your studies? Why is your face bruised? Did you fall? Your mother asked how you were. I said you were well and that your studies were going well. Why are you crying?"

Lê Oanh suggested they go to the zoo. As they sat on a bench by the crocodile pond, Lê Oanh haltingly told Hoai Nghia about what Lang had done. Hoai Nghia was so taken aback that he could not speak for a while. His eyes filled with tears. He stared angrily into the distance. Lang had committed the greatest violation of trust. He told Lê Oanh, "Go back and keep studying; don't let Lang become suspicious. Ask Nhu to find someone from the cell who knows you so that we can communicate with each other."

Nhu enlisted Bao Luong on Lê Oanh's behalf. Lê Oanh was walking with Hoang Dong Dzan's wife when Bao Luong ran into them: "Where have you been? I've been looking for you until my legs are falling off. You have a letter from home. Your mother asks you to return." Lê Oanh waved the letter at Mrs. Dzan: "Please tell others that I have to go home. My mother is asking for me." Hoai Nghia had been following the women from a distance, thinking that Bao Luong was taking a huge risk in grabbing Lê Oanh away in broad daylight. If Lang had tried to meet Lê Oanh. . . . He sighed in relief when he saw her get into a horse-drawn carriage with glass windows with Bao Luong following in an open cart. Hoang Don Dzan later reported to Lang that Lê Oanh had been summoned home. Her friend Nhu told the fourth member of their cell that she was going home to find Lê Oanh.

In fact, Nhu, Lê Oanh, Bao Luong, and Hoai Nghia repaired instead to a house near Lo Duc Street in the Red Earth area. Hoai Nghia said, "You're okay now. But we need to deal with Lang." His faith in the revolutionary cause had been shaken by Lang's actions, and Bao Luong was angry that his loss of faith was undermining her own confidence in it. She still wanted to hope for the best. The league had always treated her well. Lang was just a piece of rotting flesh that needed to be cut off before it contaminated the rest of the body.

Bui van Them and Dang van Sam had concluded their lesson in revolutionary tactics for Lê Oanh and Nhu, and were leaving when a young woman, strong and beautiful, entered. This was none other than Ngoc Anh, the daughter of Headman Hoai. She took the seat vacated by Bui van Them and launched into a training lesson for Nhu and Lê Oanh. Ngoc Anh immediately restored their flagging spirits and their faith in the future: united, they would expel the French. They needed to strengthen their will, remain steadfast in their work, and patiently harvest the fruits, however small, of their efforts. When she left, Tran Truong took her place and explained the structure of the party and the difference between theory and reality. His clear, simple language reassured Nhu and Lê Oanh. They thought, that's the way it should be. Lang was an aberration; it was better to forget about him.

More members of the party dropped in. In the morning Tran Truong came by, and he and Hoai Nghia went to buy coffee. As they passed by a tailor shop, Hoai Nghia looked in and his eyes lit up with joy. Inside, Nhu, Lê Oanh, Bao Luong, and some other women were busy measuring, cutting, and sewing. When the two men returned to the shop in the afternoon under the pretext of ordering some clothes,

Ngoc Anh told him that only she and Xuan Dieu were left; the others had gone to the countryside. Hoai Nghia was taken aback: these women worked fast! He went home by way of Mo Cay and told Lê Oanh's brother-in-law that her studies were progressing well. The brother-in-law was very happy to hear it. His area had many potential female recruits, but it was difficult for a man to get close to them. If he were not careful, he would be thought a womanizer. Hoai Nghia made no mention of the difficulties that Lê Oanh had been having with Lang.

. . .

Bao Luong's memoir is the only account of the attempted rape. She was adamantly opposed to forced marriages and could not possibly have forgotten that episode. Yet she does not seem to have brought it up at the meetings where Lang's relationship with Lê Oanh was discussed (neither Hoai Nghia nor Lê Oanh was present at those meetings). Nor does an attempted rape figure in any of the accounts that Bao Luong and others provided to the police.

In her memoir Bao Luong is vague about her movements after the attempted rape. She seems to have done a great deal of traveling, but the chronology she provided police was quite inaccurate: "I left home for the first time on the fourth lunar month [May] of 1928 to go to Saigon for a medical treatment. I stayed with my father in a furnished lodging. I returned home four or five days later, then came back to Saigon about four or five months ago to work as a seamstress. I came to stay with my cousin Tran Truong, who was then living in Phu Nhuan next to a barbershop. Tran Truong was then working for Kropff and Company. I worked as a seamstress with the intention of opening a tailoring shop. Finding that the work was not sufficiently profitable, I left after nine or ten days and abandoned my plans. . . .

"Among the photographs you showed me, I recognize my cousin Tran Truong and Tran Thu Thuy [Lê Oanh], whom I met at Do Dinh Tho's at 52 Dariès Street. I don't know those named Ton Duc Thang, Dang van Sam, Bui van Them, and Nguyen Kim Cuong."

"Where were you during the period from December 1 to 15, 1928?" the police wanted to know.

"I was in Phuoc Long at my parents'," she said.

"You're lying!" a Sûreté man charged.

"I'll tell you everything I know about this. I remained at my parents' in Phuoc Long for about three months, then at my uncle's house in Long Binh for another three months to recuperate. When I left my uncle, I went to live at Ton Duc Thang's and got work as a seamstress," Bao Luong recounted. "After a few days I went to Headman Hoai in My Tho because I had heard he had brought in a classics teacher. I went on the fifteenth of the first lunar month [February 10, 1928] and stayed there until the fourth month of the lunar year [May]. I then returned to my parents' in Phuoc Long, where I stayed a few days. I was ill so I traveled to Saigon with my father, as I said earlier. Four or five days later I went back to Phuoc Long and stayed there until the ninth month of the lunar year [October]. At that time I came back to Saigon with my brother Vien Dai, whom I put in the care of Do Dinh Tho.

"I went to live at Ton Duc Thang's house as I am related to his wife. Then my cousin Tran Truong rented a house in Phu Nhuan, and I moved in there and opened a sewing shop. Do Dinh Tho, my brother Vien Dai, and Lê Oanh joined me there. I knew Do Dinh Tho when he was an independent teacher in Phuoc Long. It was he who introduced Lê Oanh to me as a machine embroiderer and the daughter of rich parents. As I wanted to open a shop, I took her on. After ten days, my business not being profitable, I left for Phuoc Long, where I sold silks."[17]

Bao Luong does not explain why Vien Dai left Phuoc Long for Saigon, but according to their sister Han Xuan, "My father had six daughters and only one son. He was disappointed that his son frequently was truant from school. He sent him to Ton Duc Thang, who got him a job at the Ba Son factory, where he could learn how to work with machines. Ton Duc Thang wrote to report that my brother was bright, hard working, and conscientious. My father was very relieved and hoped that my brother would have a steady job."[18]

Another reason for Bao Luong's return to Phuoc Long was to arrange for fifteen-year-old Hue Minh, who was eager to follow in her footsteps, to leave home without inciting comments about her virtue or anticolonial sympathies. With the help of Ngoc Anh and Lê Oanh, Bao Luong took her sister to Cho Gao, where Hue Minh joined the cell headed by Ngoc Tho. Bao Luong was sad that her parents' three oldest children had left home, but with the French in possession of her country, she did not feel that a woman could remain in the kitchen, concerned only with cooking and sewing.

While she was in Phuoc Long, Bao Luong found that news about Lang had traveled far. Van Thong, whom she saw for the first time since he returned from Guangzhou, asked, "What about the Lang affair? Why is there so much opposition to him? If the matter is not solved, it's going to pose problems. He came here the other day. Why is he traveling so much?"

· · ·

Meanwhile, the female cells continued to work energetically. Nhu had gone to work with Lê Oanh's brother-in-law in Mo Cay, while Lê Oanh went to stay with the daughter of Councillor Ton in Ben Luc. Over time, what Lang had done to Lê Oanh became a distant memory. Everybody was busy; there was no point in obsessing about individual shortcomings. But Lang, the representative of the Central Committee, had abused the trust of the group and violated party discipline. He had sowed doubt among comrades, making them believe that the Central Committee had ordered them to no longer work clandestinely. He abandoned the demeanor appropriate for a person trying to win over others. Everyone was fed up with the way he lounged around, a cigarette drooping from his fingers, his breath stinking of alcohol, his loudspeaker of a mouth always open like a radio, revealing one secret after another. His comrades no longer respected him and now were afraid of him. While they put all their energies into nurturing the revolution, Lang appropriated their accomplishments for his own ends. He played his part well, so he continued to enjoy the confidence of the Central Committee. And the more the Central Committee believed in him, the more his comrades distrusted Lang.

Since Lang had pocketed contributions, the Southern Regional Committee had named a replacement, but Lang continued to collect the money. When he went to Ben Tre, he bumped into Hoai Nghia, who observed: "The provincial section has informed me that someone else has been appointed to do the collecting. There's no need for you to come."

"I'm going home, so I might as well collect," Lang told him. "There's no cause to stop me from doing so."

"Only that the group's orders must be followed, not those of an individual," Hoai Nghia retorted.

"I am the group; the group is me!"

"This is an abuse of power!"

"I don't care!"

Hoai Nghia went to look for Dinh, the secretary of the Ben Tre provincial section. When Dinh confronted Lang, Lang shouted back: "What do you know? Be careful not to take sides. Shut up!" Lang struck Dinh, who felt as if his barbershop, built of straw and a tin roof, was about to crumble. His eyes were bloodshot, his ears were red, and he felt dizzy from the blow Lang had landed. Dinh went to find Hoai Nghia and asked, "Why is Lang so arrogant?" Then Dinh left to warn other members, leading to an extraordinary meeting. Dinh told his comrades that Lang had spoken insolently and uttered threats to someone who was not in his jurisdiction. Dinh's friends were extremely upset. Hoai Nghia became worried at their angry reaction; he managed to cool tempers a bit by suggesting that Lang be brought in so that they could hear what he had to say. When Lang got there, he asked, "What's the meeting about?"

"We want to talk to you," the others told him.

Lang smirked at Dinh: "No way. I'm the representative of the Central Committee. You can't talk out of order."

Everybody exclaimed angrily. Dinh slammed his fist on the table: "What kind of representative are you? Down with this representative, let's overthrow him!" Lang blanched. Hoai Nghia was shaking.

Lang slinked out of the meeting and turned toward Saigon. Hoai Nghia followed, trying to smooth things over. He remembered what his young friend Bao Luong had said: "Don't make waves. Let's find a solution." How could Hoai Nghia have foreseen what just happened? Lang had made enemies, and they were bound to send protests to the Southern Regional Committee.

Indeed, the Ben Tre members drafted a petition and asked Hoai Nghia to support it at the Southern Regional Committee. While the regional committee was trying to deal with the case, it received further news of Lang's activities, which were increasingly difficult to understand. Many thought that only a traitor would act that way.

. . .

"I'm going to Cao Lanh. Don't wait for me, Truong," Bao Luong told her cousin.

"Don't leave yet," he answered. "Let's have another go at Lang. He's giving me so much trouble. Why did he change so much? Try to find the words to make him repent, then we won't be bothered anymore."

"Very sympathetic toward him, huh? Truong, have you ever been thwarted in love?" Bao Luong asked.

"Hey! I'm going to report you to Aunt and Uncle. What kind of girl are you to ask such personal questions in such a forward way? You should be spanked," he joked, trying to lighten things up.

"Tell me the truth," Bao Luong said. "If you were thwarted in love, would you wreak so much damage?"

"Well, I'd be moody," he said. "I'd be aimless; I'd be suicidal; I'd want to enter a monastery; I might go mad."

"In that case, let's pity Lang," she said. "He is mad with love."

"What are you saying? Did Lang—?"

"Yes."

"Then you have some responsibility for his behavior," scolded her cousin.

"Not I!" she hastened to reassure him. "Enough, let's go see Lang. Where does he live now?"

"Near the Thanh Xuong theater."

When Lang saw Bao Luong, he asked, "Who told you where I live?"

"You promised to train someone, then you went into hiding, so I asked Truong," she said.

"Ah, of course; he knows everybody's hiding place."

"That's his job. Where are the two female recruits?"

"I told them to go home to ask for money," Lang told her. "Their families are very rich."

"Is that the truth?"

"I'm not scared of anyone," Lang declared. "Why should I lie?"

"People know that it *is* a lie. Why bother?"

"Because I don't want to tell the truth."

"Because it's ugly?"

"Bao Luong, you're so naive. There's nothing more beautiful in life than telling a lie that does no harm to anyone," he said.

"Rumor has it that you misbehaved toward two young women. What have you got to say?"

"Even if a man married a woman with all proper rituals and exchanges of dowries and bridewealth, he would still have to coerce her. In life no one does his or her duty without being forced. Life is a long chain of oppression. The difference is in whether the oppression is methodical or random. Why do you laugh? You don't agree with my logic? Let me tell you, it's better to oppress others than to let others oppress you; it's better to abandon others than to be abandoned by them. The one who strikes the first blow has the advantage. . . . Don't worry so much, Bao Luong. The only ones to be afraid of are at the Central Committee."

After Bao Luong left for Ben Luc, Do Dinh Tho and Dang van Sam took turns trying to change Lang's mind but to no better effect.

[This is the closest that Bao Luong comes to admitting that she knew that Lang had coerced Lê Oanh into "marrying" him.]

• • •

By fall 1928 Ton Duc Thang's relations with other top members of the Southern Regional Committee had deteriorated. A cautious man, Ton Duc Thang had not sought the position of head of the Southern Regional Committee or the risks and responsibilities that went with it. "Lang and Ngo Thiem wanted me to abandon my wife and children," he later declared to the Sûreté, "to devote all my time to propaganda work, which I did not want to do. I was immediately suspected of being lukewarm toward the Vietnam Revolutionary Youth League. Soon afterward I noticed that the mistrust toward me by members of the regional committee was increasing and that I was being closely monitored by Lang, Nguyen van Thinh, and Ngo Thiem. I was discouraged and sought ways of quitting the party but could not find a way out. Then came the business of Lang's plan to marry Lê Oanh, a female trainee who belonged to the Ben Tre cell. This plan was being kept in the greatest secrecy by members of the regional committee."[19]

Lang's harassment of Lê Oanh presented Thang with the unwelcome need to take forceful action but also the opportunity to strike a blow against those who distrusted him. Although Lê Oanh had given in to Lang, she formally complained to the Saigon Provincial Section that he had compelled her to marry him. This became the principal charge against Lang. Ton Duc Thang told police: "I revealed Lang's plan to marry Lê Oanh to members of the Saigon Provincial Section. The latter, unhappy with Lang's activities, made representations to the regional committee."

While she was in Ben Luc, Bao Luong received an urgent summons demanding her immediate return to Saigon. Her friends were dismayed, complaining that such interruptions were not good for their operations. Bao Luong told police: "I returned to Saigon, where I was planning to buy more silk and resell it in Phuoc Long. This is when I met Ngo Thiem. He asked me if I knew about the [Lang] affair, without giving me any details. When I said I did not, he told me that an older comrade was harassing a young woman. I replied that even an ignorant man would not behave that way, all the more reason for an educated man not to even think of it. We parted company on these words."[20]

Bao Luong arrived at the meeting of the Saigon Provincial Section in Phu Nhuan in midsession. Every time the provincial section held a meeting about Lang, Ton Duc Thang had to call the members living in Saigon-Cholon, because a move to expel the representative of the Central Committee required a majority. This was why many were present at meetings, including Nguyen Kim Cuong and Pham van Dong, two friends of Lang's who taught at Huynh Khuong Ninh school.[21] In his capacity as communications director of the regional committee, Tran Truong presented reports from Ben Tre, Mo Cay, and Gia Dinh for Do Dinh Tho, the secretary, to read. The reports listed three proposals: relieve Lang of his position, expel him from the party, and apply the maximum punishment. The reasons given were the same: misconduct, inebriation, fraud, violation of discipline, betrayal of trust, corruption, contempt toward comrades, and indiscriminate speech. In sum, Lang was a person of bad character. If the party showed favoritism toward him, the reports said, the Ben Tre petitioners would quit and travel to every province to warn other comrades not to fall into the danger of dictatorship and abuses of power. The party would disintegrate, and its goal would not be achieved. All looked at one another anxiously. Ton Duc Thang said that reports had been forwarded to the Central Committee, and the Ben Tre petitions should be appended to them. In the meantime an investigation into Lang's actions should be started. Lang would be reprimanded and if he did not change his behavior, then would be the time to decide.[22]

Nguyen van Thinh and Ngo Thiem, both friends of Lang's, declined to lead the investigation and meting out of punishment because they might be accused of favoritism. No one, in fact, was willing to accept the task. Bao Luong spoke up: "The disease has reached the danger point. If friends refuse to conduct the investigation, they risk being reprimanded themselves. If you love your friend, go and investigate; you'll be able to get firsthand information and won't be afraid of making false accusations. When you deal with the results, you won't have regrets. If Nguyen van Thinh and Ngo Thiem are the ones who report Lang's faults, no one will dare cast aspersions against them, and the Central Committee will have no reason to reproach us." At the conclusion of the meeting Ton Duc Thang said: "What must happen, will happen."

Dang van Sam gave police his version of what happened: "About a year ago, while I was employed at the Kropff and Company, my foreman, Ton Duc Thang, asked me if I was willing to join the Revolutionary Youth League. When I said yes, Thang introduced me to Ngo Thiem, who accepted my membership and gave me the alias Nhuan. The only conditions for membership were to make a monthly contribution of 5 percent of my pay, to recruit new members, and to help one another. It was absolutely forbidden to reveal to outsiders what happened within the party. The cell to which I was assigned was comprised of Ngo Thiem, Ton Duc Thang, Bui van Them, and myself.

"Every two months our cell held a meeting in a furnished room or in the open. I remember attending only four meetings. The first was inconsequential, the second more important. Ngo Thiem informed me that I was going to be admitted into the Saigon Provincial Section along with Bui van Them. He also told me that there I would find Tran Truong, who belonged to another cell. The cell to which Tran Truong belonged included Nguyen Trung Nguyet (aka Bao Luong), Do Dinh Tho, and Pham van Dong.[23] At the third meeting Thang, who was also on the regional committee, told us about the Lang–Lê Oanh problem. He told us that Lang was trying to compel Lê Oanh to marry him, and that the support two comrades had given to his suit had forced Lê Oanh to accept. He said that at a meeting of the regional committee, Ngo Thiem and Nguyen van Thinh had agreed to give Lê Oanh to Lang in marriage. He added that he himself had refused to approve Lang's request and that Ngo Thiem had also originally voted against the marriage, but that Thiem had finally acceded to the marriage plan because he was afraid of Lang, who represented the Central Committee. Ton Duc Thang surmised that some sort of deal must have been struck between Ngo Thiem and Lang about this marriage. It was understood that Lang would render some favor to Ngo Thiem. Thang apprised us of these developments but did not ask for our opinion."

Tran Truong provided his own version of the events, though not until he had been beaten many times. Shown a photograph of Lê Oanh, he admitted: "I know this woman; she is a friend of my cousin Nguyen Trung Nguyet's. She came and stayed with me two or three times, each time for about a month. She left about fifteen days ago. I don't know where she went."

The police told him, "You are accused of having taken part on the night of December 8–9 in the murder of Lang, residing at 5 Barbier Street, together with Nguyen van Thinh and Ngo Thiem."

"I acknowledge it," he said. "Let me explain. I have been a member of the Revolutionary Youth League for about a year. It was Lang who proposed that I join it. I accepted. One evening he took me to a rented room on Courbet Street in Saigon and told me it was our duty to join the league to show the world that we were determined to no longer be miserable but to be able to eat as much as we wanted. He informed me that I needed to keep the affairs of the league in strict confidence and said that if I committed a breach, however slight, the sanction would be severe. Any serious breach is punished by death, he said. I was then assigned to a cell that included Do Dinh Tho, Bui van Them, and Bao Luong. At a meeting of the cell about a month before the murder, we talked about the Lang–Lê Oanh problem."[24]

Nguyen van Thinh, the only person who had actually approved Lang's "marriage" to Lê Oanh, tried to suggest that more people had supported the union: "Sometime in November, I went to see Lang in a tenement on Blanchy Street across from the Tan Dinh market. That's where I made the acquaintance of Lê Oanh who, Lang said, came from Ben Tre. Lê Oanh joined our group, and several days later Lang informed Ton Duc Thang, Ngo Thiem, and me of his intention to marry Lê Oanh," Nguyen van Thinh told police. "In a meeting of the group we asked Lê Oanh if she was willing to marry Lang. She hesitated at the beginning but ended up by agreeing."

"Why did Lang need the group's agreement to marry Lê Oanh?" the police wanted to know.

"Lang did not want to do things covertly because Lê Oanh was a member of the group and thus like a sister. The group then gave permission, and Lang and Lê Oanh got married," Nguyen van Thinh answered. "A few days later I heard from some comrades that Lê Oanh had complained that she had been coerced into marrying Lang, who had abused his position as leader. In fact, it was not a proper marriage. A few days after permission was given, Lang offered us a meal; that's all the ceremony there was.

"A week later," continued Dang van Sam, "the members of my cell, plus Do Dinh Tho, who belonged to the same cell as Tran Truong, held another meeting. Tho sent Bui van Them to fetch Ngo Thiem so that we could ask him to resolve, in accord with other members of the regional committee, the situation of Lang and Lê Oanh. We considered that situation scandalous because Lang was a hoodlum from Ben Tre, who, moreover, was already married and had four or five children, was about forty, and wanted to dupe Lê Oanh, who was eighteen and from a good family, into marrying him. Lang wanted to exploit his position as representative of the Central Committee to force her into accepting him. Ngo Thiem refused to attend the cell's meeting, claiming that, as a member of the regional committee, he did not have to participate and that if the cell had a request to make, it should do so in writing, and he would bring it up at the meeting of the regional committee. When Bui van Them reported this conversation, we concluded that these procedures did not follow party rules."[25]

Ngo Thiem soon changed his mind about attending meetings of the Saigon Provincial Section. Bao Luong's confession adds: "Two days later Ngo Thiem organized a meeting at my house; it included Do Dinh Tho, Bui van Them, Nguyen van Thinh, Ngo Thiem, and myself. Ngo Thiem said: 'The older man is constantly harassing a young woman whose name I cannot divulge for fear that I would embarrass her. What do you want to do?' We thought of excluding this man or at least issuing a severe sanction against him, but we realized that his power was too great, so we abandoned this idea. I knew this man was powerful because Ngo Thiem told us so. We finally settled on this decision: 'Send him back to China to let the Central Committee deal with him.'

"The next day we held another meeting at the same place. Present were Bui van Them, Do Dinh Tho, Ngo Thiem, Nguyen van Thinh, Ton Duc Thang, Tran Truong, and I. The discussion focused on the decision made the previous evening. [Ngo] Thiem proposed that we review it and we did so. During the discussion we recognized that the man in question, whose name I did not know, refused to submit. Ngo Thiem declared that the man was holding the young woman incommunicado and abusing her. When we asked the name of the abuser, Ngo Thiem demurred, saying the whole affair must be kept secret. He added: 'Let's not name the judges. Those who believe themselves capable of handling the business will agree among themselves how to carry it out.'"[26]

. . .

Ton Duc Thang chaired the next meeting. He was murmuring, "Can it possibly be so?" while staring at a still-damp sheet of paper. During the stage of clandestine action, all documents were written to look like a prescription or a story in verse. When the special compound was applied, the message that had been written in disappearing ink would become legible. Do Dinh Tho grabbed the piece of paper and read aloud: "From the Central Committee to the Southern Regional Committee: 'Do not challenge Lang. Obey the orders of the higher-ups. Keep Lang in his position. Individual shortcomings are insignificant. Lang is a good man.'"

All those present felt that a heavy cloud had descended, enveloping them in a terrifying gloom. The Central Committee clearly knew nothing of what was going on inside the group. They looked in bewilderment from the various petitions to expel Lang to the order to keep him in his position. Here was Ngo Thiem's report on his investigation; there was the report from Nguyen van Thinh on his reprimand of Lang. Both reached the same conclusion: Lang had to be dealt with. But they had failed to convince the Central Committee. The members present decided to vote on Lang's expulsion by secret ballot. When the chairman opened the ballots, every one of them read "Expel." Ngo Thiem was given the task of informing Lang of the decision to strip him of his position as representative of the Central Committee and of taking precautions against his reaction. Nguyen van Thinh would then make a report to the Central Committee. Thiem said in a trembling voice: "He'll kill me. Kill me first. Everybody, go into hiding; then Lang can be informed. When he learns that he's been expelled, he'll incriminate everyone." Although Ngo Thiem refused to tell Lang himself, the members insisted on informing Lang.

After the meeting Nguyen van Thinh, Ngo Thiem, and Bao Luong walked down the Kieu Bridge together. Bao Luong whispered to Thinh: "Thiem was just trying it on. If Lang reacts badly, we'll just play along, then see." As Bao Luong predicted,

Ngo Thiem did confront his friend, although he pretended that Lang had not yet been cast out of the Revolutionary Youth League. With a face that bore the sadness of the ages, he said, "Lang, if you are expelled, we two could go to Cambodia; food is very cheap there, and work is easy to come by."

"If I'm expelled, how can the group continue to function?" Lang challenged.

"Why would it not function?" Ngo Thiem asked.

"If I'm still in, I can behave," Lang said. "If I'm out, they're all dead."

"Come on, it's only a title!" Ngo Thiem remonstrated.

"Yes, but I cannot overlook this insult to my pride," Lang declared.

Ngo Thiem felt inexpressibly sad. Lang's intransigence was leading to a tragic showdown.

Lang eventually got wind of what had happened. Ngoc An, the student who belonged to the same cell as Lê Oanh, went to find Hoang Don Dzan in Gia Dinh. Dzan then sought out Bui van Them at the Kim Chau garage in Phu Nhuan; Bui van Them in turn relayed the information to Tran Truong and Dang van Sam: Lang was going around looking for trouble. Right then Nguyen van Thinh hurried in and said that Lang was out looking for all the meeting sites of the cells because he'd learned that he'd been stripped of his position. They immediately proposed to either send Lang to the Central Committee or eliminate him. Further discussion showed that sending Lang to the Central Committee was not a good idea. He would be suspicious if he were sent without good reason. The idea of eliminating him began to take root in everyone's mind. Five meetings were held in short order in five different places.

According to Ton Duc Thang, "The Saigon section then convened a meeting and summoned one member of the regional committee, Ngo Thiem, to attend. This meeting, which was held on a date I cannot recall [November 30, 1928], passed the death sentence against Lang, whose activities were deemed injurious to the party. The vote was unanimous except for me, as I did not raise my hand. When comrades asked why I did not vote, I observed that it would be preferable to have Lang judged by Guangzhou, since Lang was a creature of Guangzhou. My reasoning was not heeded, so Lang was condemned to death. This meeting was attended by Ngo Thiem, Do Dinh Tho, Dang van Sam, Bui van Them, Tran Truong, the woman Bao Luong, and myself."

"The sentence was reported to the rest of the Saigon Provincial Section with a request for instructions on how to proceed. Members of this section decided that the execution of Lang was impossible and that the regional committee had not approved the sentence against him, so a second meeting was convened two days later [December 2]. I did not attend it because I was sick [which was true], so I don't know what was decided."[27]

According to Dang van Sam, "[On November 30, 1929,] Do Dinh Tho informed the two cells that a tenement had been rented at 72 Paul Blanchy Street in Phu Nhuan and that another meeting was set for that very evening at seven. All the members of the two cells were present: Do Dinh Tho, Ton Duc Thang, myself, Bui van Them, Nguyen Trung Nguyet, Tran Truong, Ngo Thiem, and Nguyen van Thinh (who had been informed by Ngo Thiem of the meeting). They invited Ngo Thiem to present the Lang–Lê Oanh situation. Ngo Thiem presented it as I have related it to you, then said: 'What do you decide with regard to Lang?' It was then that Lang's fate was decided. Revolution was the priority. Sacrifices must be made for the sake of the righteous cause. Get rid of gangrenous flesh to preserve the body. Do not delay."

Dang van Sam continued: "The vote was six against two in favor of the death sentence. Only Ton Duc Thang and I objected that a more peaceful solution should be found, for example, the expulsion of Lang and the dissolution of the cells where anarchy reigned. The members at that meeting did not heed us; the comrades were too upset about Lang. We moved on to the selection of executors of the sentence."[28] (He is incorrect on this point: this meeting was held on November 30 and they were not appointed until the meeting of December 2.)

Nguyen van Thinh was one of the individuals charged with executing Lang: "One day I received a summons, and I was told that I was condemned to death because I was suspected of having been the accomplice of Lang in his relations with Lê Oanh. But I was only Lang's subordinate! I replied that I did not have anything to do with the business and was informed that I was to execute the orders I was about to receive. In that case the death sentence against me would be lifted."

"What was the motive for condemning Lang to death?" the police asked.

"When the group gave permission to Lang and Lê Oanh to marry, it was understood that they must live as husband and wife and that they must not neglect party business. But complaints had been expressed. The group that gave permission was the regional committee. Under it was the Saigon Provincial Section, which had not been informed and which had forwarded the complaints about Lang. It was members of the Saigon Provincial Section who decided to execute Lang," Nguyen van Thinh said.[29]

. . .

From the various accounts provided by the defendants in the Barbier Street case, a police inspector constructed this narrative for the bill of indictment:

> There exists in Cochinchina a secret organization whose leadership is located abroad and has branches in certain provinces of the colony. The activities of the provincial sections of this organization are controlled in Saigon by a local committee of direction.
>
> An affiliate of this organization, a woman named Lê Oanh, from Ben Tre, went to Saigon to be trained by the committee of direction for Cochinchina. A member of this committee named Lang fell in love with Lê Oanh. At the beginning, Lê Oanh seemed to respond favorably to Lang's urgent advances. However, within the committee, another member named Ton Duc Thang, also in love with Lê Oanh and jeal-

ous of Lang's authority over other members of the party, sought to derail the plans of his rival and to put in play against him the sanctions envisaged by the party.

Members of the committee of direction refused to assist Ton Duc Thang in his vengeance, but in order to avoid giving rise to criticism as a result of the promiscuity of Lang, who was an instructor belonging to the committee of direction, and of Lê Oanh, a trainee of this very committee, they decided to assign this neophyte to the Saigon Provincial Section so that she could complete her training. The separation of Lê Oanh from her lover, the comparison she could make between him and other young men, as well as the presence within the Saigon Provincial Section of Ton Duc Thang's friends, were apparently the reasons why Lê Oanh abandoned Lang and even accused him of having pressured her into becoming his mistress by the use of threats.

After listening to Lê Oanh, members of the Saigon Provincial Section held a secret meeting; they came to the conclusion that Lang had contravened discipline by abusing his authority within the Committee in order to slake his passion and decided to eliminate him.[30]

No other evidence exists, either in Bao Luong's memoir or in the records of interrogation of his coconspirators, to support the theory that Ton Duc Thang was a rival of Lang for Lê Oanh's affections, although Thang made matters worse for Lang by bringing together the regional committee and the Saigon Provincial Section.[31] Because Ton Duc Thang was sick, he did not attend the meeting on December 2, where it was decided who would carry out Lang's death sentence. Bao Luong reveals that it was she who presided over the decisive meeting:

"Let's draw ballots to decide who's going to do it," someone said.

"Don't let Bao Luong take part in the drawing," another member suggested. "There are too few women, and they're emotional; they could reveal secrets."

"Right," another man agreed. "Bao Luong, vacate the presiding chair."

Bao Luong stepped aside and watched as members slowly pulled out of a box pieces of paper that would determine who would carry out the fateful mission. Her insides knotted with anguish as she thought of her friends in Guangzhou: did they know of the dilemma their comrades were facing?

Nguyen van Thinh later stated, "I don't know who voted to execute Lang, but when I got to the meeting, the people present were Do Dinh Tho, Tran Truong, Bao Luong, Ngo Thiem, Dang van Sam, Bui van Them. As they informed me of my own condemnation, they told me that Lang must die. When I appeared before the provincial section and heard that I was being pardoned, we settled on the murder of Lang. I was one of the designated ones, together with Ngo Thiem, Tran Truong, and Bao Luong. The last two were voted in [though Bao Luong had been told not to take part in the lot drawing]; Ngo Thiem and I were selected in exchange for our pardons [for having approved of Lang's marriage to Le Oanh]."

"Who presided over the meeting?" a member of the Sûreté asked.

"I don't know," Nguyen van Thinh replied, "but it was Do Dinh Tho who read the minutes of the earlier meeting where we were condemned to death. We had a free hand regarding the murder, but we needed to carry it out without delay."[32]

Tran Truong, for his part, told police: "We judged that Lang had committed a very grave fault against the party in pressuring Lê Oanh, and we condemned him to death. We drew lots to decide who would carry out the execution. Nguyen van Thinh, Ngo Thiem, and I were designated to carry out the deed."[33]

Tran Truong omitted mention of Bao Luong; in fact, she was not expected to be directly involved in the killing, though she had been given a role to play behind the scenes.

6

The Crime on Barbier Street

On the way home from the meeting of December 2, 1928, Tran Truong said to Bao Luong, "Please undertake some errands for me." Bao Luong stared at her cousin. He must have drawn one of the marked ballots. When she arrived at Do Dinh Tho's house, she found Nguyen van Thinh and Ngo Thiem there, whispering. Thiem asked her to accompany him to the Khanh Hoi dock, where he introduced her to the man who arranged for league trainees to travel to China as stowaways. On the way back from Warehouse 5, he sighed in relief: "That's it. Bao Luong, be very careful. Don't let any woman go out in public disguised as a man; it would really cause trouble. Since you went on that trip, the folks on the boat have warned us not to repeat that stunt and so did the Central Committee. After this we should bring the Central Committee back from China. You need to pay the boat fees for two prospective trainees and bring gifts for the men who go by the aliases of A Suc and A Mui. Make friends with the Chinese, gain their support, and fill out reports on training."

"Why are you telling me all this?" asked Bao Luong.

"You'll be taking my place. It's easier for women to move around. Try to find many sets of clothes," Ngo Thiem replied, speaking without pause and as if he were never going to speak with her again.

Bao Luong listened to him in distress. Ngo Thiem was like a living training manual for the group, his memory a gift of nature. The more she listened to his advice about how to work effectively, the more keenly she felt the impending loss of a mentor and friend.

"Are you about to cry? Your eyes are all red. Don't hide it with words," he told her. "We've been taught that we need to disguise every gesture. Every facial expression betrays our actions. So you need to watch your behavior. Bao Luong, have you considered the many sacrifices that have to be made for the righteous cause? Have you ever witnessed killing for the sake of ideology? You're involved now; life and death no longer have any meaning. It is inevitable that—"

"That there will be blood and tears," she interrupted.

Ngo Thiem urged her, "Bao Luong, be as brave as you've always been."

"Who was Ngo Thiem, this intelligent, knowledgeable, dynamic revolutionary?" Bao Luong wondered. "How old was he? Where was he from? What was his real name? I knew only that he was a solid pillar in the house of theory of the Youth League. He was a gentle individual, yet he was about to be involved in the purging of evil." She never put these questions to him. Party discipline prevented her from asking personal questions. Ngo Thiem was, in fact, the same age as Bao Luong. He came from central Vietnam, as did one-third of the members of the Revolutionary Youth League active in the South.[1] Like half of those who eventually stood trial with him, he was from the city of Vinh.[2]

· · ·

The four designated executioners met to plot the murder. As Tran Truong hurried in, Do Dinh Tho asked anxiously, "You have the gun?"

"Yes."

"Oh? Are you going to pretend to recruit him for the army?" Nguyen van Thinh asked.

"Just going to Binh Loi Bridge," Tran Truong replied.

"Do we push him or does he push us?" someone asked.

"Maybe we should use poison," another suggested.

"If he suspects, we'll all be in trouble," someone observed.

"Lang went to look for Ton Duc Thang at his workplace recently [to quarrel with him]. Thang got wind of it and left by the back door. So far he's avoided Lang," Thinh reported.

"The Central Committee has not stripped him of his position. Lang is threatening that if he calls a meeting and people don't come, he'll rat on everybody. As long as he remains on the regional committee, the whole group is in danger of splitting apart," one of the men said, reminding them all why Lang had to be eliminated.

Ngo Thiem cried out to the absent Lang: "Lang, you're driving me mad!"

"He's just moved," someone mentioned.

"Where?" Ngo Thiem asked.

"To 5 Barbier Street."

"Is there a back entrance?"

"At the back there is a small yard with elephant ear plants."

"Is it a busy street?"

"No."

"Can we use the car that's in Truong's garage for repairs?"

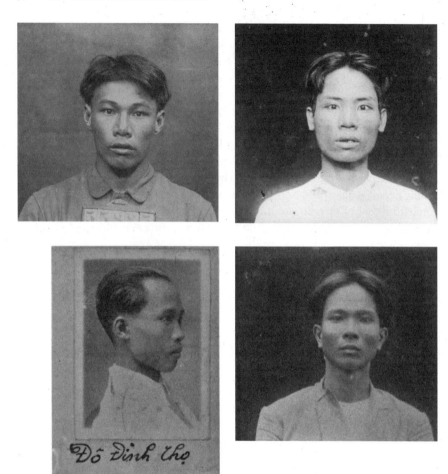

FIGURE 6 *(top left).* Tran Truong, 1929. GGI 655357.
FIGURE 7 *(top right).* Ngo Thiem, 1929. GGI 65535.
FIGURE 8 *(lower left).* Do Dinh Tho, 1929. GGI 65535.
FIGURE 9 *(lower right).* Nguyen van Thinh, 1929. GGI 65535.

"Yes. It runs very well."
"Have you got all the stuff, Tho?"
"Yes."
"Give the two knives to Truong."
The time for talking was over. Nguyen van Thinh, Ngo Thiem, Tran Truong, and Do Dinh Tho were overcome with emotion and bowed their heads to hide their moment of weakness. They held one another tight as they walked toward the Tan

Dinh market in pain-filled silence. They had always been gentle people and were unprepared to commit murder. They had imagined that if they had to, their victims would be French occupiers. This unanticipated act of cruelty, the first such mission in their revolutionary career, was going to end the life of a man who had once shared their ideals. Nguyen van Thinh and Ngo Thiem had been Lang's friends, Do Dinh Tho had once tutored him, and Tran Truong had been recruited into the Revolutionary Youth League by Lang. Filled with sorrow, they stopped every few steps to grip one another's hands as if to share their pain and shore up their courage. Every so often one of them would sigh.

. . .

Do Dinh Tho had been writing his column for *Than Chung* but put it aside to mix the drug that they planned to use to poison Lang. Tho tried to summon his imperfect knowledge of chemistry: What turned photographic developing acid into poison? What turned it into a sleeping potion? "Bao Luong is a tough cookie," he muttered as he worked. "If she had not asked that fateful question about what must be done about Lang when she presided over the meeting, perhaps the result could have been different. Why was she not allowed to draw a ballot? Lang likes to call her a she-devil, but she's more like a tigress. Why had they not just asked her to seduce Lang? It would have been so much simpler." (Bao Luong does not explain why he thought seduction would have resolved the situation.)

Ngo Thiem, meanwhile, was pacing at the end of Barbier Street. "It's six o'clock already. Why is Tho not here yet?" he fretted. "If he's become scared and has withdrawn, the whole thing will fail." Finally, he saw Do Dinh Tho limp along Mayer Street, swinging his wooden leg. He had the drug with him. The two went into a coffee shop. Tho tried to appear at ease; he took out his glasses and began wiping them, while Thiem ordered coffee. Thiem was stirring his cup when Nguyen van Thinh brought Lang in. When Lang saw Thiem and Tho, he exclaimed, "Where have you been hiding until now? It's time to hold a meeting." Thiem turned ashen: "Is it? All right, fine." He pushed the coffee cup toward Lang: "Drink up, then we can go in and talk." Tho also urged Lang, "Big brother, try this. It has an excellent flavor. It's a bit expensive but really good. Then we can talk about old times." Lang drew on his cigarette, then followed with the coffee. The taste of the cigarette and the coffee masked the slightly bitter taste of the drug.

According to the bill of indictment of March 8, 1930, the police reconstructed events as follows:

> Lang lived at the meeting place of the society, which moved frequently. According to Ton Duc Thang, Ngo Thiem and Nguyen van Thinh rented the tenement at 5 Barbier Street and settled Lang there with his propaganda materials. According to Nguyen van Thinh, either Bao Luong or Tran Truong procured a sleeping potion that Do Dinh Tho handed over to Ngo Thiem on December 8 (according to Thiem). Do Dinh Tho

also gave a vial of poison to Tran Truong, according to Nguyen van Thinh. On December 8, around 7 P.M., Nguyen van Thinh, acting on advice from Do Dinh Tho, rented a car and parked it in front of Ton Duc Thang's house. At 8 P.M., Thinh presented himself at Lang's house. Lang was at his desk. Ngo Thiem arrived shortly thereafter, then left to get three cups of coffee at a nearby stall. There he mixed the sleeping potion in the cup intended for Lang and returned with the cups. The three drank their coffee.

Bao Luong recounts how Do Dinh Tho avoided further involvement: While the others were still drinking their coffee, Do Dinh Tho exclaimed, "I forgot that I have not finished writing my article. I had better go and deliver it. The paper is about to be printed, and if it's missing a piece, there'll be trouble." Tho hurried out and got into a pedicab, urging its driver to make haste. When the three men who remained in the shop had finished their coffee, Nguyen van Thinh wiped Lang's cup clean, then poured some tea, which Thinh drank in small sips, as if nothing of importance was about to happen. Thiem said, "Let's go, Lang. How's your new house?" Thiem and Thinh walked Lang back to the house at 5 Barbier Street.

"Under the influence of the drug," the bill of indictment continues, "the unsuspecting Lang went to bed after asking his guests to wake him up when they left so that he could lock the door. While Nguyen van Thinh stood guard, Ngo Thiem went to meet Tran Truong, who was waiting for him on Paul Bert Street. The two comrades returned, arguing all the while. Tran Truong carried a vial of poison in his pocket. At this point either Truong or Thiem observed, 'People will think he died from opium.'"

Lang, in fact, did not fall asleep immediately, Bao Luong learned later from her cousin. Instead, he turned querulous. He tried several times to provoke a dispute, wanting to know who had agreed to his being stripped of his title. Ngo Thiem just mumbled evasively, waiting for the drug to work. Even as Lang was lying on the cot, no longer able to keep his eyes open, he was still uttering threats: "If you hold a meeting without me, you'll see—." There was no longer any reason to defend the decision to force Lang out, but Ngo Thiem looked at Lang as if he was an evil force that was about to be destroyed but was still trying to put on a final show of power.

Time passed. Ngo Thiem became anxious. He dropped the newspaper he was holding and went to stand by the window. He had suddenly realized that Lang might not die quietly, and Thiem was frightened. He had embraced the need for decisiveness and sacrifice for the cause. He remembered this as he gripped the bar of the window and stopped his feet from moving to help Lang as he uttered inarticulate cries and thrashed about. Thinh was pleased at the resolute stance of his friend and went off to buy more coffee. Lang, who was then semiconscious, drank the whole cup.

The two friends waited. Ten o'clock came. Looking at the silent houses, the locked door, and the sleeping man, Ngo Thiem silently cursed Do Dinh Tho: "I wish he would break his other leg. He should have used more poison. If Lang awakens, Tho will be a dead man. What kind of poison is this that cannot even kill a fly?" Nguyen van Thinh helped Lang into the inner room, then looked out into the courtyard. The sky was cloudy, the stars dim; the leaves of the elephant ear plants swayed in the breeze. Banana leaves hid the shadows on the moon. This lonely scene evoked a profound sorrow amid the sound of the crickets and the cicadas. They were not poets, but the two men reluctantly carrying out this mission were deeply moved.

Thinh went back inside. Lang's regular breathing convinced him that Do Dinh Tho had mixed a sleeping potion by mistake. Faced with this unexpected turn of events, he and Thiem had to figure out what to do. They waited some more. It began to drizzle. Suddenly, a man dressed entirely in black and wearing a raincoat and a cap turned in from Vassoigne Street and stopped at 5 Barbier Street, whistling. Thinh and Thiem doused the lights. The shadowy man stuck his head in the window, whispered something, then left. It was Tran Truong. Ngo Thiem ran into the inner room, then hurried back to the outer room and buried his head in the back of a chair. He did not know why he was crying.

Meanwhile, Nguyen van Thinh stolidly poured himself a drink from the bottle of rice alcohol that always sat on Lang's bureau and knocked it back. He lit a couple of cigarettes, gave one to Thiem, and pulled him upright, whispering in his ear: "What did you say the other day about sacrificing one's life for the cause?" The two men stared at each other, then fell into each other's arms.

"We have to get rid of a problem," Thinh said.

"Yes," Thiem answered.

"Courage!" Thinh told him.

"All right," said Thiem.

While they were trying to bolster each other's courage, Tran Truong was walking along Foucault Street, seeking shelter from the wind and the damp and muttering, "Truong, you need to be brave. This knife will cut off the problem with one flick of the blade." He stuck his hand into the waistband of his trousers to check on the knife. "I did not bring the Swiss knife with the express purpose of committing murder," Tran Truong told police at the interrogation session of August 8, 1929. "I always had it on me to make small repairs. Personally, I had no motive for hating Lang, and I regret killing him. I did it because of the league's rules, according to which I could not evade the task that I had been assigned without risking death myself." Still, Truong told Bao Luong that he knew the hour of Lang's fate was also the hour his own fate would be sealed.

Police inspectors claimed to Truong that, according to Thinh and Thiem, Truong had administered poison to Lang before slitting his throat. "I did not make him swallow anything," Truong maintained when interrogated on August 8, 1929. "Ngo Thiem locked the door, and I followed him. I don't know if Lang had taken the narcotic as Nguyen van Thinh declares. All I know is that when I got there, he was asleep. I'd gone to 5 Barbier Street with Nguyen van Thinh. Ngo Thiem went into the house to see Thinh while I waited outside. After a while Thinh came out to fetch me so that I could give a hand. You know the rest."

The city was silent, its inhabitants sleeping the sleep of those without a care. It was the most painful time for the three gentle people who had put the murder plot in motion.

As Ngo Thiem, Tran Truong, and Nguyen van Thinh approached the bed, Lang suddenly slapped down hard and opened his eyes. He looked glassily at the three men looming over him and immediately understood the danger he was in. He gathered all his strength to cry out, "Hel—." Tran Truong's knife cut off his cry. Truong wiped his blade clean, then opened the inside door. Suddenly, Lang cried out again: "Help!" Thinh and Thiem got up and looked at Truong: "What now?" Truong realized that he had not finished Lang off. "Let's tie him up," said one of the men. Truong came closer: "Isn't there a better way?"

"It's too late."

"Help! Help!" Lang cried.

"I slit his throat with my Swiss knife," Tran Truong told police on August 8, 1929. "I believe I left it there. Lang, whom we believed dead, woke up suddenly, and started to fight us off and managed to get to the door."

During a joint interrogation of Tran Truong and Nguyen van Thinh on September 20, 1929, the police asked Truong, "Nguyen van Thinh has stated that you stuck a knife into Lang's throat—is that correct?"

"Yes."

Then the police turned to Nguyen van Thinh: "You had tied him up beforehand?"

"That rope fell from the ceiling when Lang fought us," Thinh claimed, "and I don't know how it wound around him."

"Tran Truong," said the police questioner, "you plunged a knife in Lang's throat, then made a sideways movement?"

"Yes. I wanted to shorten his suffering."

"Nguyen van Thinh, you panicked and you dropped Lang, who fell from his cot."

"That's right," Thinh said. "We three were frightened and fled into the living room."

"Then you went back to Lang."

"We composed ourselves and went back, the three of us," Thinh responded.

"Perhaps because you were impressed by Truong?" the inspector asked.

"No," said Thinh, "it was because I heard whimpers, and I went to investigate."

"After being wounded by Tran Truong," added Nguyen van Thinh at a further interrogation on November 15, 1929, "in circumstances I have related, Lang managed to escape and run out of the house while we were in the living room. He fell into a bush. I went by myself to verify, and Lang recognized me. I took him back into the kitchen and told him that it was his fault that he had been condemned to death and that we too were under the same pain of death if we did not follow orders."

"We wrestled [Lang] to the ground against the kitchen wall," said Tran Truong to police on August 8, 1929, "until he stopped thrashing." He added untruthfully, "I have never since laid eyes on Ngo Thiem or Nguyen van Thinh. I learned later in the newspapers that Lang had been disfigured and his face burnt. I don't know how that happened."

Thiem and Thinh accompanied Truong to the door and watched him walk unsteadily away into the fog. Left with the corpse, the two men could not quite decide how to disguise the murder and misdirect the police. Ngo Thiem had written a fake suicide note for Lang, but his slit throat made it useless. They decided to use the "love letter" that Bao Luong had drafted as a fallback and left it near Lang.

Meanwhile, Tran Truong had gone to report to Ton Duc Thang what had happened. Thang had not approved of the murder because he didn't think they could get away with it, but he was unable to think of another solution to their dilemma. He had not expected things to turn out as they did. When he heard Tran Truong's report, he hurried to the garage where Truong worked to gather the equipment they would need to hide the evidence, and he drove Truong back to Lang's place.

"We were about to leave," Nguyen van Thinh told police on September 20, 1929, "when Ton Duc Thang arrived by car. As far as I could see, it was a Torpedo four-seater."

At the session of November 15, 1929, the police told Thinh, "Ton Duc Thang has stated that you described the crime to him and that he asked one of you to disfigure the victim. Since neither of you accepted, he ordered you to do it."

"Yes, that is correct," Thinh replied. "Thang gave me a vial and some cotton and told me to burn the face of Lang and so I did."

Bao Luong records that after they had accomplished the task—burning Lang's fingertips, stealing his ID card, and taking his pants—Truong said, "Let's take him outside."

"Where?" Thiem asked.

"Put him in a trunk and take him to Binh Loi Bridge," Truong suggested.

"It's late, it will attract attention," Ngo Thiem pointed out.

"Let's bury him in the yard," someone else suggested.

"What about [in a spot by] all that blood near the elephant ear plants?" asked a third man.

"So be it," Tran Truong declared.

"Did you burn his fingertips?" asked Ton Duc Thang.

"We took off his trousers," replied Thinh, avoiding the question.

Thang seemed satisfied. "It will look as if he was involved in a fight over a woman," he said.

"On Thang's orders," Nguyen van Thinh told the police on November 15, 1929, "we removed from Lang's house a typewriter, pamphlets in Chinese characters, and all the papers we found in Lang's drawers. We then got into the car and went to Ton Duc Thang's. Later, Thang told me he had burned the papers. He handed about a dozen brochures in Chinese characters to me. These were seized during the search of my lodging. As for the typewriter, only Thang can tell you where it is."

On July 30, 1929, Ton Duc Thang had given police a carefully edited version of his role: "Five or six days later, I learned that Lang had been murdered, first through the newspapers and later from Tran Truong, who came to tell me that the sentence had been carried out. I believe that Tran Truong took part in the deed, for I saw him return around 3 A.M. to the home that I shared with him in Phu Nhuan. I asked him to tell me what had happened, but he refused to give me any details, telling me it was none of my business. I believe that Ngo Thiem and Nguyen van Thinh were involved because they were the ones who rented 5 Barbier Street four or five days before the murder. It was supposed to be a site for training new recruits. Thiem and Thinh were its only occupants. Lang at the time lived at 17 or 27 Paul Bert Street. Lê Oanh lived with Lang at that address."

· · ·

The day after the murder, a report landed at the police station on Catinat Street in Saigon.

Police Station, Third District, December 9, 1928:

We wish to report that today at 7h15, we were advised by a Do van Cam, 36 years old, who works as accounting clerk at Painier Company and resides at 7 Barbier Street, that a crime was committed during the night against his neighbor residing at 5 Barbier Street and that his corpse was lying in the courtyard of said house. We therefore went immediately to the address given. It was a tenement comprising two rooms and a courtyard, which we immediately sealed off.

The entry door was pushed in, and the key was in the lock on the outside. We went into the first room, the living room, in which the only pieces of furniture were a small table and four chairs all made of rattan, a desk, and a bookshelf. On the table were an oil lamp and an inkpot. On the floor were scattered, burned papers and a torn newspaper. The desk drawers were open and empty. The door of the bookshelf was open, and the shelves were also empty. These two pieces of furniture seemed to have been opened and emptied of their contents.

In the second room was a cot with a mosquito net that was torn on one side. On the wooden floor by the bed, we noticed two puddles of blood; the one closest to the bed showed a footprint of about 0.25m in length. There were two more footprints near the door to the courtyard. This door was wide open; there was blood on the bolt and the jamb. In the middle of the door opening was an open, empty rattan valise. On the side of the camp bed we noticed some rolled-up pieces of mosquito netting soaked in petrol and a piece of candle. In the inner courtyard, at about one meter from the door, we observed the corpse of an individual lying on his back against the wall shared with No. 3. His right arm was bent behind his back and tied with a thick rope made of braided hemp of about one meter in length. The left arm was bent in front of the man's chest. The corpse wore only a jacket; his lower body was totally naked. We noticed that the corpse bore a deep wound at his throat, six centimeters in length and 2 cm. in depth. The larynx was sliced through. On his chest were two wounds on each side. They were not very deep and were apparently made with a narrow-bladed knife, very likely a pocket knife. The victim's face was partly burned as well as his hair; it seems that he was gagged with a piece of cloth soaked in petrol that was set on fire. Two pieces of cloth that did not burn look like linen with red stripes. The head and the top of the body lay in a puddle of brackish blood amid the calcified remnants of bloodied clothes.

The owner of the house revealed that it had been rented only a few days earlier, on November 30, by someone who called himself Nguyen van Trieu. But this man only moved in on December 3. The only person he was seen in company with was a northerner. He stayed indoors only three or four hours a day and could be seen going in the direction of Dakao, toward the cemetery. The day before his death, he told the owner that he'd inquired about installing electricity, but the rate he was quoted was too high so he was going to make do with an oil lamp.

. . .

When she heard Tran Truong arrive at her house, Bao Luong got up hurriedly and opened the door. Ton Duc Thang and Truong quickly brought in a trunk, then left just as quickly. Bao Luong called her female friends: "Everybody, go to Ben Luc. I'll follow later. I'll take care of the tailoring shop." After the women left for Ben Luc, she sat by herself, thinking hard. Her friends had not allowed her to participate in the murder, but new circumstances were creating enormous risk for her in the form of the trunk. She stared at it, thinking furiously. Perhaps Lang was lying in it. If she was arrested, what would she say? Perhaps she should say that he'd betrayed her love and so she'd killed him. But who would be the one to give him a pair of horns? What was more, someone would have had to have helped her put Lang in the trunk. Bao Luong was ashamed to even be thinking of such an explanation for the murder; it seemed so sordid. She tried out different scenarios. She still thought of turning the murder into a story of romantic betrayal but had trouble thinking of an accomplice. Perhaps it could be a robbery? She was so happy to have hit on this story line, she wanted to jump up. Yes, a robber had tried to steal her sewing equipment, she had used the bolt, and by mistake—no, it would not work. She did not know what condition the corpse was in, so she couldn't use that story. Hmm. Lang was too big to fit inside the trunk. If he'd been cut into pieces, why did no blood leak out? She had to open the trunk. Even if the sight of Lang's corpse was horrifying, she had to see it for herself so she could think of an alibi. She flicked up the two latches and the central bolt and struggled with the heavy lid. She pushed it up wide open. Inside were ropes and stones that Tran Truong had purchased some time before. The trunk looked new and smelled of varnish. Bao Luong snapped out of her nightmarish imaginings and slammed the lid shut.

Just then Truong walked in and demanded to know, "Why did you open the trunk? I brought it for you so you can keep your sewing stuff in it."

. . .

"After the crime, we three fled," Ngo Thiem claimed when he was questioned again by the police on October 31, 1929. "I left first. I don't know when the others did. I went straight to Do Dinh Tho in Phu Nhuan. The next day I left for Guangzhou."

"Three days after the murder," Ton Duc Thang had told police back in July, "Ngo Thiem went to Guangzhou to apprise members of the Central Committee of the judgment that had been pronounced against Lang."

Bao Luong recalled the chronology a little differently to the police on July 28, 1929: "Three or four days [after the murder] I encountered Ngo Thiem on the bridge of Paul Blanchy Street, and I asked him how the affair was proceeding. He answered, 'It's done. But you don't have to be kept informed.' Five days later I met him again on the bridge, and I asked him again who this influential party member was who had had to be eliminated. He told me this person was from My Nhon village [in Ben Tre] and knew how to mix medicinal herbs and that his name was Lang. As for the young woman whom Lang had harassed, it was none other than Lê Oanh. I don't remember if it's on this day or another that Ngo Thiem told me he was going abroad. When I asked where, he told me he was going to report on 'the business,' without giving further details. When I asked who had executed Lang, he replied that, having decided on a secret judgment, he had not asked for a public naming of the executioners. I have not seen him again since then."

Bao Luong implied during the same session that she learned of the motives for the murder only after Ngo Thiem left for Guangzhou: "Five days later, Lê Oanh came to live with me. I then asked her for explanations. She said she had had to submit to Lang and she felt abused."

"After receiving Ngo Thiem's report," Ton Duc Thang told police on July 30, 1929, "the Central Committee assigned two men to investigate the murder: Pham van Dong and Nguyen Kim Cuong. I reported to them on the real motive behind the murder as follows: 'Lê Oanh came to Saigon to complete her revolutionary training, which she had begun in Ben Tre. Lang was the one assigned to complete her training. He soon fell in love with Lê Oanh, who went to live with him. In order to persuade her to become his mistress, Lang did not hesitate to tell her that she had been sent to him by her comrades, who very much wanted her to become his wife. That was Lang's first lie.

"'The next day Lang told Ngo Thiem, Nguyen van Thinh, and then me that Lê Oanh wanted to become his mistress. Some time later, at a meeting of the committee, Lê Oanh complained that Lang was trying to force her to become his mistress. Nguyen van Thinh reproached Lang, but the latter threw the responsibility for the whole thing onto Lê Oanh and asked us to consider the possibility of allowing him to marry her. Ngo Thiem and Nguyen van Thinh agreed to the marriage, but I requested that this issue be taken up by the Regional Committee of Ben Tre, to which Lê Oanh still belonged. Nguyen van Thinh replied that, in order to avoid problems within the committee, it would be better if I gave my assent to the marriage of Lê Oanh and Lang. He also advised me to behave like a new man and to rid myself of old-fashioned ideas.

"'I did not agree to their plans, but I was outvoted. A contract was drawn between Nguyen van Thinh and Lang, according to which the marriage would take place after a month's leave for Lê Oanh, so that she could go to see her family in Mo Cay. This marriage had to be kept secret from other comrades, and it was also specified in the contract that Lang must not neglect party business under pain of death. Lang violated every clause of this contract. I informed the Provincial Committee of this fact, and it then met to decide Lang's fate.'

"After I made this report to Nguyen Kim Cuong and Pham van Dong, I was summoned to Guangzhou by the Central Committee, about three months ago. Pham van Dong transmitted the order. I did not go. I was too happy to have a reason to leave the party, and I did not want to leave my family."

Ton Duc Thang had by then decided to launch a new group, called the Southern Workers' and Laborers' Association (Nam Ky Cong Hoi), in competition with the remnants of the Revolutionary Youth League and bucking the nascent movement toward the formation of a communist party.

· · ·

As the police initially had difficulty establishing the identity of the dead man or motives for his murder, the conspirators began to believe that they had succeeded in covering their tracks. Bao Luong recalled: "Newspapers portrayed the Barbier Street murder as a horrifying event and embellished it with sensational details such as the story that a beautiful woman had come by car that fateful night to administer the drug to her lover and then assassinated him with the help of a third person. Or that the adulterous pair murdered the pitiful husband. Or that this was a settling of accounts between gang members—they had not shared fairly the loot they had stolen. The adulterous pair was heard sobbing gently. According to rumors, neighbors on either side of the house had heard the couple quarrelling and the wife sobbing loudly. Public opinion seemed to agree that this was a crime of passion, which made the perpetrators sigh with relief."

After the conspirators were arrested, the police fed suspicion that Bao Luong was the mysterious woman of the rumors. Both Ngo Thiem and Nguyen van Thinh, however, denied she was present at the scene. "Ngo Thiem," the police said to him on September 20, 1929, "Nguyen van Thinh has stated that you came a few minutes after him, that you went to fetch three cups of coffee in a nearby shop, and that you put the cups on a table in front of each of you."

"I don't recall."

"But on December 6, at 4 P.M., you went to Tran Truong's house in Phu Nhuan, and you met some comrades there, including Do Dinh Tho. Bao Luong was in the other room. You were in the kitchen. Tran Truong was at the door. You asked Do Dinh Tho if it was necessary to drug Lang before killing him. Bao Luong's brother [Nguyen van Dai] overheard this."

"Do you know Nguyen van Dai [Vien Dai]?" asked another inspector.

"I don't know him," Ngo Thiem said. "I might have met him but without realizing it."

"Do you know Bao Luong?"

"I know her, but I cannot tell you in what context," Ngo Thiem said.

Nguyen van Thinh also denied that Bao Luong had been at 5 Barbier Street. Still, Bao Luong was portrayed as an evil seductress who had used her wiles to detain Lang on the afternoon of his death, to make sure that he would be at home when his assassins came to kill him.

. . .

For seven months after the murder, things seemed to be back to normal. "Of course, the French Sûreté investigated vigorously," Bao Luong wrote, "but the ranks of the Youth League tightened and its work continued. It can be said that the years 1927–28 were its golden age. Except for Kim Oanh, Ton Duc Thang's wife, who took her children back to Vinh Kim, everybody stayed put and set the various cells to right. Ngo Thiem, Nguyen van Thinh, and Tran Truong went into hiding for only a few days. Meeting sites had been moved since before December 8, 1928, and aliases had also been changed. Those who had gone into hiding soon went back to their usual activities. The women's cell could no longer meet at the tailoring shop in Phu Nhuan so it relocated to Ben Luc.

"Internally, we were going through a crisis, but our will was not shaken. We all hoped that this experience with violence would teach those who had embraced revolution that it began with them; those who acted in the name of the nation and the people to expel the invaders and held positions of leadership must be totally upright. They could not be corrupt; they could not be dictatorial and monopolize power. If they shut their eyes and only opened their ears to flatterers, how could the revolutionary work proceed? But this work failed for a variety of reasons, which illustrated the multifaceted meaning of the term *unexpected.*

"One day Ton Duc Thang received news that the whole leadership of the regional committee had been replaced. All those who had taken part in the murder of Lang were punished with a six-month suspension and forbidden to hold meetings. We were not upset because we thought it was reasonable that, having contravened orders from on high, we would be disciplined. We calculated that by the June assembly, we would be able to resume our communications with the Central Committee. We would then be able to report on our progress in inducting new members. But this did not come to pass."

Instead, beginning in June, the dissolution of the Southern Regional Committee of the Youth League began. Bao Luong's account ties its dissolution firmly and exclusively to the murder on Barbier Street. There were, however, forces that would have led to the same result, even if no murder had taken place. This was the emergence of a dissident movement within the Revolutionary Youth League that sought to steer it in the direction of overt communism, while Ton Duc Thang was becoming more interested in syndicalism. At the May 1–9, 1929, meeting of the Central Committee of the Revolutionary Youth League in Hong Kong, a faction urged the formation of a true communist party in line with the ultraproletarian policy of the Comintern. Its representative in the South was Bao Luong's former suitor, Nguyen Bao Toan, who had been released from prison in February 1928, at the same time as Lang.

7

The End of the Revolutionary
Youth League

Bao Luong was not willing to marry Nguyen Bao Toan, but she was nonetheless fond of him. She notes in her memoir: "Among those who put their faith in Nguyen Bao Toan were Uncle Tran van Trieu's wife and her sister-in law Aunt Tran Ngoc Vien, Tran Sum [Tran Truong's brother], Van Thong [Bao Luong's neighbor and fellow trainee], and many others. One could say that in the Long Binh and Phuoc Long areas, those who had joined the revolution considered Nguyen Bao Toan as a shining star. He was good looking and better educated than most and was good at explaining revolutionary theory. If patriotic young women did not consider him their Prince Charming, at least they held him in great esteem, for Toan was never crude or flirtatious but always behaved courteously. Since Tran Truong and Nguyen Bao Toan had supported my bid to go abroad, I felt a debt of gratitude toward the man I called 'Fifth Brother.'"

Bao Luong had seen Nguyen Bao Toan again a few months after her return from Guangzhou and his own release from jail. He told her, "Bao Luong, work hard. I'm going on another trip abroad, and I won't be back in the South for a long time." Bao Luong had felt a nameless sadness at his words, but she could not give in to her curiosity. Her cousin Truong enlightened her: "Didn't you know? Nguyen Bao Toan was recalled to China to be reprimanded for allowing his personal feelings to cause him to reveal secrets. But when he got there, he found out that the reports about him were inaccurate. He asked to confront the person who had accused him, and everything was sorted out. But when the Central Committee asked him to go to the North, he accepted right away so that the suspicions that he had been led astray by personal feelings could be allayed. And do you know who was said to be the object of his affection?"

"No, how should I?" retorted Bao Luong, although she knew well how Nguyen Bao Toan felt about her.

"I've often advised you to settle your marital status," Tran Truong went on, disregarding her denial. "Twice the Central Committee has suggested men of good character and enthusiasm for the cause to you; you should pay more attention."

"At Tran Truong's words," recalled Bao Luong, "I was overcome with disappointment and anger. It looked, after all, as if revolutionaries were ordinary people and not saints. I felt sorry for Nguyen Bao Toan, for he was full of revolutionary fervor. Still, whether he operated in the South or in the North, he would still belong to the same movement, still pursue the same mission. People who really knew him would not stand in his way. But now it was June 1929 [seven months after Lang's murder], and Nguyen Bao Toan was back in the South with the mission to dissolve the southern branch of the Revolutionary Youth League."

When he got to Do Dinh Tho's house, Bao Luong was happy to see him and called out, "Fifth Brother!" The thought ran through her mind that this meant he was allowed to resume working in the South. Her joy had not yet dissipated when Toan asked her to sit by him and began scolding her for allowing the Barbier Street affair to occur. She tried to explain, but he continued to scold her. He was visibly exasperated with the Revolutionary Youth League. He said, "Bao Luong, I have to tell you that there will be many more similar cases. If we want to stop such instances of failure that undermine the revolutionary will, we need to transform the party."

"Yes, of course, but when?"

"Tonight, at the meeting," he told her.

Her feeling of gladness was gone. She went to find Ngo Thiem. After the Barbier Street affair Ngo Thiem had assigned her to escort recruits to the boat, and Tran Truong had put her in charge of communication under the guise of selling packets of miscellaneous goods. But after things had settled down, she had quit those assignments. Now, after learning what Nguyen Bao Toan planned to do, Ngo Thiem asked her sadly, "Bao Luong, have you met Nguyen Bao Toan? What kind of man is he?"

"He is a good man, full of zeal," she replied. "For the rest, how can I know about the unexpected factors that push individuals into certain courses of action? People are not made of steel, and even steel cannot withstand time."

"So in whom can we put our faith?" Ngo Thiem wanted to know.

"In ourselves and in our own will," she answered. "We need to have faith that we will overcome all difficulties, that we will fulfill our mission as though we were guided by heaven."

"Bao Luong, even when facing death, you'll be full of optimism. But I can't help worry about the future of the party," Ngo Thiem said. "It looks unstable in the current trend."

"Let's not worry about it," she said. "Let's go to the zoo."

Ngo Thiem and Bao Luong met up with Tran Truong and Nguyen van Thinh at a drinks stand in the zoo. The thoughtful expressions of the two men showed that they had already learned from Nguyen Bao Toan what the meeting was going to be about. When she saw Thiem's funereal expression, Bao Luong decided to leave them and walk along the river by herself. The silence helped her remember those days full of enthusiasm and optimism at the Central Committee.

. . .

Everybody was present at Do Dinh Tho's house that evening. Nguyen Bao Toan arrived after seven and told those assembled that the Revolutionary Youth League must dissolve because it was too amateurish to lead the revolutionary movement. He slowly recounted what had happened at the Central Committee in Hong Kong. Of the founders of the Revolutionary Youth League, Phan Boi Chau had been arrested by the French on the way from Shanghai to Guangzhou in 1924, and Nguyen Ai Quoc [Ho Chi Minh] had been pursued by the Guomindang general Zhang Fagui. Ho had had to flee to Hankou and thence to the Soviet Union. Other original leaders of the league were now heading the Central Committee: Lam Duc Thu, Hong Son (who had been released from jail), Ho Tung Mau, and Le Hong Phong (who had returned from Moscow). Ho Tung Mau had organized a general meeting in late 1928, but he was arrested at the beginning of 1929 by the Chinese government. Despite this, another general meeting was held in Hong Kong on May 1–9, 1929, with representatives from the North, Center, and South: Ngo Gia Tu, Nguyen van Tuan, and Tran van Cung. These three representatives declared that the majority thought that the half-nationalist, half-communist propaganda was misleading, and that the organization's name should be changed to the Vietnamese Communist Party. The Central Committee and other representatives argued that it was premature to openly advocate socialist ideas. As long as Vietnam was under colonial rule, revolutionary nationalism would be an effective rallying cry; there was no need to resort to communist rhetoric, which was unfamiliar to peasants who had a capitalist mentality. The revolutionaries needed to proceed slowly. However, aware of majority sentiment in the North and in central Vietnam, the three regional representatives went back to Vietnam to begin agitating. Almost overnight members of the Youth League in northern and central Vietnam were gathered under the banner of the Communist Party; the Youth League had become an empty appellation, and the Central Committee had no authority over this new party.

Nguyen Bao Toan asked those present at the meeting for their reaction to his report. They all said they were willing to stop taking orders from the old Central Committee but wanted to see the new party in action before deciding whether to join it. Toan asked Tran Truong to accompany him on a tour of the provinces to sound out the opinion of the local members. On his return Toan reported with irritation that the provinces still liked the Revolutionary Youth League, wanted its leadership to relocate inside the country, and wanted to go on operating as before. Bao Luong told him that the reason people still liked the league was that its mission was not yet accomplished and its modus operandi remained best suited to current conditions. "Since that is the case," asked Bao Luong, "why not let it continue its work?" Toan replied, "Bao Luong, you must be joking. I have the job of dissolving the Revolutionary Youth League. What will happen if I fail?"

"Is the new party really sincere?" she asked.

"Truly and completely. It will be extremely active," he assured her. "It will shake the colonial regime to its foundations, and in a not-too-distant day it will chase the invaders from our country. It will take over power and bring happiness to our people. Bao Luong, if this appeals to you, help me find a solution."

.   .   .

Bao Luong had just gone inside the house when Do Dinh Tho, his eyes red, his hands shaking, his wooden leg unsteady, gripped her hand and said softly, "I was just about to go and look for you all to tell you to go into hiding. Bao Luong, tell the female members to go back to the countryside. You, come with Phan Xuan Dinh [a league recruiter] and me to Laos. There is a revolutionary cell there." Tho's voice was unsteady and full of tears. Bao Luong tried to reassure him: "All the sisters have gone and are safe. As for me, I'm staying here to oversee Tran Truong, my brother Vien Dai, and Lê Oanh as they learn martial arts. Who is going to harm you? If they do, you won't be able to accomplish your mission, that's all."

"Bao Luong, don't joke. I have only one leg left, I won't regret losing the other one as well [if I should be caught]. But if the group falls into the police net, it will be disastrous. Please tell Ton Duc Thang and Tran Truong to leave," Do Dinh Tho begged her.

"Thang's wife and children have gone back to the countryside," she told him. "As for Thang, he is fine."

"When will you be ready, Bao Luong? My bags are already packed," Do Dinh Tho said.

"I'm not going anywhere," Bao Luong replied.

"Bao Luong, please listen to me and leave."

Do Dinh Tho's warning was like a bell tolling an impending tragedy. Bao Luong looked at him carefully. He was slight and somewhat taciturn; he had many good ideas when writing for *Than Chung* and could do math at record speed. Despite his wooden leg, he traveled from North to South tirelessly for the revolutionary cause. This knowledge persuaded her of his profound sincerity. "Tho, don't worry," she said. "We should fear only informants and being arrested by the French. How can we hide from committed revolutionaries?"

"Bao Luong, you don't understand," Do Dinh Tho told her. "It's not that Nguyen

Bao Toan is out to do us harm, but one party has to be overthrown in order for another one to rise up. The Revolutionary Youth League owns the nationalist label, and that is its appeal for the masses. Of course it's an obstacle for the new party! In the North and in central Vietnam, economic conditions are pushing people into joining the proletarian revolution without the need for persuasion. It's not like that in the South, with its plentiful rice and plentiful fish. Every so often people here engage in revolutionary activity like so many amateurs. They make patriotic speeches; they can lie in their courtyard spouting [reformist scholar] Phan Boi Chau's poems for a whole month without fear of reprisals. If their insides are full, their limbs are not going to move. Do you agree?"

"Yes, of course." Bao Luong said.

[The Sûreté seems to have agreed with Do Dinh Tho's assessment that a revolution was not likely to succeed in the South: "In Cochinchina, the terrain was less favorable (for the supplanting of the Revolutionary Youth League by the Indochinese Communist Party). The three delegates who advocated forming a communist party did not have connections there. They sent a trusted member from the North [Nguyen Bao Toan] to explain the viewpoint of the new party."][1]

"This is why," Do Dinh Tho told Bao Luong, "Nguyen Bao Toan claims that the Youth League must be dissolved, and right away. But the majority does not agree. They say stirring up the masses is like pushing them to run before they can walk; they'll fall and they'll turn away from the revolution. It will be difficult to establish trust in the new party in areas where the league is present. And you know that the league has established a presence everywhere. If only Phan Boi Chau or Ho Chi Minh were still on the Central Committee, none of this would have happened—"

"It sounds good but you're all wrong," she interrupted. "Even Phan Boi Chau may have been a reluctant sacrificial lamb."

Bao Luong and Tho fell into a prolonged discussion of the rumors that Phan Boi Chau had been betrayed to the French in 1924 in return for a large sum of money by someone eager to establish the Revolutionary Youth League. She was unwilling to think ill of anyone in the Central Committee, but Tho pointed out, "You, Bao Luong, when you went to the Central Committee, you were provided with food, clothing, and books; who knows whether these were not bought with the money that came from the sacrifice of Phan Boi Chau? Well, anything can happen. Let me shake your hand a last time. Personal friendships can no longer flourish in the garden of struggle. Flowers, plants, and even insects will perish, and only stones and gravel will remain."

Bao Luong tried to refute Tho's suggestion: "I asked Nguyen Bao Toan about Phan Boi Chau's arrest; he said he'd been caught in a Sûreté sting—"

"Of course," retorted Tho, "which revolutionary does not exploit circumstances? Moves and countermoves—how can one really know what goes on? If one day we are arrested, it will be said that it was because of the Barbier Street affair. Who will investigate to find out the truth and assign blame? So, if you're not coming to Cambodia or Laos, let's shake hands and say farewell here."

That evening Do Dinh Tho, Nguyen Bao Toan, and Bao Luong had dinner together. Tho looked sorrowful; Toan was silent and pensive. Bao Luong jokingly asked him, "So, Toan, how do you propose to 'cook' the Youth League? Are you going to make a curry out of it?" Toan, who had been lost in thought, looked at her vaguely. She switched metaphors: "Toan, if you jump onto a brand new boat and pilot it for a few impressive turns on the water, you'll attract a lot of passengers. What is there to be sad about? Experienced sailors will avoid drowning; you don't need to worry about not having enough passengers."

"Bao Luong," replied Nguyen Bao Toan, "don't make fun of my misery. I need to find a way out."

Do Dinh Tho observed, "Bao Luong, you will remain naive unto death. You'll still be joking in prison." He got up and went to the back of the house.

Toan asked Bao Luong, "What did Tho tell you?"

"You yourself talked about dissolution," she answered, "but if the majority doesn't want to join the new party, and you don't approve of the method of pulling people in, then what we've been discussing for fun will become the reality, isn't it so?"

Nguyen Bao Toan put his chopsticks down with a frown.

· · ·

Those who met at Ton Duc Thang's house that evening agreed that they needed to go into hiding, even though they were willing to work with the new party when it proved itself better than the Youth League. To show that they were not partisans, they cut off communications with the Central Committee. Ton Duc Thang said, "I have the feeling that something bad will happen. It's very difficult to overthrow a movement that has the trust of the people during a phase of secrecy. It's important to avoid the colonial police, and to avoid arousing popular ire. The best solution in that case is to throw everyone into the net. Getting the Sûreté to do your dirty work is tidy and quiet."

"So what do we do?" asked Tran Truong.

"Let's disperse," answered Thang. "Don't come back to the old places, suspend operations for a while. Take care to protect your families. If you join the new party, it will be like going on an airplane. It can fly fast, but death is also quick. Bao Luong, go back home."

Bao Luong was not worried. Her sister Hue Minh was with her friend Ngoc Anh in Cho Gao. As for her brother Vien Dai, he was a man; he could take care of himself. But she was disturbed by the thought that one revolutionary movement might use the colonial regime to get rid of a competitor. It would be like committing suicide. It was, after all, not easy to attract someone to the cause and train him, she thought. To then lead him into prison had to be either a crazy idea or the diabolical scheme of a double agent. She did not heed Ton Duc Thang's advice and stayed where she was at Do Dinh Tho's house. She also continued to engage in debates with Nguyen Bao Toan. Gradually, Tho's own anxiety abated, and he stopped talking about going to Laos.

[We know from the police file that Do Dinh Tho took in a lodger early in the summer of 1929. Luu van Phung, a twenty-six-year-old from the North, provides some idea of what life in Tho's household was like from mid-June to mid-July (he moved out, ostensibly to join his wife, two days before the police moved in—a coincidence or was he a plant?). A few days after Phung moved in, Do Dinh Tho quit the newspaper and "spent his time doing housekeeping chores together with me and the other Vietnamese living in the house," Phung said. "[Tho] also sewed on the sewing machine that was in the house. The first few days he did not go out at all. Then after a few days he began going out."

According to Luu van Phung, four others were living in the house: Tran Truong, Vien Dai, Lê Oanh, and Bao Luong, whom he knew only by their aliases. After a couple of weeks, they moved out after "some disagreement regarding a woman; at least that's the feeling I got. I cannot swear to it, since . . . I was not part of discussions. . . . The day they left . . . they all seemed to be angry; they seemed to have been angry for several days, but in front of me they refrained from showing their feelings and did not utter a word." The man he knew as Sixth Brother, Tran Truong, returned that afternoon and never mentioned the three who had left.]²

They were in fact tense rather than angry; the net was closing. Lê Oanh went home. Tran Truong and his cousins Bao Luong and Vien Dai went to live in another tenement. At some point Bao Luong went to see her parents. On the way she stopped in Cho Gao. "It was a happy place where comrades were enthusiastic in their work. They knew me only as a fellow student. I did not tell them about my worries, just as I had not told them about the Barbier Street affair. I only advised them to beware. I went to Mo Cay in search of Lê Oanh. Her brother-in-law went to fetch her in Ba Vat and gave us a lot of fabric, which Lê Oanh and I used to make Thai-style clothes in case we had to join our comrades in Siam. Then Lê Oanh went to Go Den, and I went home to Phuoc Long. I sold fabric along the way so that people got used to me and became less suspicious of my movements."

· · ·

When she saw her home, Bao Luong was dazed with pity for her parents. The plants in the courtyard looked desolate, the tiles were broken, one screen had a big gash on one side. When her mother heard Bao Luong's voice, she ran out, followed by her younger sisters, who asked, "Where are Third Brother Vien Dai and Fourth Sister Hue Minh? Why are they not back?" Their mother, Chau, silenced them: "They're still at their studies, why do you ask?" She then said in a low voice: "Your father is also absent all the time, going after them; it's really hard."

The sound of horses' hooves alerted them to Nham's return, and they rushed out to welcome him home. After a joyous feast Bao Luong and her father played chess as in the old days. But without Vien Dai and Hue Minh there to shout, "You're not allowed to move your piece after you've set it down!" it was not as much fun as before. Nham called for a glass of medicinal wine and began humming poetry. "Trung Nguyet, respond to my verses so that we can relive those days of your childhood, when the influence of Eastern morality was still strong in you." Her father's words triggered memories of the days when Bao Luong had learned about the literal and figurative meaning of words. It was eight years ago already. "Trung Nguyet," Nham suddenly said, "be careful when talking about love, lest you be thought fast. Truong told me that you went against the wishes of the group and refused to get married—why is that?"

"Father, I'll think about marriage later," she replied.

"Later, later, until some indefinite time. . . . But that's all. I'm going to keep my promise not to decide for you," her father said. "When are you leaving? Don't let things slide. Nguyen Bao Toan was here; he told me you were safe and that the party was going to change. He talked a lot to your cousin Tran Sum and your friend Van Thong. I suspect there is something afoot. I went up to Ton Duc Thang several times to visit you. Where were you every time? And where are your brother and sister? I did not dare ask for fear I would be laughed at."

Bao Luong tried to prepare her parents for the worst: "Father, when you're involved in anticolonial activities, it's not uncommon to be imprisoned or executed. Just think like that and you'll accept fate better. Be careful. Have faith that we three will not bring shame to our family."

Since her father had brought up Nguyen Bao Toan's name, she sought her parents' advice: "Father and Mother, Nguyen Bao Toan said to me, 'When victory is ours, please return my love.' What does that mean?"

"It means he is trying to cover up his disappointment that you refused him," her father replied. "When will the struggle end, after all?"

"We were composing poems. You told me that love is not pity, so I did not—"

Bao Luong was using a word, *thuong*, which meant both affection and pity in Vietnamese. Chau was uncomfortable with talk of romantic love. She frowned at her daughter: "You are about to say things aloud that you should not. If you have not made promises, it's fine. If you don't feel sorry for him, he does not have to feel an [inferiority] complex."

"Who says anything about complexes?" her husband interjected, surprised at Chau's use of a newfangled word and thinking back on their own arranged marriage. "Your mother has made great progress in fancy speaking," he told his daughter. "Let's compose some more poetry."

"For three days," recalled Bao Luong, "we stayed close to one another. My parents told stories about their own parents that were better than legends. We killed many chickens, for friends and relatives kept on coming. On previous visits my mother had not appeared very sad. But this time she often cried as she looked at the clothes I had put aside in a pile as if preparing for travel to a faraway place. In the end, I did not go far, but I did not return home for eight long years."

Bao Luong went back by way of Cho Gao, where her sister Hue Minh was living in the big house belonging to Councillor Ton's mother. An easygoing girl, Hue Minh had quickly made a place for herself in the circle that included Bao Luong's friends Ngoc Anh and Ngoc Tho.

[Bao Luong and Ngoc Anh spent their time talking about poetry, the miserable conditions of tenant farmers, how to deal with robbers, and Bao Luong's grandfather, who was her ideal of honor and patriotism. During one such conversation, Bao Luong gave Ngoc Anh her secret account of what had happened on Barbier Street on December 8, 1928.]

When Ngoc Anh finished reading Bao Luong's account, she did not sound particularly distressed by the murder but asked, "Bao Luong, you have not become disenchanted because of the Barbier Street affair?"

"My faith is as hot as a flame and as vast as the tide," Bao Luong responded. "We are all tiny bits of dust in the workings of a piece of machinery as it starts to break gravel to pave a road. The Barbier Street affair is like a little impurity in the oil. Any more of it and the machine would have had to stop but only for a while. The history of revolution proves that failure is the mother of success, and everything, however insignificant, contributes to success, thanks to the lessons drawn from experience."

"When are you leaving?" asked Ngoc Anh.

"Right now," said Bao Luong. "I leave my sister in your charge."

Ngoc Anh saw that Bao Luong was anguished at leaving the Revolutionary Youth League for another party. Was it the right thing to do? Bao Luong had not yet crossed to the other side, but the wish to do so was there, and it was like betraying a lover. Her sadness seemed irrational, but it was still sadness. If Tran Truong had not called her back to Saigon, she would have stayed on with her friends. "Which ideology one chooses, which party one joins depends on the capabilities of the people," said Ngoc Anh. "You know you always have to adapt yourself to new circumstances. It's not up to you alone to decide. If the majority wants to cross over to better fight the enemy and you don't, you'll be left all alone by the side of the river."

"No, I'm going to go along with the majority," replied Bao Luong. "I'm going to cross the river and join the new party. I cannot let my personal feelings get in the way. Perhaps one day we will be able to stand under the same banner. Farewell!"

. . .

Back in Saigon in July 1929, Bao Luong still hesitated to carry out her decision. Tran Truong told her, "Bao Luong, stop reciting poetry all the time. Let me tell you: Nguyen Bao Toan is still here in the South. He's confirmed that, according to plan, all members of the Youth League will be brought into the new party, and this new party will operate on a larger scale. It will be effective, and it will build a powerful movement that will reach the majority of the population. What do you think of that?"

"I believe that it will work if Nguyen Bao Toan is willing to bring people in gradually," she said. "The Youth League tries to treat people as if they were toddlers: only when they can be steady on their feet would it release them to walk on their own. But according to this new direction, people must learn to walk as soon as they can stand up, however unsteadily; even if they fall, they must get up again and keep on practicing walking until they are used to it. My feeling is that we should not avoid walking out of fear of falling. We need to put what we have learned into practice. Only through experiment can we adjust our methods. We must engage in struggle right away."

"It's settled, then," Tran Truong said. "Tonight I'll talk to Nguyen Bao Toan and suggest we hold a meeting."

"Were you waiting for me to hold it?" Bao Luong wanted to know.

"Of course. We had decided on this a long time ago."

"Does Nguyen Bao Toan know this place?" she asked.

"No, but he'll know tonight because he is supposed to give me some guns."

"Why guns?"

"Toan said someone wants to sell them; he bought them for me. I want you to learn to shoot."

"Buy them for yourself," she said, "I don't want them; it would be too difficult to hide them. How long have you been in this place?"

"Ton Duc Thang rented it four days ago. It's very convenient. Champagne Street is wide and quiet," he said.

"You brought my trunk and my sewing machine here; if Do Dinh Tho knows about this place, then Nguyen Bao Toan must know it as well."

"It's your brother who helped me move. Tho was not home. Why are you afraid?" Tran Truong said.

"I don't know why—"

"Bao Luong, I have to tell you, I am beginning to be afraid of the future."

Bao Luong was so taken aback that she dropped her newspaper and stared at her cousin: "Truong, please don't put me to the test. Even though we are being subjected to disciplinary action, we don't need to stop our activities. But if you are sad because of that 'business,' get over your weakness."

"You do not have blood on your hands, Bao Luong," he replied. "You cannot understand the pain that gnaws at my insides. I had been prepared to kill the enemy but not to start with—"

"Truong, it doesn't matter. There is no morality or ethics in conquest. Love and friendship are so many obstacles in the path of the hobnailed boots that tread on blood and bones. They [the French] used violence to rob a whole people of its life and called it glory, a civilizing mission, the sacred mission of the more advanced nations. As for us, we need to have a means of defending ourselves against this oppressive regime and against collaborators and traitors. How could you not punish Lang?"

"If only he had not repented—" Truong said.

"He repented only at the last minute, when he could no longer do any damage; it was useless repentance," Bao Luong argued. "There is no book that teaches you how to wage revolution; it all depends on the society one lives in. If you are giving in to pessimism—"

Tran Truong interrupted, "Ngo Thiem and Nguyen van Thinh are here already. Let's get to work."

"Let's work to bring the Central Committee back closer to the people. It would be great if the Central Committee also joined the new party," said Thiem.

"Thiem, you're dreaming. It's because the Central Committee did not approve of the new plan that Nguyen Bao Toan came south and that we are about to cross over and join with the opposition," said Tran Truong.

"Vien Dai, stay here," said Bao Luong to her brother. "We three have something to do."

. . .

Bao Luong, Tran Truong, Ngo Thiem and Nguyen van Thinh left the house together. As Truong walked ahead with Ngo Thiem and Nguyen van Thinh, Thiem said, "I feel sorry for Bao Luong."

"Lower your voice—she's catching up," Tran Truong hissed. "Why do you feel sorry for her?"

"She's naive to the point of stupidity," said Thiem. "She believes in the Central Committee and in her comrades. She does not know that danger is beginning to surround us."

"She knows but she says we can avoid external threats but not internal rot. If the French had had no help from Vietnamese, would they have succeeded? If there had been no one to snitch, they would not have found their way around and conducted sweeps. If you are in a boat and a fellow passenger wants to sink it and kill everybody in it, don't even try to avoid death; it cannot be done."

They kept on walking among the prostitutes who moved in the shadows in search of customers. As Thinh and Thiem were detained by some streetwalkers, Bao Luong and her cousin forged ahead without them and became engaged in a spirited discussion of prostitution and poverty. Tran Truong then went off on his own. When Ngo Thiem and Nguyen van Thinh finally succeeded in freeing themselves from the prostitutes and caught up with her, Bao Luong said, "We need to work fast. Truong has become downhearted. Let's say good-bye here. I'll stay with Sixth Aunt [Tran Thu Cuu], then leave from there."

"Wait. We still need to meet with Nguyen Bao Toan," said Ngo Thiem. That afternoon Tran Truong was criticized during the meeting at Ton Duc Thang's house. Truong knew that Bao Luong had mentioned to Dang van Sam and Bui van Them, their fellow cell members, that he was dispirited. He laughed as he said to Thang, "There are bound to be clear skies after the storm, no?" Thang retorted, "What if the storm is followed by a typhoon? Be careful." Truong looked at him worriedly. This austere and patient man had often guessed correctly how events would unfold. If he spoke of typhoons, he must have seen one gathering force in the horizon.

. . .

Back home, Tran Truong tried to cheer up: "Bao Luong, compose some *vong co* stanzas, please. It does not matter if they're not very good."

"I have some at the ready," she said. "But don't you have to meet Nguyen Bao Toan?"

"No, he's missed meetings twice, so I'll go to him tonight." Tran Truong and Vien Dai began to play their stringed instruments and to sing.

"Your playing sounds so sad, Truong," observed Bao Luong.

"It's not just your opinion," he replied. "Ngoan in Long Binh said the same thing. I also feel that my playing carries the sadness of ages. I won't play anymore." He threw his moon lute down onto the wooden platform, breaking its strings. Bao Luong stared at him. Bui van Them and Vien Dai burst out laughing.

That night Truong went to meet Nguyen Bao Toan, and Toan gave him the two guns he had bought for him. Truong paid for them, then returned home. It was exactly midnight, July 12, 1929.

"Does Nguyen Bao Toan know this place?" asked Bao Luong.

"Of course. You need only go to Ton Duc Thang's workplace to find out where he lives," Tran Truong said. "When he gave me the guns, Nguyen Bao Toan saw me turn into this street."

"Bao Luong, prepare your luggage; Vien Dai, you, too," said Tran Truong.

"Why?"

"Ultimately, Nguyen Bao Toan is committed to revolution, to the point of blindness," said Truong.

"When will we depart?" she asked.

"Seven o'clock."

Suddenly, someone knocked at the door and asked for electricity money. Tran Truong saw two Frenchmen looking at the electricity meter and went to give them the money. One grabbed him by the shirt, and the other went in and opened the trunk. Bao Luong grabbed his arm and yelled, "Are you trying to rob us?" The tall, thin man with blue eyes and a sharp nose dropped Truong and laughed. "I'm Inspector Bazin and I have a search warrant," he said. The two men searched the house from top to bottom and did not find anything, so they rubbed their hands and made their excuses. But at the door Inspector Bazin suddenly turned around: "Where are the guns?"

"There are no guns," said Tran Truong.

"We've been informed that you do have guns," Bazin replied.

The two men pushed the trunk aside, took out the tiles, and dug up the gun. "To whom does it belong?" Bazin demanded.

Truong said, "It's mine. I keep it against robbers."

Bazin said, "Fine. In that case, come back to the station. You, miss, and the young man, come along, too. You'll be released after we've taken your statements."

In the car Bazin said in Vietnamese, "Don't talk, okay?" Bao Luong was dismayed that he could speak Vietnamese. She disregarded his order and said to her brother: "Don't worry, the gun belongs to cousin Truong; you are here only to apprentice as a worker." Vien Dai nodded imperceptibly. Truong said calmly, "You two will be released this afternoon. I bought this gun without papers; I'll be put away for five years, probably. Vien Dai, learn to be a good worker. Bao Luong, you'll excel as a seamstress." Vien Dai and Bao Luong caught his meaning. "I told you not to speak," repeated Bazin. "When did you buy the guns?"

"At midnight."

"Liar. If you bought the guns at midnight, how could you be arrested by morning? The informer told us you had the guns for several days already. Have you made use of them yet?"

Truong laughed out loud: "I'm telling the truth. I bought them from a Chinese friend who needed money. I got them for protection, and I brought them home at midnight."

"All right, then, you'll get two years," Bazin said. "As for the young man and the young woman, I'll let them go this afternoon."

8

The Road to Hell

"During the colonial period," Bao Luong recalled, "nothing was more terrifying than to be taken to the police station, and especially to the main station on Catinat Street. To be kept there was worse. When it came to 'procedures' inflicted on the body, one would need to have recourse to some extraordinary new language to depict the torments suffered in that police station; in Vietnam under French rule it was like the tenth circle of hell on Earth. For a long time we had heard that people were tortured to death in that building. We three were there now. Beginning on July 13, 1929, we were about to know real pain."

Bao Luong did not realize for some time where she was being held. She had not yet come to grips with the reality that she was in prison. She was as befuddled as when Tran Truong and Nguyen Bao Toan had taken her to the boat and put her in the hands of A Suc, back in September 1927. But that trip, intended to forge a future full of hope, lay in the past. What was happening to her cousin Truong and her brother Vien Dai? And what would happen to a woman? Bao Luong sat on the tile floor, worried about whether she could defend herself against rape. She was about to take the penknife she had seen between the pages of a book when a gofer named Ton came in and told her, "Miss, please sit over there, some people are coming to work here." She thought happily that this meant she was about to be released. The window was thrown open. Three men walked into the room, sat down at a desk, and began writing steadily as if no one else was present. Behind their desk were two leg shackles connected to an iron bar. It looked like the room had recently been occupied by a prisoner. But she did not own guns—the charge against her cousin— so why should she worry about being put in shackles? For two hours she sat in silence, reassured because she was in a room with people who were working. She was

FIGURE 10. Nguyen Trung Nguyet, 1929.
GGI 65535.

sure that she would be going home in the afternoon. Naively, stupidly, she refused food, thinking she would eat once she was home.

"Ton, ask her why she is not eating," a Sergeant Thinh told the gofer.

"She says the shrimps smell bad, she'll eat at home," Ton replied.

Time passed; no one paid attention to Bao Luong. Suddenly, Ton ran to Sergeant Thinh and whispered in his ear. Sergeant Thinh looked at her and said to Ton, "It doesn't matter whether it is about guns or something else. Bring the prisoner over to your area. But it's strange."

"Yes, indeed," answered Ton. "I don't know why they called for vans and spread out in all directions and brought back so many people that the cells below are overflowing."

"There are people who are well known, like Ton Duc Thang, who lives near the sawmill that belongs to my aunt," said Ton.

"It can't be the Heaven and Earth secret society or a reprise of the Phan Xich Long case," observed Sergeant Thinh. (Phan Xich Long was the head of a Heaven and Earth Society gang that had staged riots in 1913 in Saigon. In 1916 some of his followers tried to free him from jail by again staging riots.)[1]

When Bao Luong heard them refer to Ton Duc Thang and mention other names, she understood that Dang van Sam and Bui van Them had been arrested and that the party cells in both Saigon and the provinces were compromised. She remembered that Inspector Bazin had observed, "The informer says there are guns." She would have to think up logical denials of her role in the Revolutionary Youth League.

"A girl who's involved with guns, she must be a hardened case," one guard said to the other.

"I heard she grabbed the arm of the inspector. That must mean she's guilty."

The men left, closing the door behind them. In the dimming daylight Bao Luong could see only gofer Ton sitting in the chair previously occupied by Sergeant Thinh. Ton was staring at her. Her brain was panicked, like a horse lost in the jungle. She was afraid that she would not have the strength to defend herself against rape. And if she banged her head against the wall or bit her tongue off, she might not die; instead, she would be permanently disabled and would become a burden to her parents. She fingered the penknife but decided not to use it. She felt dizzy and put her head between her knees. As panicked thoughts were chasing one another in her mind, Ton approached Bao Luong. She got up, pulled out the penknife, and said, "Does this belong to you?" Ton replied: "Please, won't you eat? You'll go hungry. Please keep the penknife." With these words he left the room. Bao Luong stayed where she was, bewildered by his kindness. Her brain felt as if it were shrouded in a thick fog; she did not know what to think. Those whom she had believed to be wonderful had turned out to be evil. Those whom she suspected of being as black as coal might turn out to be as pure as water lilies in a pond.

Ton returned, holding a package wrapped in paper. "Here is some bread—eat quickly. I'll give you some news. Is Vien Dai your brother? Is Tran Truong your cousin? I bought sandwiches for them and for the others." Bao Luong, still suspicious of Ton's intentions, did not speak up or eat the sandwich. She was afraid it might be laced with a drug—and if she were drugged, she was afraid of what might be done to her.

"Please, miss, eat it. I've given sandwiches to everyone, not just you. If you're not involved in the affair of the guns, you don't need to be sad. Eat to keep up your strength."

"Why do I have to keep up my strength if I'm not incriminated?" she demanded to know.

Ton bowed his head as if to hide something. He rewrapped the sandwich and went out. After a while two Frenchmen came in, looked at her with insolent eyes, and ordered: "Shackles!" Ton put her legs in the shackles. After the two Frenchmen had left, he gave her a large piece of oiled paper and said, "Put it underneath your back. You can also lean your head on the book and use it to shoo away mosquitoes."

Bao Luong did not eat for two days. She did not feel too bad from lack of food as she was staying in one place, inactive. Two mornings after her arrest, Sergeant Qui came in early. He was about the same age as her parents and had a rather arrogant air, which Bao Luong attributed to his working for the French. And yet he was kind. He looked at her shackled legs and clicked his tongue. He stood next to her and said, "Please eat this sandwich I just bought for you. Don't be afraid that anyone will come in. I've bought sandwiches for everyone, even cigarettes. You only have to fear the French, not us." With that he left. Gofer Ton took up where Qui had left off: "Eat up quickly—don't think of us like dogs or buffaloes, using tricks to make you confess. I'm only a gofer who escorts prisoners to court and back, that's all. There is no drug in this sandwich. The food vendors here are horrible. I only want to help those unfortunates who have ended up here to eat properly so that they will be able to withstand the horrible torture that will be inflicted on them. Please eat up."

Sergeant Qui stuck his head into the room. "Eat, eat," he said. "Then get rid of the wrapping paper. If they see it, it will be trouble for us!" Gofer Ton went to get Bao Luong some drinking water. When he came back, he announced, "Big trouble, miss! It's said that the people who were arrested were involved in the Barbier Street murder and that you are the main culprit. Is that correct?" She remained silent.

Another day he said to Bao Luong, "Tran Truong asked me to tell you that it is settled that the Barbier Street affair was about a rivalry over a woman, you don't have to worry about it anymore. But there is an order for your hands to be manacled!" In the afternoon he brought her a bowl of rice; in the rice were hidden a fried duck's egg and a Chinese sausage. He explained, "I gave money to the cook so that all your friends would have the same food. Let me open your handcuffs and shackles. No one will come in; you can lie down on the table. If you hear the sound of keys, let me know. You've been awake for several nights already—" He was about to put his own head on the table when Bao Luong spoke: "Put my legs back in shackles before you go to sleep." Ton exclaimed, "Oh, god! I am showing you some kindness and you refuse it? How weird; I've never seen the like." When he shackled her legs, Bao Luong brought the handcuffs close to her body. She did not want him near her. He had helped her cope with the cold in her back and mosquitoes; he had not drugged her food to make her confess; he had not done anything wrong. But whom could she trust now?

At night she lay down on the cold floor, bothered by the shackles. It was uncomfortable lying down under the gaze of three men. She wanted to put her hair up, but she was afraid that Ton would be disciplined if he opened her handcuffs, so she let her hair become all tangled; now she wished it was short, as Ly Tu Trong had advised in Guangzhou. Heartrending screams filled her with apprehension. Despite everything, she had no regrets. "Why didn't I follow Do Dinh Tho to Laos?" Bao Luong wrote in her memoir. "Because only a dark, uncertain future awaited a single woman who went away with two men without a support system, without membership in an organization. In a strange country I would have to take one of the two men as husband, and all I would be left with would be a bunch of children."

Perhaps, she mused, her friends were badly tortured before revealing the Barbier Street affair. So a case of illegal guns had turned into a murder case. When would it become a political one? Would her friends who were still at large be able to hide? If the police suddenly turned up at meeting places that had not yet been discovered, those friends might all be arrested. The Barbier Street affair involved only three people; yet many had been arrested. Maybe it was about something else? The main reason must be revolutionary politics. And since they had all been arrested on the same day, the question was not why but who was the informer?

[Bao Luong never answered her own question, even though the hints are fairly obvious in her memoir: she suspected Nguyen Bao Toan.]

. . .

"What is this case that has attracted such a crowd?" asked one of the sergeants.

"I heard that it even involves members of the Tan Viet Revolutionary Party of Nguyen Dinh Kien," the second sergeant said.

"Is this woman involved?"

"We don't know yet," said the other sergeant. "She has not yet been subjected to the electric shock treatment or the breathing in of fish sauce, or the airplane—"

Ton interrupted, "The French called for her to be shackled tightly. It's up to us to choose the size of the shackles. I told them there weren't any shackles in small size left. If they want her to fill them, let her eat well."

"If she's incriminated in this case, her limbs are going to swell without the help of food," said one of the sergeants. "Ah, they're coming."

Bao Luong had been faking sleep throughout this grim conversation. Three Frenchmen came in and woke her up, yanking at her shackles and yelling at Sergeant Thinh, who replied to them heatedly. After they left, Sergeant Thinh said, "Miss, the red-faced man is Inspector Monnier. He is brutal, and he is an expert at torture. He beats you in such a way that there aren't any marks and he can deny that he did it. The fat one is Bertin; he is kinder because his mother and his wife are Vietnamese. But how can he go against a real Frenchman? As for the old fox, that's Bazin; you know him already. He speaks Vietnamese very well, and nothing gets past him. Do you know about this murder? Did you live in the same house as Tran Truong? He's been informed against; it was in a letter. So has Ton Duc Thang. Perhaps the informer was someone in their confidence? If someone who has your trust betrays you, there's no way to escape from the cage."

Bao Luong had been detained for ten days. As far as the three men working in the room were concerned, whoever had been arrested must be guilty. And yet their attitude toward her was still deferential; this made her feel unsettled. Although they made quite a bit of noise, they could not cover the screams emanating from the upper floors and from the front of the building. Startled by the cries, Bao Luong would get up on all fours, but she was hampered by the shackles, so she would sit down again. But whether upright or sitting down, she shook at the sobs she heard: "It hurts, have pity on me, this is so unjust!" followed by labored breathing and heavy blows. These heartrending cries echoed through the cold nights and into the sunny days. One day when her spirits were low, the gofer Ton brought her up the spiral stairs, telling her, "Please tell them everything, miss." He then left her standing near Inspector Bertin.

"Whose guns are they?" the inspector asked.

"I don't know," Bao Luong replied.

"Living together, you must have known," Bertin insisted. "Tran Truong has confessed. Why do you keep on lying?"

"I only came to Saigon to sell my sewing machine," she said. "If the guns are his, that's his business."

"Were you the wife or the lover of Lang, who was murdered on 5 Barbier Street?" Bertin demanded.

"I don't know anything about that case," she said.

"Ngo Thiem said you were the one who drugged Lang," Bertin shot back.

Bao Luong knew that Bertin was trying to trick her, for it was not the truth. This gave her back some confidence: "I don't know anything."

"Let's call your brother and your cousin; then you'll know right away."

She suddenly remembered that, according to gofer Ton, Tran Truong's story was that the murder had been committed over a woman. Did Ton tell her that to reassure her or for some other reason? And even if Ton had tried to reassure her, this comfort was short lived, for this was only the beginning.

"Where were you at the time of the murder?" Bertin wanted to know.

"I have a sewing shop here in Saigon. When things are tight, I go back home," Bao Luong told him. "Why should I remember things that happen when I'm not here?"

"Do you know Dinh from Ben Tre? And Hoai Nghia? And what about Dong in Cho Lon? They all said you were Lang's lover." Bertin was persistent.

From that line of questioning Bao Luong became more confident that the Sûreté did not have any proof regarding the Barbier case.

Ton escorted her back to the cell and put the shackles back on. Sergeant Thinh, Sergeant Qui, and gofer Ton asked many questions and were glad to see that she did not have bruises and bumps. "Just keep on saying you don't know anything, miss. If you confess to even one thing, you'll go to hell." But no sooner had she sat down than she was called again, and she made her way back up the spiral staircase. Inspector Bertin laughed as soon as he saw her: "This time you've got to know. Here is your brother." He turned to Vien Dai: "So, at the time of the Barbier Street murder, where was your sister?" Vien Dai took three steps into the room. Bao Luong did not dare look at him; she had seen at a glance that he'd been tortured. She bit her lips and looked at the floor. Vien Dai said to her, "I remember you were at your sewing shop in Phu Nhuan."

"I don't remember. But what has that case to do with us?"

Vien Dai stared at his sister. Perhaps he thought she had confessed. "That's all I saw," he said. "They thought I knew something."

"You don't know?" said Inspector Bertin. "You'll know soon enough."

Tran Truong was brought in next. His clothes were in tatters, his face drained of blood, his limbs shaking. He said to his cousins: "Don't worry, this does not concern you."

It seemed that Inspector Bertin was willing to let them talk in order to learn more, and therefore did not interrupt them. Tran Truong told Bao Luong and Vien Dai, "We were tortured by electricity. I saw the letter in which the informer said that we three [Nguyen van Thinh, Ngo Thiem, and Tran Truong] were the perpetrators of the Barbier Street murder. You don't know it, but it's about the prostitutes on Lo Duc Street, that's all."

[Unbeknownst to Bao Luong, Tran Truong was, in fact, trying to misdirect the police and limit their investigation. On August 6 he "confessed": "I acknowledge being the owner of the handgun which you discovered at my house, 361 Champagne Street. I have owned the gun since July 12. I bought it that very day from a European who also sold me the two boxes of cartridges that you seized together with the gun. I bought the whole lot for twenty-five piasters. The European man was tall, heavy-set; he had a long face, beardless. He wore a gray linen suit and a black fedora. I went to Jean Eudel Street in Khanh Hoi one day to look to buy a gun. By chance I met this European man I just told you about in the street. I asked him if he could procure an automatic weapon for me. He said yes. He fixed an appointment for July 12. This happened on July 10 or 12. I did not want to use the gun, just to resell it for profit. This was the first time I was involved in gun trafficking."[2]

On August 16, 1929, Than Chung reported: "The number of people implicated in the Barbier Street affair now runs to twelve. On Monday morning [August 12], the so-called murderers were brought to No. 5 to reenact the crime for the benefit of Prosecutor Lafrique, Judge Grosse, and the Head of the Sûreté. A camera was brought in. One of the murderers played the role of the victim. They told the story from the beginning to the end. In it is implicated a woman.

"According to the newspaper Opinion, this is a political murder. The woman was used as a decoy. It seems that six members of the group will be brought to the court at its next session."]

After Vien Dai and Tran Truong had left, Bertin smiled at Bao Luong: "Your brother and your cousin are protecting you, but there are many who are saying that you were the cause of the murder. So, was Ngo Thiem your lover boy?"

"Who is Ngo Thiem, and what do you mean by 'lover boy'?" she demanded.

"Don't lie!" Bertin told her.

Bao Luong was taken back to her room. The sergeants were surprised to see her unharmed. Gofer Ton said joyously, "I'll bet you'll be released soon." Bao Luong was not so sanguine. Tran Truong had said there was an informer's letter. So much was certain. Was Truong so naive as to believe that the Sûreté was interested only in the murder on Barbier Street? The arrest of so many members of the Tan Viet Revolutionary Party suggested that dissidents within the Revolutionary Youth League had manipulated the French into arresting their own colleagues as well as members of other parties so that a new communist party could emerge without competitors. How could Truong think that the police would stop at investigating the murder? Bao Luong felt she had to protect those still at large; she could not give away their names even under torture, but she was terrified at the thought of electric shocks. Truong, who was normally so healthy and strong, had been reduced to a shadow. No matter. Death ended everything.

Contrary to her fears, Bao Luong did not die. Instead, she was called upstairs a third time. As she emerged from the stairs, Dinh, the man who had tangled with Lang over contributions in Ben Tre, ran over to her and grasped her hand, exclaiming, "Comrade Bao Luong!" She shouted, "Idiot!" Then she looked at him: his face was black with bruises, his hair matted, his whole body emaciated. The poor man stood stock still before her, belatedly realizing that he had revealed too much.

"So the girlfriend of Ngo Thiem and Lang was this woman?" asked Bertin. Dinh did not reply. Bazin said from the corner where he was sitting: "It's really bad for revolutionaries to fight over girlfriends to the point of committing murder." Dinh went red: "Don't insult us. The Barbier Street murder was not a crime of passion. It was the elimination of a counterrevolutionary." He turned to Bao Luong: "It's no use denying, Luong. They've made a full report already."

After Dinh left, Bertin said to Bao Luong, "You see, you have not been beaten since coming here. But the proof is all here; confess and everything will be over."

"I don't know anything," she insisted.

"Who is Bao Luong?"

"I don't know."

Bazin laughed and shoved a small photograph into her face: "You're sure you don't know this person?"

"Of course. It's my father."

"What about this picture?"

"I don't know," Bao Luong told Bertin.

"You're not going to avoid being beaten," the inspector told her. "You stayed with this person, ate his food, you persuaded his daughter to join the revolution, and now you say you don't know him? You really deserve a beating. I'll give you five minutes to think it over."

Bao Luong went out to the corridor. How had they gotten a picture of Headman Hoai? He was not involved in anything. Had his daughters Ngoc Anh and Ngoc Tho been arrested as well? Her mind awhirl, she walked back into the room.

"So do you know whether Dinh is your comrade? When did he join the party?" Bertin asked her.

"I don't know."

Inspector Monnier always sat in the middle when interrogations were being conducted. This time he got up and went to stand on one side of Bao Luong, and Bazin stood on the other. Bertin looked solicitous: "They've confessed everything. It does not matter if you say something or not, except that they'll beat you and pour fish sauce into your nostrils. It hurts a lot; you'll cough blood right away."

"Why should I be treated this way since I don't know anything?" she asked.

With that Monnier slapped her hard on the temple with fingers as large as bananas. He and Bazin took turns slapping her. Bao Luong became dizzy. Outside the window the sun seemed to turn round and round. After a while she felt complete quiet, as if she'd gone to sleep.

· · ·

"Miss, miss, wake up and eat."

Bao Luong vaguely heard someone talking to her but could not open her eyes; her jaw was locked, she could not speak. She heard Sergeant Thinh say, "Here, here, get some salt to rub on her. Get some water so she can drink this pill; she needs to cough up blood. Otherwise it will stay in her lungs and she'll get TB."

"If she did not do anything, why was she beaten so badly?" Sergeant Qui asked.

"Qui, you only began working here yesterday?" Sergeant Thinh replied. "Has anybody ever confessed to robbery? But we must have pity for her; she has not made a confession."

"So did someone confess and implicate her in the Barbier Street murder?" Qui asked.

"The police did not beat it out of them," Thinh said. "The informer had pictures from China—how could they deny anything?"

Bao Luong took in everything they said. Pictures from China! That meant the Central Committee had also been searched. She felt hot, then cold, as if she had a fever. Only an informer within the Central Committee could have led the Chinese police to the incriminating pictures.

"Don't shout, miss. Drink this medicine. Are you awake?"

She opened her eyes to see the two sergeants looking at her with apprehension. Her face was swollen and her jaw askew. She was taken upstairs again. Inspector Bertin said: "You have a new friend today." Bao Luong turned and saw Nguyen Kim Cuong, the teacher who was a friend of Lang's. Bao Luong did not know exactly how Cuong had been tortured, but he had to be held up by two men. He looked at her with glassy eyes. Bertin showed him a bunch of photographs and asked him to tell about each person in detail. Nguyen Kim Cuong looked at Bao Luong again with immensely sad eyes as he talked about joining the party and said that the Barbier Street affair had been a political assassination.

"Is this Comrade Bao Luong?" Bertin asked him.

"Yes."

She erupted: "Don't talk rot. You did not succeed in harassing me, and now you're throwing accusations at me!" Cuong's face turned green, and he fainted. Bertin turned to Monnier, and the two men laughed aloud. Bertin asked, "Are you mad at him? He's sick because he told the truth. He was not beaten!"

"He's sick for the same reason I'm sick. French people are liars."

"I tell you, miss, that the murder has been reenacted," Bertin informed her. "You weren't there, but do you know who else was there? And how many members were there in the party? Where are they now? You'll get a reduced sentence if you talk; you might even be released right away. Think about it."

Bao Luong knew the inspector was lying. If the scene of the murder had been reenacted, they wouldn't be asking her about it. She thought that if she denied that she had information about the party, she would have to have witnesses to support her story. If she confessed to being a party member, the whole base would be destroyed. She put her hands on the low wall in the corridor and tried to gather her thoughts. Nguyen Kim Cuong and Dinh were fervent believers in the cause. If the police had not had specific and detailed information, Cuong and Dinh would not have confessed, even under torture. And her cousin Truong was tough. He had been willing to admit to committing a crime of passion. Dinh, however, had said this was a political assassination. The French had used the crime to defame the revolution by claiming that revolutionaries were depraved and had been fighting over mistresses.

It was already too late to protect the organization, thought Bao Luong. Too many members had been arrested and tortured. She recalled the eyes of Dinh and Nguyen Kim Cuong, full of hatred for the French and full of bitterness, and realized how much she loved the organization to which she still belonged. They must have been informed against, with full proof they could not deny.

"Whose picture is this?" they asked again.

She said nothing.

"And this?" As Bao Luong looked at the pictures of Truong Phong and Thanh Huyen, her heart was full of sorrow. These were friends who had crossed the sea with her in search of guidance. She could die over and over, but if she were to live another eighty years, how could she live with the guilt of betrayal? She would die in order to avoid shaming the name *comrade*. This decision made her feel better. She remained silent.

"You deserve beating," Monnier warned. "Don't blame me if you get one, my child."

Why did he have to call her "child"? It reminded her of Hoai Nghia. From Hoai Nghia it sounded so sweet, but from Monnier, the fat colonial invader, it was an insult.

"Hold her down," Monnier ordered.

Bertin told her in a voice full of concern, "Lie down. Confess, or you're going to get it."

Bazin aimed at her spine, using a stick made of two pieces of rattan that had been nailed together to make the weapon wider. At first it did not hurt. After a while it itched. But after the fifteenth stroke or so, Bao Luong could not have said whether it hurt or itched; she felt feverish and her head ached. When she kept stubbornly silent, the Frenchman got mad. He pulled her up by the armpits and lifted her right up. She felt a sharp pain in her chest; a blessed darkness descended. Sometime that night Bao Luong woke up from her coma and vaguely noticed someone sitting by her and wiping her mouth. Although she was only semiconscious, she knew right away it was gofer Ton.

"Miss, wake up and take some medicine and let me spread some salt," he told her. "You have blood on the tiles."

Bao Luong wanted only to die, but when she heard "blood on the tiles," she panicked and looked. There was indeed something on the floor that looked like chicken blood.

"Do you need to change your clothes?" Ton asked.

She said nothing.

"I stayed up all night, because I took off your manacles and was afraid they'd see it," Ton told her.

Still she did not respond.

"How do you feel, miss? At dawn, when the two sergeants come in, they will bring medicine, they know about you," Ton said.

Gofer Ton thought Bao Luong was unable to speak, so he did not ask any more questions.

"Someone's coming," he told her now. "Give me your hands quick so I can put the manacles on."

The manacles felt heavy and tight. They rubbed against the places where the skin had broken. The smallest move hurt. Ton took his handkerchief and wrapped it around Bao Luong's ankles, muttering, "Those cruel bastards. Oh, Mr. Qui has arrived."

"Miss," said Sergeant Qui, "you were tortured badly, right? I told my wife about you, and she cried. She sends you a pair of trousers and a short-sleeved top; if the French ask, you can say that when you were arrested, you wore two outfits; that is quite common, and you will be fine. Ah, Sergeant Thinh has come. He probably has some medicine."

"What's this blood?" asked Sergeant Thinh. "Ton, clean it up quick. Get some water for the medicine. There's some vegetable soup in the small canteen in the corner. Be careful how you go about. This is a very big affair; there will be many more interrogation sessions. There's someone who was beaten so badly his eye looked like snail stuffing. He's kept in a solitary cell; he looks awful. Are you Miss Hai? Ton Duc Thang has stated that he is your relative by marriage; you don't need to be afraid to acknowledge him. You need to acknowledge insignificant details. I type up the confessions of all your gang, so I know everything."

In those days of suffering at the police station, these three men went to great pains to help Bao Luong surreptitiously. Their faces took on an anxious air every time some papers came down from upstairs for them to type up.

"We feel very sorry for you because you're a woman," one of them told her. "You

were forced to act as courier, and so you got arrested with them, weren't you? In
that case it won't matter much."

Gofer Ton told her, "There were also women involved in the Phan Xich Long
case. As long as you live, you can still go home."

"Ah, here is Ton Duc Thang's confession," Sergeant Thinh said. "He's a tough one.
He says he is a member of the Communist Party but had not started to be active
because he just joined. Tran Truong, Vien Dai, and Trung Nguyet are relatives of
his wife; they stayed with him a short time. He was not in any way involved in the
Barbier Street murder."

"So he's in the clear," Sergeant Qui said.

"How can he be?" Sergeant Thinh said. "Others have implicated him."

As Bao Luong listened to the men, she decided that she should avoid confirm-
ing anyone's story.

· · ·

"Could I take a shower?" she asked one day.

"The sky will fall! No one has ever asked for a shower here!" Ton replied. "There
are showers, but of canings, of blood, of fish sauce."

"Well, we'll be demoted and won't be escorting the prisoners to the tribunal,"
said Qui. "You need to have a heart of stone to work here. All day long, your ears
are inured to cries and screams. If we can help those in peril here just a little bit, we
can preserve something of our own humanity. The money I gave to you for the male
prisoners, I hope it's not wasted?"

"This month I won't be able to hand over money to my wife," Thinh said. "I am
supporting several guys so that they can withstand the torture. I put sausage in the
bread. Mr. Qui, give me some money to buy milk. There are some who can't open
their mouth to chew bread."

"Ton, how is Vien Dai, my brother?" interrupted Bao Luong.

"That kid? He's well fed," Ton said. "He was the least badly treated."

"He'll probably be let go," one of the sergeants added. "No one has implicated
him. Pretty good job, living with murderers and people who joined the Communist Party, and yet no one got him into trouble."

Bao Luong repeated her request: "Please ask permission for me to take a shower.
The smell of blood is so bad!"

"Wait a bit—when they come in, you can ask," Ton advised. "Right now, they
come in all the time, so I cannot open your manacles."

"Please go quickly—right away. If you don't, I'll shout for permission and you'll
be scolded," Bao Luong warned.

"All right, you are bold! I'll have to be, as well. They won't kill me, if they don't
give permission, that's all there is," Ton said.

Not long after Ton ran out, Inspector Bertin came down and said with a smile,

"So you want to take a shower? Fine, fine. Ton, open her shackles and take her to the fountain. Stay there and watch her, then bring her back in."

Inspector Bertin went to stand at a distance from the fountain while Ton helped Bao Luong to walk there by slow steps. To get to the back door, she had to pass by several cells, and she tried to look inside them for people she knew. She saw Ton Duc Thang, Bui van Them, and Dang van Sam; they were shackled to the same iron pole. The room was dark, but she saw clearly the skeletal bodies of her friends. Their eyes were red and swollen, their faces gaunt; they sat with their knees up in an attitude of despair. Dang van Sam saw her and cried out, "Bao Luong!" Bui van Them immediately slammed an elbow into him. Ton Duc Thang said with difficulty, "How are you two?" Bao Luong wondered if the men were bitter when they saw her walking outside. She did not want to look at them for long, afraid that she could not maintain the pretense that she did not know them. She also feared that, if she showed any difficulty in walking and other signs of damage, and especially if she cried, she would cause them pain. So she tried to appear strong. In the other cell she saw Nguyen Kim Cuong and Dinh. If they were being held together, it meant that they had already been interrogated. As for Tran Truong and Vien Dai, she was unable to find out their location.

At the fountain she washed her feet and started walking back. Inspector Bertin scolded, "Why did you ask for a shower but only washed your feet? You think I have the full authority to let you come out here?"

"Men are not allowed to take showers, but you choose to let a woman? And why is that?" Bao Luong asked.

Inspector Bertin laughed and told Ton to stand in the corner. Bao Luong called out, "Ton, please lend me a sarong." On Bertin's nod, Ton gave her a sarong and the packet of clothes that Qui had brought in from his wife. After she had finished washing her clothes, she saw a hand sticking out from a cell, waving at her. Peering into the gloom she was able to discern her cousin Truong.

. . .

As soon as he saw Bao Luong, Inspector Bertin smiled. "Today everything is definitely going to be concluded. Sit down, you are not going to be interrogated again because there is now sufficient evidence. You are Bao Luong, you went to China to plot against France. So whose picture is this?"

She did not respond.

"It's a picture of Headman Hoai; you stayed at his house for quite some time," Bertin said.

"I never met him," she maintained.

"Oh, really?" Bertin said. "Here he is."[3]

Headman Hoai moved out from behind the door and called out, "Nam!" This was one of Bao Luong's aliases.

Inspector Bertin laughed: "You persist in your denial? He's recognized you."

"No," she said, "I don't know this man."

Headman Hoai's legs were shaking from a combination of old age, weakness, and torture. He said, "Perhaps you don't know me, miss, because you studied far away; I used to go around teaching martial arts."

"Why did you say yesterday—?" demanded Bertin

"I thought it was someone else," the old man replied.

"Which someone else?"

"A friend of my daughters'; I'm not sure," he answered.

Headman Hoai left. Bao Luong's feeling of relief was short lived. Inspector Bertin showed her another photograph: "Who are these?"

She said nothing.

"Let me say it instead of you: this is Ton Duc Thang, whose name in the Communist Party is Dinh Cong Thang, head of the Regional Committee of the Revolutionary Youth League. You don't know him, but you were present at the meeting where it was decided to sentence Lang to death? And here, a picture of Luu Hoai Nghia; you went with five other people [to Guangzhou]. Who are they? Where are they? And here is another one. You had your picture taken with four Chinese women. Who are they?"

Bao Luong felt suffocated, without means of escape. It was only a photograph, but as she looked at it, her insides knotted painfully. To her the photograph was sacred, for it marked her entry into revolution. In the picture she stood solemnly between Ly Tu Trong and Ly Tri Thong. Bao Luong's hair was in braids, and she was wearing the cheongsam that Duc had given her. The picture had been taken at the ceremony in front of the tomb of Pham Hong Thai, where she had sworn loyalty to the revolution and had felt like a bride.

"Let me ask one last time," said Bertin. "Is Thang your relative by marriage?"

"He is my relative by marriage in such a distant way as to be meaningless," she responded.

"He is pretty dangerous, isn't he? He's pretty involved in revolutionary activities, isn't he?" Bertin queried.

"I'm only distantly related to his wife, so how could I know anything of his activities?" Bao Luong shot back.

Now Bertin changed the subject: "In the Barbier Street murder, you gave the poison and there were five people involved, isn't that so?"

"I wasn't involved in that business," she said.

"Well, Tran Truong and Ngo Thiem also said you were not involved, but there are reports that a woman's loud sobs were heard that night," Bertin said. "Were these the sobs of Nhut, also known as Lê Oanh?"

"Who's Lê Oanh? Where is she?" demanded Bao Luong.

"Don't you see? If there was no one to give us a lead, how would we know the whole story?" Bertin pointed out. "If Tran Truong and Ton Duc Thang had not seen the informer's report, why would they have confessed? Do you want to meet them?"

"What for?"

"So that you can believe that French people do not lie," Bertin told her.

Ton Duc Thang was brought in. He calmly told Bao Luong, "There's nothing to worry you. We've seen the informer's report, and we know whose handwriting it is."

"What does it mean?" she asked.

"We just have to accept the evidence," Ton Duc Thang replied.

Bao Luong understood him to mean, confess to things that you cannot deny. After Ton Duc Thang was taken away, Inspector Bertin took out a photograph of Hoai Nghia. "Tran Truong is about to come up," he said. "You'd better say it now. You went to train for revolution with this guy, didn't you?"

"I don't know him," said Bao Luong.

"You're going to know right away," Bertin declared.

But it was Nguyen Kim Cuong who was brought in.

"Speak up," Bertin ordered. "Yesterday you said that Bao Luong went with many people. Who are they, what are their names, where are they?"

Bao Luong stared at Cuong. He looked conflicted: "I only heard about it."

"What about joining the party?" Bertin asked.

"I also only heard about it," Cuong claimed.

"Who told you?"

"It was Lang, who was also known as Le van Phat," Cuong replied.

"He's dead; easy for you to put the blame on him!" Bertin shouted.

After Nguyen Kim Cuong came Tran Truong. He was badly injured. He said, "Bao Luong, we have reenacted the murder. The gun business is of little significance. As for joining the party, it involves only a minority and it's unimportant."

"Truong," asked Bertin, "did Bao Luong associate with these people?"

"I don't know for sure," her cousin replied.

After Tran Truong came Dinh, the man from Ben Tre. Bertin showed him the picture and asked, "Did Bao Luong associate with Hoai Nghia?" Dinh grinned: "Hoai Nghia said he went to China with Bao Luong, but I don't know if that's the truth."

"We're going to have to deal with these two, Dinh and Cuong," Bertin snarled. "It shouldn't be that easy to retract confessions!" Listening to Bertin, Bao Luong understood that Nguyen Kim Cuong and Dinh had been duped into believing that she had confessed. They were caught out when they found that she had not. The regret that hollowed Cuong's eyes, and the half-smile, half-grimace produced by Dinh when the two men realized their mistake filled her with pity.

"Hoai Nghia is going to come up," Bertin told her. The informer really had not spared anyone! It was useless to keep secrets.

Hoai Nghia looked at Bao Luong with studied indifference. Inspector Bertin asked him: "Do you know this woman?"

"No."

"This is the limit! She said she went with you to China to wage revolution, she had her picture taken, and she went with four other people," Bertin lied.

Hoai Nghia fell for Bertin's trick and got mad at Bao Luong. He yelled into her face: "How many beatings did they give you to make you confess everything, Bao—"

"Bao what?" she cut him off. "I don't know you. What am I supposed to have confessed?"

Despite this byplay, they could not fool the professional detective's eyes of Inspector Monnier. Bao Luong's phony denials and Hoai Nghia's misunderstanding only confirmed the sad truth.

"When did you join the party?" he demanded.

"Ask her; I don't know," said Hoai Nghia.

"How many people went to China with you?" Monnier pressed him.

"Ask her."

Hoai Nghia seemed unaware that Dinh and Nguyen Kim Cuong had already told the inspectors everything about him. Bao Luong decided to say, "I had made a promise to a Minh Huong Chinese; I followed someone I knew to China to look for him. When I was on the boat, I met this Chinese man. When I got to China, I took pictures with relatives of this man." Bertin waved his hand: "We need witnesses, not liars like you. Your cousin Tran Truong and others have already said enough about you."

Bao Luong was taken back downstairs. She was hoping that, if Headman Hoai was able to remain unscathed, her friends in the My Tho area would not be implicated; and if Hoai Nghia did not confess, then those who had gone to China with him and her would also be out of danger. She returned to the clerks' room and lay down in the old spot. She tried to ignore the discomfort caused by the swellings and bruises and the sores where her flesh had burst open from the beatings and to concentrate on reviewing the situation. Ngoc Anh, Ngoc Tho, and Lê Oanh, as well as the student and the civil servant who had been in the same group and some of the newer recruits, were not at risk; that was some relief. As for her, she just had to endure and wait for the tribunal.

[*Bao Luong seems to have telescoped several scenes of interrogation, giving the impression that they took place within a very short period. In reality, her confrontation with Hoai Nghia apparently took place months after her arrest and after she had been transferred to Central Prison. According to the bill of indictment, "On January 3, 1930, Nguyen Trung Nguyet, alias Bao Luong, confronted Nguyen van Ngoc, alias Hoai Nghia, and said to him: 'The rot comes from within our party. I was not the one who denounced you. I only confessed after being confronted with the avowals of others who spoke before me. You were in Guangzhou with me. I said so.' Nguyen van Ngoc then said: 'I acknowledge belonging to the Revolutionary Youth League, and here are the circumstances that led me into this revolutionary organization.'*"[4]

Hoai Nghia then gave an account of his introduction into the league by Ton Duc Thang, his trip to Guangzhou on the Telemachus *with Bao Luong and others whom he named, his opening of a jewelry shop in Ben Tre to facilitate his work of propaganda, and the steps taken to bring him into the Southern Regional Committee, which were suspended when Nguyen Bao Toan arrived in June 1929 to dissolve the Revolutionary Youth League.]*

· · ·

A few days later the accused saw each other at the courthouse, where they had been transported to have their mug shots and fingerprints taken. Ngo Thiem told Bao Luong, "There are three heads that are not going to stay atop their necks." Nguyen van Thinh and Tran Truong, who stood nearby, smiled faintly. "Bao Luong, don't be sad. Do you know who the informer is?"

"Why say his name out loud?" replied Bao Luong. "The deed is done. Are people on your side okay?"

"Yes. I have not seen anyone from the party cells under me," Tran Truong replied.

Nguyen van Thinh laughed: "We've got people to continue our mission; we can close our eyes right away and die." Ngo Thiem added, "Anyone who has someone to follow him can be said to have someone to close his eyes for him." Bao Luong was relieved: it looked like this meeting at the courthouse was not going to be an occasion for bathos.

Vien Dai, who had a sunny nature, smiled as he told his sister, "When I get to go home, I'll shout to let you know." Upon hearing this, Truong laughed: "And when they guillotine me, I'll also call so that you can make a cheering noise, Bao Luong." Then he took out a small comb and gave it to her: "They'll be shaving our heads. Please take this comb." Bao Luong was overcome with sorrow as she recalled the many times when Ton Duc Thang's wife had combed her long hair. She wondered how Kim Oanh and her two girls were faring while her husband was incarcerated.

As the group headed back to the police station, Dang van Sam's mother and his wife walked by his side; they gave him food and supplies, such as a toothbrush and a towel, all the while crying piteously. His mother hid her face in her hands and sobbed, then fell on the ground. Dang van Sam tried to soothe her: "Mother, please go home, I'm fine." His wife, whom he had married less than six months earlier, cried as if at his funeral. She rushed forward to be closer to him, and abandoning decorum and restraint, she spoke the passionate words of a young wife who had been torn from her husband: "If something happens to you, I'll follow you; if you die, we'll die together. You are so gentle; who sowed poison against you? Heaven, look down on us, take pity on us." Then it was her turn to fall on the ground; her mother-in-law pulled her up, then the two fell again. Dang van Sam gazed at his wife and mother in anguish, his feet turned to lead, his face aflame: "Please take Mother home, dear; I am okay." Nguyen van Thinh smiled faintly as he looked on.

Tran Truong joked, "If your wife were here, she'd make the same scene." Thinh retorted, "No way. We've got three children. We're set."

As Bao Luong passed the fountain, she thought at first that she was seeing things. Kim Oanh, Thang's wife, was sitting propped against a wall, a baby in her arms, waiting for her husband. When she saw Bao Luong, she called out, "Little sister, little sister!" Then she choked up and could not continue. Bao Luong hastened to ask, "So you already gave birth?" "Yes, a boy!" The two women looked at each other with tears in their eyes. Police officers came to hurry the prisoners inside the police station, cutting short their conversation.

. . .

"Miss, miss, tomorrow I'm getting you a sponsor at Central Prison," said gofer Ton. "You'll be better off there. The fish is smelly, the food greasy, but you won't be shackled. But I have to sponsor you, otherwise the wardens and the *caplans* [cell overseers] will be really hard on you."[5]

"You're escorting me there?" Bao Luong asked him.

"Yes."

"Thank you and the two sergeants."

"Don't. Your case is not settled yet; you'll be back here several more times," Ton told her.

"Why is that?"

"Because your interrogation file is still missing information. I think you'll be asked again about Headman Hoai," Ton said.

"But I don't know him!"

"If you said you did, you'd be done," Ton told her. "When did you arrive here?"

"July 13. And now it's August 8. It's already twenty-five days!" she exclaimed.

"It's when you're in prison that time seems long. 'A day in prison is like a thousand autumns outside.' Let me ask you directly. The business is over. Why not confess? Did you engage in revolution like Phan Xich Long?" Ton asked.

"What would that look like?" Bao Luong countered. "How can I know?"

"So you're keeping secrets to the end?" Ton asked.

. . .

Bao Luong was brought upstairs again. Thanks to the outfit sent by Sergeant Qui's wife, she was fairly comfortable, except for the smelly blood in her hair and the itch caused by the bleeding as the tight manacles and shackles rubbed against her wounds. Walking up the spiral stairs now exhausted her. When she got there, she was greeted by the cruel faces of Monnier and Bazin: "You were Lang's lover? And there were many others involved in this affair? It's not possible for only three men to have carried it out," Monnier declared.

Bao Luong was defiant: "I could have done it by myself; three is too many."

Bertin, who was translating, gave her a fierce look and said, "Be careful. Think before you reply."

"You need to be examined by a doctor," Bertin said.

Bao Luong gathered from this statement that the Frenchmen wanted to combine a story of politics and lust as the motive for the Barbier Street affair so as to portray the revolutionaries as depraved individuals who should not be emulated. Meanwhile, her goal had changed. Originally, her comrades had decided to disguise the elimination of Lang as a crime of passion; Bao Luong had even been willing to play her part by penning a "love letter." But clearly the Frenchmen had not bought that story. Could she just let their hateful accusations stand? She thought that since they had reenacted the murder scene, they would have trouble connecting her to it. Perhaps she should say the same thing as Dinh. She hated the police attempt to portray her as a woman of loose morals and her fellow revolutionaries as scoundrels.

Suddenly Bazin asked, "What about Lê Oanh? She was Lang's lover as well. Where is she?"

"Who's Lê Oanh?"

"Lê Oanh, who used the alias Nhut; she is even more implicated in the murder than you!" Bazin said. "You know Lê Oanh better than anyone else. You must confess; otherwise you will suffer worse than the last two times."

"Even if it's ten times worse, I can only die once," Bao Luong retorted. "You need to tell me who Lê Oanh is."

"It's your fault," Bazin warned. "Don't blame French people for not 'striking women with flowers' and instead hitting you with a stick. Lie down."

Bertin said something to his two colleagues, then got up and told Bao Luong, "Follow me." Halfway down the spiral staircase, Bao Luong asked, "Where are you taking me?"

"To the doctor. He'll see if you are still 'intact'; then we can figure out what to do."

Bao Luong was all bravado: "All right, let's go." Bertin led her all the way to the back door, then looked her in the eyes and said, "Let's go back up."

She had lost her fear. Being interrogated and tortured, that was to be expected at the station. As for verifying her virginity, that too was not surprising. An unmarried girl working among men would not be expected to keep her maidenhead long. At least, that must have been a French assumption. Bao Luong suddenly burst out laughing.

"You laugh? What do you have to laugh about?" Bazin demanded. "Where is Lê Oanh? It's because of her that there was a murder, isn't it?"

"The other day you said it was because of me, now you say it's because of Miss Lê Oanh; another day you'll say it's because of someone else," Bao Luong told him. "How would I know?"

"The informer said it was Lê Oanh and that you knew her very well," Bazin said.

"Bring the informer here, then everything will be clarified," Bao Luong said. Bazin wasn't the only one who could bluff.

"You're clever. You know the informer wrote a letter and cannot be produced in person to confront you," Bazin said. "Here is a photo; who are these two women?"

It was a photograph of Ngoc Anh and Ngoc Tho, taken when they were children. So they had been unmasked.

"I don't know them."

"Are you telling the truth?"

"I don't know them."

Headman Hoai was brought in to confront Bao Luong: "Here, whose photo is this?"

"My two daughters, Ngoc Anh and Ngoc Tho," Headman Hoai told Bao Luong. "You studied with them."

"I studied with many people," she said. "I can't remember them all."

Headman Hoai caught her meaning. He could not go back on what he'd said, so he tried to bluff: "It's true—the school is large and has many students who come and go as they please. There's no need to remember all of them."

"Silence! You led these two women astray and who else? You'll see that you're lying and you'll get a well-deserved beating. Don't you know who I am?" Bazin demanded.

"I don't know, I don't know."

When the men from the Sûreté threw Bao Luong down to administer more beatings, the eyes of Headman Hoai filled with tears. He stumbled down the stairs on unsteady legs, his sleeve over his face. Bao Luong's wounds from the previous beating had not healed yet, and the new strokes added to her hatred of the colonizers. They were determined to extract the names of troublemakers through torture. But they would fail! Those who defied death had gathered the courage to endure iron pincers, strokes of the cane, fish sauce through the nose, electric shocks. Mere mortals could not beat information out of them. But the photographs of Ngoc Anh and Ngoc Tho had brought up so many memories. This was the most painful night Bao Luong had spent in prison.

"When so many fervent revolutionaries like the members of the Revolutionary Youth League were sacrificed," she wrote later, "when the league's direction was still appropriate for prevailing circumstances, yet suddenly they were pushed into the net of the French colonizers, it led to much puzzled dismay over this policy: Perhaps the gains thus achieved must be enormous? If my hypothesis was 90 percent correct, should I bear grudges against those who were implementing it? Anyway, there was nothing I could do about my resentment. Those who had fallen into the net often found their resolve dulled, like the Old Man of Ben Ngu [Phan Boi Chau]. But I had to be sure about my feelings to accept the fate of the one fallen from the moon down to Earth. A blood sacrifice to provoke a strong revolutionary wave; to move on to a new plane; to achieve a more effective movement against colonialism and feudalism; to ignite a movement that would terrify the colonizers; to shake the very foundations of the invaders' regime; to forge ahead, ahead, to move forward all the time until the goal was achieved."

It was ultimately too large a sacrifice to ask for, Bao Luong decided, but the sacrificial lambs could not protest; they could only accept their fate without hatred and resentment. If one day, thanks to the energy released by this policy of sacrifice, independence flowered and showered beauty and glory over the whole country, then perhaps her suffering would not be in vain. This thought eased her mind. She only needed to bear whatever pain came her way, however many times she returned to the police station, so long as she did not harm Ngoc Anh and her other friends. During the night, as she heard the clank of shackles, hers and those of her friends, she sought solace in lines of poetry.

· · ·

"Miss, will you be all right?" Ton asked.

"Yes. What do you mean by 'turning intestines inside out'?" Bao Luong replied.

Gofer Ton put his head in his hands and said, "When fish sauce is poured in your nose, it causes bleeding. It's less damaging than electric shocks. If you're subjected to electric shocks, you'll be crippled for life. But with the 'airplane,' your lungs are damaged, you can burst a vein. Then there is turning your intestines inside out: your head is brought close to your heels and you are beaten on your chest. Even buffaloes would scream and wood would turn to mush."

Sergeant Qui interrupted Ton: "Your babbling will lead to a demotion. I think I forgot my raincoat here." Ton grinned, handed over the raincoat, and took the packet of goods that Qui had brought for Bao Luong. "Why are you so nice to prisoners?" she asked.

"It depends on the case," Qui replied. "If it's theft or robbery or counterfeiting money, we won't help. In fact, we'll make their life even more miserable. Miss, how can a mere girl defy the French? Even Phan Xich Long could not."

Bao Luong taunted, "It's because men do not that women must. If men had prevented the French from coming in and brutalizing women, we'd have stayed home happily." Ton was thoughtful, then whispered behind his hand, "Vietnamese cannot compete with Chinese. There was discord. If there had not been, you would not have been in this mess."

"What mess? Was there a traitor?" she asked.

"It's even more serious than that!" Ton told her.

"Sometimes disagreement leads to misunderstandings," Bao Luong said. "But there are still many good people, like you three."

· · ·

Bao Luong was anxious every time someone told her that she would be leaving the station. Here she was beaten and shackled. During the day she heard torture; at night she heard cries and sobs. She had given up the dignity of being clean. But at least she and her friends were all together. Tomorrow she would leave this place she was calling the ninth level of hell. To which depth would she fall? And would her friends be deported to Con Son, Lao Bao, or some faraway island hell?

When the sun went down and she was left alone with her weaknesses, far from home, she gave way to sorrow and tears. Her arms and legs in shackles, her body covered with sores, her hair full of dried blood, she was afraid that she would forget what she needed to remember and focus only on herself and her sufferings, ignoring the suffering of others. She berated herself: How could she neglect to think of Kim Oanh and of Dang van Sam's wife, who were worse off than she? They did not know whether their beloved husbands were alive or had died under torture without being able to say a few last words to their wives and children.

"Would you like to write home? I will open the manacles so you can write and I'll buy some stamps for you," Ton offered.

"Thank you," she replied. "I'd like to reassure my parents. But I have nothing else to tell them."

"Miss, I've heard they're conducting searches throughout the provinces."

"Who else is there to arrest? They've already got too many innocent people."

"Usually, people confess to anything under torture; and when they go to court, they retract their confession. So they're brought back for more beatings! Some cases are reviewed, but they're very rare," Ton advised. "You're a woman, how will you stand it? When you go to court, deny everything and you should be okay."

"There's nothing for me to contest," she said. "I have acknowledged things I could not refute. But is there anyone who has accused me?"

"No one did, miss. But there was a letter. Here are three more pills. Take them all. You won't be able to bring anything into Central Prison, not even a handkerchief. Perhaps a comb, but that will certainly be taken by the *caplans*."

"What do I still have?"

"Your blue outfit that is torn and your identification placard," Ton said. "Miss, let me help you get up and walk back and forth so that your feet will feel less painful. You'll have to walk from here to Central Prison."

"When?"

"It could be right away or tomorrow."

"Thank you. If I cannot walk, I won't go immediately. Don't go to trouble for me."

Sergeant Thinh grinned. "Right, and they'll take you to hospital: Cho Quan Hospital."

Gofer Ton explained, "If you go there, you'll be with the crazies, they'll spit in your face all day long, and you'll end up nuts just like them. You're better off listening to me and getting up."

"You act as if you are familiar with what goes on there," Thinh said, mocking him. Turning to Bao Luong, he said, "Miss, I've recommended you to people over at Central Prison."

Sergeant Qui frowned. "Is your recommendation good? The wardens and the *caplans* there are supposed to be real toughs. Just performing massages [for the *caplans* and their subordinates], cleaning floors, taking out garbage, carrying water, and generally serving them are enough to make you ill."

"Please don't worry about me," she said. "I'm sure things will work out. There's no point worrying about things one cannot change."

"You are right, miss, as long as you live, you will get out one day," Qui said. "I have a daughter just like you, that's why my wife cried when she learned about you and has been so concerned."

Ton said, "I don't know why I am so sad about you. Is it also true for you two?"

"Of course! We work for them because we need to," Thinh said. "I needed the money, that's why I became a clerk. Since coming here, one ear has gone deaf. I wish I were deaf in the other ear as well, so I would not hear the screams and cries."

While they were talking, an order came to bring the Barbier Street gang to Central Prison. Inspector Bertin came in, and Ton opened Bao Luong's shackles. She walked out slowly, holding onto a chair for support. Sergeants Qui and Thinh kept their heads down, typing as if they were unconcerned about what was going on. Bao Luong looked with emotion at her shackles, at the book that she had used as a pillow, even the spot where she had laid down, and finally at the door. In the corridor her friends were already lined up. The two sergeants and gofer Ton seemed to want to say goodbye, but how could they dare to look up?

· · ·

Bao Luong had been at the police station only one month, but when she came out into the open, the sun blinded her and her steps faltered. The men were manacled in pairs; as the only woman in the group, she went last and without handcuffs. The prisoners did not pay attention to the passing scenery; they looked around only to verify that they were all there, that no one had died. Tran Truong, Nguyen van Thinh, and Ngo Thiem were handcuffed together. Truong kept looking back, while Bao Luong tried to move ahead to catch up with him. Truong said, "As to us three, our fate is sealed. I am only worried that you will not be able to bear it, Bao Luong. Do you understand? Are you sad?" Ngo Thiem laughed out loud: "Why be sad? When you're alive, you have to toil. Dead, you can rest. Bao Luong, write a funeral orison for us, will you?"

"No, I'm too sad," she said. "I'm going to give up poetry."

"How will you survive if you give it up?" Ngo Thiem asked.

Nguyen van Thinh winked: "Tomorrow, when we go to court, we'll be sitting for a while. We can have a long talk then."

"Hoai Nghia, how are you?" asked Bao Luong.

Hoai Nghia appeared angry at her. "Don't. I don't know you anymore," he said. "You can say whatever you want."

"It was Dinh and Nguyen Kim Cuong who talked, not I," she explained.

Cuong overheard her and turned around, his face sad. He said after a long silence, "Don't be angry at me, Bao Luong. Let me go because—." His voice trailed off.

Truong also slowed down in order to urge her: "You need to show some sympathy; don't harbor grudges against Cuong and Dinh. I know everything. Try to protect yourself, because you're a girl. I hope your friends are all right?"

The group in chains had stopped under the grimacing face carved on the gate of Central Prison. Bui van Them commented, "The goddess of justice is weeping because there is no justice here."

"No, no. It's the head of a person who's been condemned to death," said another man. "Even those who are not sentenced to be beheaded will die here, of a slow death, of hunger, of illness."

The iron gates opened with a creaking noise. The soldiers hurried the prisoners in. They were inside the first circle of Central Prison.

9

Down among Women

"Anyone who has money or other property, bring them over for safekeeping!" a guard told the new arrivals at Central Prison.

Bao Luong took out the gold chain that Lê Oanh had given her, the little heart from her friend Ngoc Anh, and the ring with the square face from her cousin Tran Truong; she put them in a little package and handed them over. She then went to receive an identification tag, a wooden placard about three fingers wide. She took it without bothering to read the inscription, then waited for her friends to complete their procedures and get their own identification tags.

It was difficult to believe that this place, where "one day felt like a thousand autumns," as the saying went, could look so beautiful. Atop the iron gates sat a sculpted head that reminded Bao Luong and her friends of the executions that took place in front of the prison. Across from the gates was a bell tower. It was located in the dead center of the prison compound and was the highest point of this infernolike universe. A spiral staircase led to the top of the tower. Somebody was leaning over the rail of the balcony, looking down. Around the tower were planted flowers whose purple, pink, and yellow petals brightened the whole edifice and made it look like a giant vase. Two courtyards, paved with tiles in various designs, were lined with grass like a park. Rose bushes were in bloom, and in the distance other flowering bushes gave off a heady perfume. On the right was a long building several stories high with high walls, bars, and iron gates. It was painted a pale yellow at the top and black at the bottom. Thick blinds covered the openings; the building was shrouded in silence. In front of her was a similar building with similar blinds. On the left was a building that she guessed housed the kitchen since smoke rose from it. Farther away was a row of low buildings with doors; she could not determine the purpose of those buildings.

[Central Prison of Saigon, which was built between 1866 and 1890, housed both European and Vietnamese prisoners. In 1929 only two cells were reserved for female inmates. On October 26 Than Chung reported that the prison was full, with no space for additional inmates. By July 1930, when Bao Luong went on trial, the prison population had swollen further as a result of the mass protests that had begun in April.]

"Everything's done," said the Indian clerk as he waved his hand, and the monitor ordered everyone to go down into the cells. Bao Luong's male friends went through two iron gates, crossed the flower garden, and walked on the path to the bell tower. She sat and watched as they disappeared into a portal topped with a half-moon and adorned with flowers and greenery, like the gate to paradise. She was frightened and anxious. She felt that she had gone from the wolf's lair of the police station on Catinat Street to the tiger's den of Central Prison: "I had believed that human feelings withered and died in that place of torture, where flesh was torn and bones broken, and the whole building echoed with screams of pain. And yet individuals might have their limits, but humanity did not. Even here there might be some vestige of human kindness. Would it enable my beloved friends to endure pain?"

The head of the prison was a bald Frenchman named Agostini. He looked at Bao Luong and called out, "Mr. Lac!" Mr. Lac, a tiny man who served as interpreter for the prison director, translated: "The boss says that for a girl, you are really tough; you've dared to plot against French authority. But you've lost and you'll have to be shackled." Bao Luong became angry and retorted, "Of course, those who lose get this treatment." Mr. Lac laughed and translated. Agostini bent down and shouted into her face: "It will be a long time before the French are defeated! Right now, I advise you to follow the discipline of the prison."

"Let's go, miss." She followed the white-suited jail boy *(boi ron* or *boy-geôle).*[1] This was the name given to prisoners who had received light sentences and had connections or had bribed the regular staff and were literate enough to do clerical work. They escorted prisoners to the courthouse or to the infirmary; they took care of everything, brought cigarettes for the guards and did small services. In return, they had greater freedom of movement and enjoyed better food than the other prisoners. Bao Luong followed the jail boy across the lawn to the third row of buildings and went behind a blue fabric screen. To the left was a staircase leading to storeroom for clothes and bedding for the prisoners. The jail boy told her to stand next to the screen, and he took away her ID. He came back with a wooden box that held a blue uniform and told her to change into it and to put her own clothes in the box. He also gave her a new identification tag to wear. After she had changed, she handed the wooden box to the jail boy. He gave her a small straw mat but then stared at her: "Oh, my god! Why is this outfit so torn that your arms stick out from your elbows down, and it's mended everywhere? Warden, give her another uniform!" While she waited for her new garb, Bao Luong began to feel like a nest of ants was crawling all over her body. She hurried to take off the new clothes and beat them against the tiles. Bedbugs and fleas flew in all directions. She was still beating the clothes against the tiles when the warden came back with another uniform. The warden was about forty years old and skinny, with a pock-marked face. He had smiling eyes. "Please also give me your inside jacket, miss," he said. "When you go in, they'll take it from you anyway and I'll be scolded."

"I'll worry when I get there," Bao Luong said. "Right now, I'd like to ask you a favor. When I tried to get rid of the bugs, I tore the clothes some more."

The warden reassured her: "Just wear these, miss. Your ID has the letters *M-A-P*. You will surely get different clothes."

The jail boy took Bao Luong to the French guard and his Vietnamese warden. They pushed her into cell 18. Immediately, a Chinese woman of about fifty jumped down from her bunk and came over. She passed her hands all over Bao Luong's body, undid her hair, rubbed her back, and stared at her identification placard. As she finished inspecting Bao Luong, the door closed with a clang. Bao Luong stood there, disoriented. The black iron door was the dividing line between light and darkness. Her universe had shrunk to a few square meters of concrete floor; her life was now enclosed within these four walls. She leaned back against a wall, dazed. A woman in rags, smelly and disheveled, lurched into the latrine. Bao Luong looked down at herself: the same blue rags, the same ID tag hanging from a jacket button, a straw mat in her hand. She had truly become an inmate, yet another anguished denizen of cell 18.

Unlike cell 17, which housed prisoners who had already been sentenced, cell 18 held female inmates, both old or young or even children, whether they had been sentenced or were still awaiting their day in court. Its *caplan* was the Chinese woman who had greeted Bao Luong. Unlike the jail boys, who were serving light sentences and were allowed to roam the prison, *caplans* ran their cells and came from the ranks of inmates serving the longest sentences. The Chinese woman was serving a life sentence for slitting her husband's throat. She looked well fed and tidy in her outfit of black taffeta. She ordered Bao Luong, "Go over there!" Bao Luong took her mat and went to sit on the edge of the little concrete bath and looked around. She was lucky to have gone through the *caplan*'s inspection without trouble. If she had had gold teeth, she would not be sitting quietly on the edge of the bath.

The cell was full to overflowing. Some inmates lay on straw mats spread over the wooden platforms lining the walls, others lay on the concrete floor, head to head. They had tried to leave a path for walking, but they were so crowded together that reaching the latrine or the cell door was like negotiating an obstacle course. The odor of damp, sweaty clothes, mixed with the smell of unguent and of the urine and feces of the children, was more than the nose could bear. And yet what else could she do but breathe in the foul smell? The garbage can was next to the latrine.

Because the cell was full, some inmates had to sit next to it and endure the odor. Bao Luong was in a corner, next to a cistern of drinking water and two buckets of water. She sat there, looking at the dim light filtering through the blinds that masked the window openings and bathing the cell in drab gray.

"It's nap time! Lie down, everybody. Anyone who whispers will have her mouth split open!" Everybody fell silent at the order from the assistant *caplan,* a woman named Binh, who was in prison because she'd taken part in a knife fight that had resulted in fatalities. She was tall, had a loud voice, and wielded more authority than a general. Under her was a whole raft of enforcers *(anh chi)* more brutal than the head *caplan,* whom the other prisoners called Chinese Mother.[2] Prisoners did not even dare to cough for fear of incurring Binh's wrath.

Suddenly, they heard repeated knocks. Binh put her ear to the slit in the door, then waved her hand for silence. A guard opened the door of cell 17. Curses and shouts rang out for a good while. Then a man in a yellow uniform dragged a woman of about thirty out by the hair, slapped her several times, and threw her to the ground. The woman shrank against the retaining wall of the courtyard. The cell door banged shut. "To the isolation cell! This time you'll be in isolation for thirty days!"

When the clank of keys had faded away, the *caplan* put her mouth to the slit in the door and called out to the caplan of cell 17: "Nga, Nga, what was that about?"

"It's my cook. She was not watching the door. The French came in while the fire was on, with oil and cotton sitting out for all to see. She really deserves it," Nga replied.

"You should try to get her out of solitary," the Chinese woman replied. "She's your cook, after all; it was just bad luck!"

"How can I ask?" Nga said. "She was caught red-handed!"

"In that case, don't serve as *caplan* for convicted inmates!" the Chinese *caplan* advised. "You've already had your sentence pronounced; you don't have to be afraid of having time added to it."

When the guard had opened the door of cell 17, cell 18 had been abuzz. Pasty-faced women in blue rags and hair like rats' nests staggered to their feet, looking like denizens of hell. Others stayed wrapped in their mats like so many bodies in a graveyard. The *caplan* repeated, "Lie down, it's nap time." Bao Luong spread her mat next to the bath, leaned her head against its side, and gazed at the nails in the walls of the cell; hanging from them were bread and bananas, as well as a variety of pouches.

· · ·

"Come here, you!" It was Binh, the assistant *caplan.* As Bao Luong walked toward her, several pairs of eyes watched her, fearful on her behalf. "What are you in here for?"

"Guns."

"You're lying," Binh said. "You would not be having those three letters on your tag merely for guns."

"No, no, it's the truth. It was guns."

"If it was, you would only get two letters. What does the letter *P* mean?" Binh wanted to know.

"I have no idea."

"You don't even know what you're in here for? Maybe it was for sexual shenanigans?"

Chinese Mother called out, "Don't talk dirty, Binh. Even promiscuity would get her only two letters."

"All right, I'll let it go. Are you willing to be my 'baby sister'?" Binh asked Bao Luong. "Can you read or are you an imbecile?"

Bao Luong looked at the floor, wondering what being her "baby sister" entailed. She felt as if she had been traveling on a well-marked road and had suddenly fallen into this hellhole. She needed time to divine its ways and its language. As she pondered how to answer Binh, she felt a woman of eighteen or nineteen discreetly scratching her back.

"So, are you willing?"

"Let me think it over."

"What is there to think about?" Binh wanted to know. "It needs the accumulated merit of generations of your ancestors for you to become my 'baby sister.' Tu, make her sweep the barracks this afternoon!" The person who was thus charged with making Bao Luong work was a woman in her early twenties, one of the baby sisters of the assistant *caplan*. She was tall and had prominent cheeks and a sharp mouth. She fully deserved the nickname Tu the Cruel.

. . .

"Slut! Are you built like a horse that you kicked my mat?" Thus scolded, the eighteen-year-old who had scratched Bao Luong's back earlier was trying to make herself as small as possible next to her. The woman who had yelled at her was spread out on a whole mat rather than the half mat that others were using. She wore taffeta trousers and a silk blouse and had rings in her ears and on her fingers. Her legs were stretched out for two of her minions to massage. She was another *caplan*. She ordered Bao Luong to come to her: "Bring your ID over here. I've never seen these letters before. What did you do? And whom do you want to serve? Chinese Mother? Binh, the assistant caplan? Or me, Chin Xich; I'm big and I know martial arts. So who?"

"What does it involve?" Bao Luong asked her.

"It depends on what you can do. If you're skillful and gutsy, you can take out the gold teeth of the new prisoners. Or you can take away the food received by the prisoners who have visitation rights and bring it to me. If we're found out, you can go to the isolation cell instead of me. I'll share with you so you don't have to eat leftover food. If you're really clueless, you can bring in the food when it is served, sift out the sand from the rice, and cook all the food again for me, and you will need to keep an eye on the door. You will also wash my clothes and massage me. When you're free, you can write letters for other prisoners; you can rid the mats and clothes of bedbugs. When I'm asleep, my 'baby sisters' can rest. In return, you won't have to work hard, and you'll eat well because there is always a good deal of leftover food."

"How should I address you?"

"Ah, you can call me Sister Chin or Brother Chin, because I have a wife."

Thunderstruck by this statement, Bao Luong looked at Chin Xich again: jade earrings, hair in three buns—a length of hair hung from one—and especially a woman's voice. Bao Luong had never encountered a lesbian before; she was still gazing at Chin Xich in bewilderment when Binh, the assistant *caplan*, came over, cackling. She threw herself on the ground and shouted, "Oh, my sides! She's so funny! Brother Chin, leave this goody-goody to me! I took notice of her when she came into the cell."

"Really? Scoot!" replied Chin Xich.

Bao Luong crawled back to her place by the bath and covered herself with her mat, adding her body to the graveyard scene. Suddenly, she felt someone creeping up from the bottom of her mat and tensed. But it was only the girl who had scratched her earlier. She put her hand over Bao Luong's mouth and held her. Bao Luong tried to speak, but the girl closed her eyes and shook her head. Bao Luong followed her lead and fell silent.

. . .

The bell rang in the tower, signaling that it was time to open the doors of the prison. The girl began to speak: "I feel so sorry for you; you remind me of myself when I first came into the prison."

"So we can speak now?" Bao Luong asked.

"Yes, when the bell rings, we can talk," she said. "My name is Dzung; I was in service, and my boss accused me of stealing a watch. I've been here two months already. I was so scared when I came in that I agreed to be a 'baby sister' to Binh. But I have no special skills so I've been assigned the job of getting sand out of the rice and washing dishes. I scratched your back to warn you not to follow my example."

"What is there to fear?"

"Please, don't set yourself against them!" Dzung warned. "One word from them, and your life won't be worth living. Fold your mat, and make a mark so that you can recognize it. When you hear the sound of keys in the distance, put your mat in the pile, then stand in a line so that Mme Lecuir can count the prisoners. Then you'll be allowed to sit in the eating courtyard. You'll be going to the courthouse this afternoon, right? Don't worry, I'll keep some rice for you."

. . .

Bao Luong followed the messenger and went to the "office." Her friends, especially her cousin Tran Truong, Hoai Nghia, and her brother Vien Dai, followed her with dead eyes. When she reached the outer door, the director of the prison shouted, "Mr. Lac, Mr. Lac!" Mr. Lac turned to Bao Luong and translated: "This is really bad. Please go back and change into different clothes. He said you are too lazy to mend your clothes. He will punish you and scold Mme Lecuir." Bao Luong received another outfit, which was somewhat less tattered than the previous one.

Once they were all inside the courthouse, they were able to talk to one another. Ton Duc Thang told Bao Luong that many members of the Tan Viet Revolutionary Party had been arrested, including Nguyen Dinh Kien, its head, and Tran Huy Lieu (the reporter who had once urged Bao Luong to give speeches), and many others whose names and faces he did not know. He glanced at Tran Truong, then looked down at the ground. Bao Luong understood his meaning and blurted out, "But they have not heard our case yet!" "Not yet," he said, "but it won't make a difference." Her heart clenched at his answer. She threaded her way to the three men, held their hands, her throat working. Tran Truong joked, "What's this? Can't you swallow unmilled rice?" Hoai Nghia said, "Bao Luong, you can write poetry to allay your sorrow. In prison there's all the more need to write poetry, to see it as your friend. When you get out of prison, you'll let me read it, all right?"

The prisoners took turns sitting on a chair to have their photograph taken and their fingerprints recorded. When this was done, police officers came to handcuff them in pairs and return them to the prison. On the way four or five high school students ran along and shouted, "Sister Nguyet, Sister Nguyet! We've come all the way from Ben Tre!" Bao Luong shouted back, "Move away! Don't give me anything, go away!" Dang van Sam's mother and wife were crying again, though not as much as last time.

Bui van Them said to Sam, "I told you that marriage brought trouble! Single guys like me have nothing to worry about!"

"That's not a given," retorted the harried Sam. "Although it's painful, at least I have the solace of knowing there is someone to weep for me, to feel pity for me; it shows that human kindness still exists and that life is still worth living."

"It's too painful to see," Bui van Them said. "It's enough to make you want to die in order to avoid these separation scenes."

"We've been to the courthouse twice," observed Sam. "I wonder how many more times we'll be back."

"Why do you want to know?"

"So that I can tell my mother and my wife not to come and see me," Sam said.

. . .

Bao Luong returned to cell 18 dragging her feet, her heart heavy. After she had been inspected by the *caplan*, she was allowed to retreat to her corner with her mat. The lights had been turned on in the cell. Whispered conversations sounded like the buzzing of bees. She sat by the edge of the bath and counted the number of women receiving massages. Six! Two were on the benches; that presented no problem. But how to negotiate past the other four?

"I kept some food for you," announced Dzung.

"Thanks." Bao Luong took a small bucket containing about two bowls of brown rice and a couple of pieces of dried meat so spoiled that they disintegrated. She began picking at the food.

"Can you eat brown rice on its own just like this?"

"I have no choice," Bao Luong replied.

"Ah, let me bring my mat over and I'll tell you what needs to be done in the cell," Dzung said. "I wish I had money to bribe the *caplan* so that you would not have to work. The work is hard, but worse are the shouted orders and the urgings to hurry up."

"It doesn't matter," Bao Luong said. "I could not enjoy idleness when others labored so hard."

"It's easy to say, but the work is really hard," Dzung said. "They don't care for you. Indeed, they behave as if they were your grandmother."[3]

. . .

"Why aren't you singing your baby to sleep? A woman with a child and you made alcohol illegally! You're preventing everybody from sleeping. If you can't quiet your baby, you should not have married!" As these harsh words fell as bitter as gourds and as fiery as chilies from the mouths of the "enforcers," the women with children hastened to hold their babies to their shoulders, softly humming lullabies as they walked up and down by the wall leading to the latrine. But the babies were bothered by the heat and the mosquitoes and by hunger; because the mothers' bellies were empty, they had not produced enough milk. The babies cried even louder, disregarding the authority of the enforcers.

"Why are you not calming your babies down?" The sound of the *mata* soldiers' knocking on the door spurred the *caplan* to even more demands. She sent one of her minions to one of the mothers and ordered, "If you can't soothe your baby, give him to me, I'll take care of him!" The "baby sister" yanked the baby from his mother's arms. The baby immediately started yelling and grabbed at his mother's hair. The panicked woman grabbed her son back and ran inside the latrine. The sharp-mouthed "baby sister" heard her *caplan* shout: "Drag her out and beat her up to make an example!" Obeying her *caplan* to the letter, Tu the Cruel pulled the mother out of the latrine and slapped her hard: "You'll learn not to let your child cry." The other women who had children were green with fright. There was no more vivid image of suffering womanhood than these mothers who stayed up night after night, consumed with sorrow and worry, their hair and their clothes in utter disarray, their bodies increasingly emaciated. "You'll see," observed Dzung. "The poor woman will have her food ration reduced. The *caplan* will tell the Frenchwoman, who will report to the chief. [The mother] will be punished. She'll have to sit apart, and she'll have only one meal; she'll be given a handful of rice as punishment for allowing her baby to cry."

"Even with two meals a day she does not have enough milk for her baby," Bao Luong said. "He's bound to cry even more tonight. Could she perhaps chew the rice and feed it to her baby? How can we help nursing mothers?"

"All right, I'll try to bring more rice in," Dzung said.

"Tomorrow," continued Dzung, "you'll be going to the courthouse. I'll see if someone has money or food to bribe the *caplan* for you. I'm afraid you won't be able to cope with the work."

"Don't worry, Dzung. I should be able to carry water. You'll see," Bao Luong assured her.

"How will you do it? The water is not carried in tin buckets but in huge wooden ones. You break out in sweat just looking at them," Dzung recounted. "After you've carried the water, your whole chest is afire and aches. I worry because from your ID placard, it looks like your sentence will be heavy. Mine is for three months, and I've already served two."

. . .

The nights in Central Prison seemed endless. Bao Luong told herself that she did not have a baby to put to sleep, she was not in shackles, and she had a mat to cover herself: for a prison inmate, she was in good shape. And yet she kept tossing and turning. She had beaten her clothes to death to rid them of bedbugs, but she had forgotten that some insects were smaller than bedbugs and even worse. A long time ago she had seen some coolies from a French-owned rubber plantation who had escaped to Saigon because they had not been able to endure life there. When they were caught, their French overseers had tied them together with hemp ropes and made them wait at the train station to be taken back to the plantation. As she walked past them, Bao Luong had noticed they could not bear the tiny bugs that had transferred to their clothes from the ropes. So they had taken their clothes off to look for the insects. The same insects were crawling through the blue outfits, maddening the inmates. Not a second passed that one was not bothered, to the point of wanting to strip naked. The women were covered in sores from head to toe. Bao Luong had originally thought it was because they were dehydrated; she had not considered that these pests could be even more lethal than mosquitoes and bedbugs.

"Take my clothes," Dzung told Bao Luong. "I have a way of dealing with the pests. I'll put the clothes in the bath and spray something over them." While Dzung was acting on her words, someone shouted, "Dzung, you are so clever! You can't take care of yourself, but you wait on her? Tomorrow, you'll have me to deal with!" Frightened, Dzung dropped Bao Luong's clothes and went to hide beneath her mat. She whispered, "She'll give me hard work tomorrow. Never mind, I'm used to it, but you are a novice."

Suddenly, from the convicts' cell came urgent calls: "Mata, mata, open the door quick! Hurry up!" The Chinese woman and the enforcers from cell 18 vied to ask, "What is it? An epileptic seizure or an opium overdose?" The door opened and a woman came out, crying to the heavens and hardly able to walk. She was holding a child of about two whose eyes were rolling back in its head; its mouth was foaming, its body in spasm. Nga, the *caplan* of cell 17, asked for permission to escort them to the building that served as the infirmary. After the door closed, Chinese Mother chuckled: "Nga is a great one. She's always asking to escort the sick. But it's not the sick whom she loves!" Thanks to Dzung's explanations, Bao Luong had gained some understanding of prison life and its strange ways. She was discovering a whole different way of being.

. . .

The next day was the day of Bao Luong's court appearance. The members of the Tan Viet Revolutionary Party went to court separately, as did Hoai Nghia and many others. Only Tran Truong, Ngo Them, Nguyen van Thinh, Ton Duc Thang, Dang van Sam, Bui van Them, and Bao Luong were part of the same case. The group was taken to the judge's chambers. This meant their case was a grave one. The judge's office was where depositions taken at the police station were checked. "Can we retract our confessions, Sam?" Bao Luong asked.

"Sure, it should not be hard," one of her friends said sarcastically. "First, we'd have to tear up the photos taken in front of Pham Hong Thai's tomb and our files at the Central Committee; then we'd have to swallow the letter that lays out the whole network of the league. Then we could begin to deny."

"So what can we do?" Bao Luong persisted.

"Those who have confessed can try to retract; those who were the target of confessions can try to deny. It depends on each case," the man said.

"It's going to be a very long time before we meet again," Bao Luong said. "So let us talk to the end, give me your advice, let us share confidences."

"We are being held in the same place. Your brother Vien Dai is held upstairs with Headman Hoai. I believe that when the case is over, he will be released," Ton Duc Thang told her.

Tran Truong whispered, "Bao Luong, if prison conditions lead to your death, then so be it. But if you receive a heavy sentence, I suggest you think of it as going into a wilderness full of evil spirits and poisoned water, where you can still wage revolution. I tell you: it's easier to deal with danger and hardship than with sorrow.

To combat depression use your skills in the service of revolution: proselytize among your fellow prisoners so that when they are freed, they will be receptive to activism. If you can convert even one person, you will have done well."

Bao Luong was skeptical. "I am afraid that things will change drastically in the outside world; instead of just guessing, it would be better to stay silent than to talk inappropriately."

"We know that," replied her cousin. "Still, go ahead and proselytize, even if you receive a heavier sentence."

Bui van Them said, "If we go to Con Son, we'll be able to see the blue sky and the vast sea; a water death is quite refreshing. But we worry about you, Bao Luong. Listen to us: turn poet for a few years, hone your skills."

"Don't worry about me," she said. "Do you want some lines of sad poetry to follow you? You'll get them without asking because this is the only way I can memorialize my friends."

They were taken back to the prison. Tran Truong was given another identification tag, which brought his total to three; as for Bao Luong and the others, they had two each, the number of tags reflecting the severity of their crimes. The men returned to their cells by a different route. Bao Luong followed the one she had taken earlier, which took her past the courtyard. There was a slit though which one could see below. She was immeasurably glad to see her old friends sharing a bucket of rice. She inserted in the slit the comb that her cousin had given her when they'd had their mug shots taken at the courthouse, and they nodded to signal that they understood what she was telling them: her location in one of the two cells reserved for women.

· · ·

When Chinese Mother saw the two wooden placards hanging by Bao Luong's armpit, she stared at her for a while; she called her "baby sisters" over, then grilled Bao Luong about the crime that had earned her the two placards.

"Tell us the truth," Chinese Mother demanded. "You look frail but you must be really dangerous to have two placards."

"Possession of guns—and someone's accused her of taking part in a murder," one of her baby sisters said.

"Really? Well, even with ten placards, you could only get a single heavy sentence," another woman observed. "Leave her alone!" said the first baby sister. "What business is it of ours?

"I just wanted to know," Chinese Mother said. "We're all the same here."

Dzung too looked at Bao Luong's tags and tears sprang to her eyes. "Even one is hard to bear. When will you get out with two? Will there be anyone to welcome you?"

"My family is in Rach Gia," Bao Luong told her. "They don't know yet."

"Ask to be allowed to write to them," Dzung advised. "You'll get permission right away."

"I won't. I want to keep it from them as long as I can; why make them sad?"

"So who will provide you with food?" Dzung asked.

"Whoever jails me has to feed me!" Bao Luong said.

"Sure they will—with unmilled rice and greasy fish."

Bao Luong ate her rice with the salt Dzung had given her; then she drank some water and felt things were not too bad. She could cope.

Soon the bell rang. Each person put away her mat and stood in line by the wall. Mme Lecuir opened the door and gave her keys to Chinese Mother. The sharp-mouthed "baby sister" Tu ordered Bao Luong to sweep the floor. Bao Luong did not think it was difficult, except that the gang leaders did not bother to fold their mats, and she had to be careful not to spread dust and dirt over them. So it took her some time to gather up the garbage and put it into the can. Dzung had asked to work with Bao Luong, so the two of them took the can out to the courtyard.

The courtyard where women ate their meals was next to the prison gate. Along-side was a hedge that prevented the women from looking into the dungeon where the men ate theirs. Cell 17 had a communicating door outside. Mme Lecuir's chair was outside the door, and next to her chair was a screen preventing inmates from seeing the gate, the execution site, and the offices. The garbage area was outside Mme Lecuir's small kingdom. There, one could look up and see the upstairs, where French prisoners were held and the offices were located. Farther away were the kitchens, the infirmary, the execution site, and the minors' cell.

After days and nights of breathing the fetid enclosed air of the cell and the sour smell of sweat, being able to breathe clean air was an unforgettable experience. That was one of the reasons why the *caplans* and their enforcers vied to carry out the garbage: to be able to feast their eyes and clear their lungs. Another, perhaps more important, reason was that the French prisoners would toss cigarettes from their upstairs cell, and love letters flew up from the dungeon cells. So why had they al-lowed Dzung and Bao Luong to take out the garbage can? This pair had no idea of how to take advantage of their opportunity and merely took the can back in with-out looking right or left. The voice of Nga in cell 17 rang out: "Chinese Mother? Why did you let two strange girls take out the garbage? Have you run out of un-derlings?" As she spoke, she came out and took the can back out and pretended to exchange it for another one. Meanwhile, she had made hand signals to prisoners both upstairs and down below. Bao Luong did not understand this sign language and burst out laughing. "What are you laughing about?" Nga asked. "Madame, look at her. She's just arrived and already she's flirting with the men below!"

Mme Lecuir waved Bao Luong over. "What's your name? What case? Whom were you looking at?"

"My name is Nguyet," she responded. "I'm with the Barbier Street case. I was looking at my cousin and my brother upstairs."

Mme Lecuir, who oversaw female prisoners, looked like a kindly woman. She spoke Vietnamese fluently. She always wore black and always brought her sewing. She also relied on the *caplans* to maintain order in the cells. She was about to grill Bao Luong about her "violation of prison discipline" by daring to look at men when they heard a *caplan* shouting, "Everybody inside!" The enforcers went back behind the communicating door. The *caplan* left the door ajar and announced, "The macaques have left. Someone count the food." The name *macaque* was given to inmates who served as cooks. Someone had explained to Bao Luong that the macaques were afraid that they would be locked up again once they had finished cooking and would not have time to eat, so they ate as they cooked; because they were afraid that the monitors would notice their eating on the job, they stuffed their cheeks with food, which made them look like monkeys.

As soon as the *caplan* asked, Binh came forward. "Here I am, a real toughie. Can I do the counting, Mother?"

Mme Lecuir immediately pleaded with her: "Binh, please, don't go behind the screen, you'll make me lose my job. Go in, go in. It will be better for Thu's mom to do the counting!"

Binh grinned. "You're so clever. How did you know I have a lover among the macaques that you forbid me like this?"

"I know everything about you," replied Mme Lecuir. "I know you have three lovers and that love letters keep flying about. If you have to go to the isolation cell, I won't lift a finger. But if I am scolded by the boss, I'll be very embarrassed."

The men who brought the food were prisoners who had received light sentences. When they came, they looked and winked at the women. The *caplan* of the macaques, seeing Binh standing outside, had put food beneath the rice in order to strike up an acquaintance with her. Binh stayed outside for a long time on the pretext of hanging clothes to dry; she looked at the upper story and made signs. Frenchmen began sending down cigarettes. Binh also knew someone below and threw down a blue outfit for him. She had a Chinese lover as well, so she enjoyed protection. She did as she pleased and even often outfoxed Chinese Mother, her ostensible boss.

After the buckets of rice and fish had been laid out around the courtyard, ten inmates went to sit around each bucket. Those who enjoyed the favor of the *caplans* and their enforcers were the only ones allowed to dole out the fish. They put two slices per prisoner along the rim of the rice buckets; sometimes they poured the sauce over the rice, sometimes they drank it themselves. They chose the biggest slices of fish and took them away to serve to the *caplans* and the enforcers. They skinned the fish slices, and marinated them in fish sauce, chili, cayenne pepper, and oil supplied by the macaques. They then took three empty cans of condensed milk, dipped cotton wool in oil, lit a fire, and stewed the fish. They even had molasses and fish sauce for dipping and vegetables. As for ordinary prisoners, they had to content themselves with rice, the leftover slices of fish, and whatever salt had been smuggled in.

"Have you finished eating? Bring out the buckets. The macaques are here. Bring in the tea!" a *caplan* commanded.

Bao Luong was overjoyed at the prospect of tea as she longed for some hot water. But it was not easy to get from where she sat to the bucket of tea. One had to be careful not to walk on fish bones or on the rice that the children had thrown about, all made filthier and greasier because the fish bucket had tipped over and emptied sauce on the ground. After each meal the courtyard looked like a wasteland. By the time she got to the bucket, the tea was gone. In the blink of an eye the "baby sisters" had transferred it into bottles for their *caplans* and enforcers.

· · ·

The sharp-mouthed devil Tu ordered Bao Luong, "Today, you'll sweep the courtyard with another person." Dzung knew the drill. She helped Bao Luong put the buckets away and held out a broom. Bao Luong swept the ordure into seven or eight piles and tried to push the skins of cucumbers and gourds into the waste bins. But her broom was too big for the bins and she had to use her hands. When Dzung tried to help her, Tu yelled at her: "It's not your turn. Did you take a bribe? No one is allowed to perform work for someone else here."

"She's new; she's not used to it," Dzung explained.

"Ah. Was she indolent, then, when she was outside?" Tu demanded.

Despite that scolding, Dzung helped Bao Luong push the fish bones into the waste bin and helped her take it out. Bao Luong had tied her *ao dai* at her hips and folded up the legs of her trousers. But the bucket was heavy, and she was still hungry. Sweat beaded on her forehead, but she still had to wash the courtyard and wipe it dry. Two women brought a bucket of water and tipped its contents out, yelling, "Sweep!" Bao Luong's broom flashed out, driving the water into the gutter, while the prisoner who was supposed to help her stood to one side. Unfortunately, some water flowed back toward the chair where Mme Lecuir sat. The enforcers started shouting, "Flood! Flood! Get up, ma'am. Those two! You only know how to eat but not how to sweep? You call yourselves women, but you don't even know how to wipe floors! All you know is lying down."

Mme Lecuir hastily got up to avoid getting her shoes wet and scolded, "Binh, you're nice and fat; why don't you sweep instead of letting a skinny girl do it?"

Binh got mad. "She's the one who got your feet wet: punish her! Why are you telling me to do her work? *Caplans* never do it!"

"You eat too much, you've gotten fat," retorted Mme Lecuir. "The *caplan* is the Chinese one, not you. Why do you call yourself *caplan*? Are there dozens of them? I only recognize Chinese Mother and Nga."

Meanwhile, Bao Luong and her helper had run around the courtyard sweeping away the water. They were out of breath when they got back into the cell, dropped their brooms, and leaned against a wall. But Tu the Cruel immediately threw two sacks at them and shouted, "Wipe the floor dry! Are you going to stand there un-til it's time to count the prisoners?" It should not have been difficult to wipe the courtyard dry, but Bao Luong's shoulders were aching. She thought that it was be-cause she was hungry, forgetting that she had been in shackles for a whole month without exercise. Or perhaps, she mused, it was because of the torture she had en-dured. After she had finished the morning's work, her outer clothes were soaked and smelly from the fish and the other garbage. She rinsed them, hung them out to dry, and went to sit by Dzung. "When can I wash my clothes?" she asked. "They smell so bad!"

"Only on Thursday, when we are allowed to take a shower," Dzung replied. "If you do it now, you'll get a caning."

. . .

Thursday was an important day in the lives of female prisoners. It was their op-portunity to take a bath and get rid of filth. In this manmade nest of disease, no one had the slightest interest in providing adequate medical treatment to prisoners if they were not French. When we think about bathing, we think about privacy, about modesty, some minimal attempt at safeguarding one's self-respect. But in Central Prison keeping one's dignity was impossible. When the *caplan* issued her order, Bao Luong was struck dumb. She badly wanted to bathe but not in a communal bath, totally naked in the middle of the day under the eyes of a hundred other women all waiting impatiently to jump into the water, afraid to lose their chance if the doors closed before they had taken their turn. They had no compunction about eying other inmates' bodies and commenting on every one of their features. Bao Luong sat in the corner, ignoring Dzung's call, and wondering how to escape this ordeal.

A group of women had rushed naked into the bath and were sitting with two fingers' worth of soap, waiting for the *caplan* to throw water on them. The *caplan* threw the contents of one jug on each woman, while her assistant held a stick, ready to hit anyone who moved or made a fuss. This usually happened because the bath was crowded and the women's hair was invariably soapy, but the *caplan* doled out only three jugs of water for each woman, the first to wet her hair and body, the sec-ond to wash off the grime, the third to rinse off. If someone complained that her hair was still full of soap, down came the stick, along with insults: "You think we're your slaves? Get out quick so that others can come in." Some women came out of the bath with their hair still foamy, their backs full of welts, their ears torn, and bumps on their heads. When it was the children's turn to bathe, their screams echoed through the cell. Bathing worsened their sores; the soap that clung to their bodies irritated their skin. They had to get out before they had truly finished bathing and had to put on the blue uniforms before their bodies were dry. And then it was time to eat. They wiped dirty hands on damp clothes. Was it any wonder that the already smelly clothes smelled even worse? No wonder people used the expression "filthy like an inmate." It was different for the *caplans*. After their meal the *caplans* ordered their minions to hold up mats to shield them, while other "baby sisters" washed their hair and scrubbed their backs. Their bath completed, they would then go to sleep.

Bao Luong decided that communal bathing was not for her. She asked Dzung whether one could get some water from the cistern in the latrine. "You want to die? What will happen if you fall? Why did you not take a bath this morning? Your bashfulness will kill you."

"Just look out for me," Bao Luong said. "If someone comes, I'll jump down." She took her clothes into the latrine along with a bucket and a jug. She could not swim, but she excelled at climbing trees. In a flash she was on the third rung of the iron bar and opened the top of the cistern. She passed jugs of water down for Dzung to pour into the bucket. Dzung was laughing and poked her in the side. "All right, but it will take another thirty generations before you should do it a second time. I saw Warden Xuyen look into the hole of the door. It's a good thing I was able to sit down quickly and you were up high; otherwise he would have seen you."

"He would not dare open the door to the latrine!"

. . .

"I think you'll spend a long time in prison, since you have two placards," Dzung said one day.

"Don't worry, Dzung. As long as we live, we'll meet again," Bao Luong told her.

"If only I could be sure that you would be able to cope, I could go home easy in my heart," Dzung said. "If you don't obey the enforcers, they'll make mincemeat of you."

Bao Luong shrugged. What else could the French, the enforcers, and *caplans* do to inflict more pain?

When Mme Lecuir came into the cell, Chinese Mother told her that Bao Luong had refused to eat. The Frenchwoman turned to Bao Luong and asked why. "I'm not used to eating with my fingers. I want to be allowed to eat by myself." Mme Lecuir looked thoughtful. The enforcers crowded around her.

"The sky will fall before she's allowed to eat by herself."

"She can eat by herself when she goes back to the outside."

"Perhaps her butt is itching for some caning."

"Maybe she wants to visit the isolation cell!"

They were all certain Bao Luong would be punished. They did not know the value of struggle, even through hunger strikes. Mme Lecuir called and Agostini, the director, arrived, his face like thunder and a stick in his hand. Bao Luong walked out of the cell and greeted him calmly. Through Mme Lecuir he demanded to know what she wanted. "I want a pair of proper chopsticks, a tin cup, a small bucket of rice, and some fish sauce and chili pepper," she told him.

Instead of berating her, Agostini replied, "Some time ago, female inmates used all the chopsticks for firewood and hit one another with their tin cups. That's why they now have to eat with their fingers. If you want to use a cup and chopsticks, you have to promise to return them after every meal. If you take them back into the cell and they're used for fights, you'll get thirty days in the isolation cell."

"I'll return my tin cup and my chopsticks to the kitchen after every meal," she promised. "As for any other that might be inside the cell, I have no idea where they came from." Agostini nodded and turned again to Mme Lecuir. She translated, "The director says that you are a political prisoner. He's giving you special treatment because you're political." Bao Luong had no idea what *political* meant. But at least, she had gotten her way. Dzung was even more glad that Bao Luong would be allowed to eat separately. She brought over the bucket of rice, the fish sauce and chili, and said softly, "Having fish sauce in prison is a real luxury. Now, how can you avoid having to do chores?"

· · ·

On Sundays prisoners were allowed two pieces of fatty meat. But before they could enjoy them, they had to clean the room. At five in the morning they piled up their mats and swept the floor; then they spread sand over it. Every prisoner, armed with a broom about twelve inches long, scrubbed the sand across the concrete floor. Of course, the *caplans* and the enforcers did not have to get their hands dirty; neither did those who were in prison for debt because every week they received money and bribed the *caplans*. The debtors wore civilian clothes and shared those with the *caplans*. By the time the other prisoners were finished scrubbing and their arms felt as if they were about to fall off, they would pour water over the floor to flush away the sand, and then they had to dry the floor. On that day the floor gleamed and felt fresh. No one bothered to spread out her mat; instead they lay on the bare floor.

Bao Luong had only just lain down when Chin Xich, the biggest of the enforcers, called out to a woman named Sau Xim. The latter was serving a twenty-year sentence for breaking the neck of a child in order to steal her necklace and for throwing the child into a well. Sau Xim had originally been sentenced to hard labor but had gotten pregnant by one of the wardens, so she had been sent back to Central Prison, where she had given birth. Her son was now two years old. "You think just because you're serving a long sentence that you're in clover and you can protect someone else so that she can be idle?"

"No, of course, I don't," Sau Xim replied. "Did you see that I have any 'baby sister'?"

"You think you can throw sand at my eyes?" Chin Xich demanded. "Where are the taffeta trousers that the woman who owes money brought in?"

"Here they are. If you can take some, so can I. I am here for a long time, I need clothes to change into, and the trousers were given to me," Sau Xim said.

She had not finished talking before Chin Xich's "baby sisters" came over, pulled

Sau Xim's baby out of her arms, and held him down on the mat while they kicked her, then yanked her up by the hair and slapped her back and forth. Chinese Mother tried to intervene but in vain. Sau Xim called out for the *matas*. Chin Xich dropped her and took the trousers and the packet of salt that Sau Xim had stashed in the belt. The *matas* arrived and took Chin Xich to the isolation cell. Two minutes after she'd gone, two of her baby sisters started pummeling Sau Xim. The *matas* came back and took them off to the isolation cell as well. Then two more baby sisters hit Sau Xim, and they too were escorted to the isolation cell. Xuyen, the guard, was angry at having been disturbed and threatened everyone with no food and a beating the next day. He grumbled, "What kind of *caplan* is this that cannot keep order?"

The woman who shared her mat with Chin Xich and whom Chin Xich called her "wife" was named Muoi Thinh. She was serving a ten-year sentence for having killed a man after coming to the aid of her husband in a fight. Now she sat silently on the mat, chewing betel and smoking. Although she was one of the enforcers, she was a placid woman and did not go about beating other prisoners very much. But she was the most cunning and thus the most dangerous. She said little, so others had trouble predicting what she would do and were even more afraid of her than of Chin Xich. Muoi Thinh was the only one who could control Chin Xich and whom Chin Xich heeded. So after Sau Xim was beaten three times, she crawled over to Muoi Thinh's mat to beg, "Please help me. When Chin Xich gets out of the isolation cell, she'll kill me."

"Tomorrow, go and ask for Chin Xich to be let out of the isolation cell, and everything will be fine," Muoi Thinh advised.

"How could I ask that of the boss?"

"That's not my business."

That was when Bao Luong understood fully the tyranny of the enforcers even within their own ranks. They all competed to protect their interests; the strong prevailed, the weak lost out. Those who were part of a large group got together to take advantage of new inmates; they took bribes and they sucked up to the ones who had power and kicked the ones who had less. Within this world of only a few square meters, oppression had not disappeared. This gave new meaning to what her cousin Tran Truong had once said to her, "Don't blame it all on society. We need to think of our own responsibility and how we can contribute to making things better."

After three disturbances in one night, Agostini showed up with his familiar rattan stick as soon as the door opened. He told Mme Lecuir to order all the prisoners into the courtyard where they ate meals. An inmate named Tu Thanh tried to hide, but Agostini saw her, pulled her back by the hair, and beat her with his stick. Mme Lecuir called out, "Sau Xim and the women with children, get into the cell." Bao Luong ran to the screen partition and sat down. Dzung kept hinting for her to go into the cell, but she did not want to. She figured that, if Agostini came close to her, she would run to the flower courtyard. Once the women with children had gotten into the cell and the door had closed behind them, Agostini ordered the rest of the inmates to stand against the wall and started to hit everyone from their heads to their toes. When he got to Tu Thanh, he pulled her out by the hair and threw her down on the ground, shouting, "Thug!" He did the same to Binh, hitting her until she spit blood and calling her a hoodlum. After he got tired of wielding his stick, he went to where Chinese Mother was standing and pointed it at her face: "Have a care!"

Then he came over to Bao Luong and asked why she was sitting there.

"Because I did not take part in the fight," she replied.

"And why did you not obey orders but sat back here?"

"Because I'm scared of your stick."

Mme Lecuir laughed. "A political prisoner who is afraid of being beaten? Why did you get involved in politics then?"

Bao Luong looked back at her innocently: "I did nothing!"

Agostini slammed his hand down on the vat that stood close by and yelled, "Don't imitate them or I'll grind your bones."

After Agostini left, Muoi Thinh complained to Mme Lecuir: "Only some of the women were involved in the fighting, but you let the boss beat up everyone. Why didn't you intervene?"

"I wasn't inside the cell, how could I know who was doing what? Why didn't you tell the boss?" she replied.

Bao Luong guessed that Mme Lecuir had wanted to protect Sau Xim and Chinese Mother. She disliked the enforcers, and as for others who gave her trouble by quarrelling, she did not care to shield them from blows. Once order was restored, however, Sau Xim explained to Mme Lecuir that, if Chin Xich was left in the isolation cell, it would make life very difficult for her. Mme Lecuir understood how things worked in prison. On her way home she stopped by Agostini's office and told him that if he did not want a bloody feud among the inmates, he should release Chin Xich. That afternoon Chin Xich returned to the cell.

To Bao Luong this incident showed that the director and the guards were comfortable with the way the prison system worked. They allowed the enforcers to wield power and to form cliques; they used inmates to spy on other inmates and relied on *caplans* to keep order in the cells in the guards' absence. The whole cell had suffered an undeserved beating, but it did not matter to Chin Xich. Many came to intercede on Sau Xim's behalf, but Chin Xich, who knew martial arts and who was strong and fearless, listened only to her "wife," Muoi Thinh.

According to prison convention, the *caplans* were the inmates serving the longest sentences. So Chinese Mother stood above everyone because she was serving a life sentence. Next should have come Sau Xim, who was serving a twenty-year sentence, but Binh had muscled in to become "assistant *caplan*," which gave her the right to exploit others. Within a few days Chin Xich was talking and laughing with Sau Xim and even playing with her son. But the upshot was that anyone who entered the cell had to give over their goods for Muoi Thinh to decide how they should be parceled out. Binh tried to get Chin Xich and Muoi Thinh to move to the cell of the convicts next door, but the two found ways to remain in cell 18 because it had a steady influx of new inmates who brought in goods that they could confiscate.

. . .

[A French lawyer named Giaccobbi was retained to defend Bao Luong, her brother Vien Dai, and her cousin Tran Truong. Bao Luong does not state when Giaccobbi began to help with their defense. The police records first note his presence on November 21, 1929.]

As she entered the room next to the iron gates, Bao Luong saw Truong sitting on a chair. He smiled. "Our families have retained the services of Mr. Giaccobbi for you, Vien Dai, and me." No sooner had he finished speaking than a Frenchman came in. He put his hand on her shoulder and signaled for her to sit down. Bao Luong, who still nurtured an implacable hatred of all things and all people French, was bewildered by his friendliness and kept her head down. Giaccobbi was accompanied by a gangly interpreter who introduced himself: "You don't know me, but I'm Phan van Gia. We're like family."

So this was Phan van Gia? Bao Luong knew of him as Van Trinh, the author of a series of stories about Central Prison that had been published in Than Chung, the newspaper edited by her uncle by marriage. Earlier, Than Chung had published a series by Phan van Hum based on his two months in Central Prison. After the authorities stopped publication of Phan van Hum's stories, Than Chung had immediately followed up with Phan van Gia's own "Paris–Central Prison–Saigon."[4] And when that series too had been suppressed, the newspaper had immediately begun serializing Phan van Gia's travel account "Saigon-Shanghai-Yokohama." Bao Luong thought that his articles were somewhat superficial, but at least they showed that Vietnamese students who had gone to France retained their love of country even as they absorbed new ways of thinking and being. She had gone to the offices of Than Chung a couple of times to express her admiration to him, but each time he'd walked past her, saying, "Excuse me, I need to look for some papers." So when he introduced himself, she nearly blurted out, "Brother Gia!" as if he were a relative. But she stopped herself just in time and looked down self-consciously at her faded blue prisoner outfit.

Phan van Gia was raising issues unconnected to his role as the lawyer's interpreter: "Miss Nguyet, I'd like to support one of your younger siblings, would that be all right with you?" This was not something Bao Luong could decide on her own and she told him so. Gia replied, "Don't you know? Your father has been arrested. Your family is in dire straits, with your mother left alone with four young daughters, the youngest of whom is only two months old. That's why I decided to raise one to lighten your family's burden."

[Bao Luong does not record whether this was the first time she heard the news of her father's arrest. Her sister Han Xuan recalls: "At the beginning my father did not think that the arrest of Bao Luong and Vien Dai would implicate the rest of our family. Not only was he not sad, he was actually proud of his children. On the main pillar of the house he kept pictures of people who were involved in 'national affairs.' The large one was of Phan Boi Chau. On the table in the middle of the house was a group of small photos under glass: Phan Chu Trinh, Nguyen An Ninh, Phan van Truong. On the wall by the tea tray was a picture of my sister that my father had taken from the journal Opinion. *It was taken on the day my sister had walked from Central Prison; she wore a black* ao dai *and walked between policemen. Underneath was a caption in French: 'Return of Princess Trung Trac?'[5] My father was very happy as he explained its meaning to my sisters and me. Then one day someone came to give him some news. My father immediately moved the family to another place. A few days later we heard that my father had been arrested and taken away in manacles."*

An editorial in Than Chung *on November 7, 1929, read, "It will be remembered that Miss Nguyen Trung Nguyet is suspected of being an important member of the Communist branch in Saigon. Her actual 'crime' has not been determined, but news comes that her father, Nguyen van Nham, a landowner in Rach Gia, has been arrested. He is not the only one arrested in Rach Gia. Two brothers, Tran van Sum and Tran van Hoe, landowners in Phuoc Long, were arrested at the same time."*

Than Chung *did not mention that Sum and Hoe were Tran Truong's brothers. They seem to have been detained only for a very short while. At first, Nguyen van Nham's family was unsure what had precipitated his arrest. Bao Luong's other sister, Van Trang, recalled, "Like my brother, my father sometimes absented himself from home. No one ever asked why our menfolk went or when they would return. One day, while my mother was waiting for my father with dinner all prepared, news came that he had been arrested. At first she thought it was the member of the local council taking revenge for my father's defending his servant last year. But that was not the case. It had to do with the Barbier Street murder. As for revenge, it began right away. After half a month, when he saw that my father was not coming back, the councillor sent his tenants to catch fish in our ponds and to kill the [rice in the] paddy on both sides of the irrigation ditch. Aware that my mother was busy with her new baby and with arranging for a lawyer, he sent his henchmen to destroy all our crops and with them our family's livelihood. My mother could not cope with four young children all by herself and took us to Ca Mau, where her nephews Tran Sum and Tran Hoe helped her build a large straw hut. They then hired a sampan to bring all her furniture to Ca Mau, so she was abandoning everything my father had worked to build since coming to Phuoc Long with empty hands thirteen years earlier."]*

At that first meeting Giaccobbi asked detailed questions of both of Tran Truong and Bao Luong and told her specifically, "Deny everything you have confessed. It will make it easier for me to defend you." Bao Luong remained suspicious of the

Frenchman. She was puzzled by the advice he gave in the form of questions: "You were beaten, that's why you said what you did, isn't it so? You were lured into going to China, but you did nothing there, right? As for the murder, you just followed the majority; whether you agreed or not was immaterial, right?" While Giaccobbi reviewed all the indictments that would be presented to the court, Phan van Gia said softly to Bao Luong, "Do you think it's wrong to make revolution?"

"Of course it's right."

"Then it will be prison for you," he said.

"That's certain," she agreed.

"What do you think about your father?" Phan van Gia asked.

"He has three children who have left home; that's why he's fallen under suspicion; I don't think he is in danger," she said.

"Are you sure?"

"He's old," she pointed out. "How could he be involved in the Revolutionary Youth League?"

When Giaccobbi turned to Tran Truong, he laughed: "I don't know why my family has retained you. It's no use at all."

"It is quite useful," the lawyer explained. "We can get you permission to receive family visits and packages."

"No, I don't want to create problems for my family," Tran Truong said. "Please tell them not to go to any trouble so that I can be at ease."

After Truong was returned to the dungeon, Phan van Gia asked softly, "Do Communists hate the French?"

"They hate all imperialists," Bao Luong responded.

"Do you hate the French?"

"There is a collective answer to that, and it applies to you, too," she said.

"Ah, you think I'm trying to worm information out of you? No, I ask in all sincerity, as of a close friend, to learn about the opinion of women about the situation of our country," he explained.

"Since our country was conquered, there can only be one point of view, regardless of gender," Bao Luong replied. "The difference is whether or not one is prepared to act."

Lawyer Giaccobbi took his leave; Phan van Gia lingered behind. He gave Bao Luong a package containing a loaf of bread. Inside the loaf were half a pencil and some toilet paper. When she returned to the cell, Bao Luong gave the bread to Dzung. She inserted the half pencil in her straw mat and folded the toilet paper, then tore it into pieces. She sewed the pieces together with needle and thread that she had borrowed from Dzung, silently saying, "Gia, do you know that what you've given me is more precious than gold?" She would be able to write poetry to while away the boredom of prison life.

· · ·

Truong had told Bao Luong about conditions in the cells underground, although at the beginning he'd been held in isolation. Dzung had sketched for her the layout of the prison, telling her the location of each part of the facility. So after the second visit from the lawyer, Bao Luong asked the warden to allow her to return by the circular way. A walk along that path revealed in full the inhumane conditions in which the French kept Vietnamese prisoners. The circular route was lined with pots of flowers, like the road to heaven. But it masked a hell underneath, a hell of darkness and filth. The prisoners were naked, their skeletal bodies covered in sores, their hands gripping iron bars, their legs in shackles. At first glance they looked like a tribe of miserable monkeys. They had lost all appearance of humanity except when they called out: "Miss, it hurts so much!" Could she really grasp the torment of their souls and crippled bodies as a result of their inhumane treatment? She was thinking about writing the story of the prison beneath the circular path in her booklet of toilet paper, but she was interrupted by an order to take clothes for mending.

Mending clothes should not be difficult, Bao Luong thought. Dzung brought in five blue outfits and some rags. She hurried Bao Luong: "Quick, thread the needle and spread out the outfits; if we're not finished by the time they're collected, we'll be in trouble." As she looked at the uniforms, Bao Luong became anxious. They were torn everywhere and had been badly washed and insufficiently dried. They smelled of mildew. The rags gave off dust that bothered her nose. When she spread out the clothes, bedbugs and fleas scattered in every direction. Panicked, she beat them against the iron bar used to anchor the shackles. Dzung cried, "Focus on mending the clothes and forget about the bedbugs. They're coming to collect them soon." Bao Luong squatted, keeping the clothes away from her, and grumbled under her breath. The needles were rusty and the clothes damp; it was hard to pull the thread through. By the time the clothes were collected, she had mended only three outfits. Dzung turned pale at the sight. She folded the uniforms that had not yet been repaired and mixed them in with those that had been; then she took the lot to Binh. They were lucky: Dzung was her subordinate, so Binh did not bother to check.

. . .

The enforcers were taking notice of Bao Luong. She took her meals separately and ate better food, and she had escaped the collective beating. Just before the collective beating was to be administered, she had told Dzung to go to the end of the line, get into the bath, and squat down facing away. So when Agostini began striking prisoners, Dzung was not hurt much, and the stick did not touch her face. As other prisoners cried and writhed, Dzung took advantage of the confusion to run toward the bell tower. When she returned, no one ratted on her, so she also escaped reprisals. Dzung mentioned her good fortune to Binh, who decided she could make use of Bao Luong. Binh sought to persuade her to join her gang of baby sisters: "You won't have to do any chores, just write letters for me, okay?"

"I cannot be of use to you," Bao Luong said. "I still need to worry about my own situation. I don't mind doing chores alongside other prisoners."

"All right, if you don't want to join my group, that's okay," Binh responded. "But you will write letters, won't you?"

"I don't mind writing a letter every couple of weeks."

"What? Five or six a day is more like it!"

"If the letters are intercepted, who will go into the isolation cell?" Bao Luong asked Binh.

Binh laughed so hard her eyes disappeared. "You're so naive! Someone will be going in your stead."

So in the end Bao Luong had to write love letters for Binh. She wrote to a man named Lung upstairs who was in prison because he had fought with knives and hammers. The coarse and crude love words of this prostitute embarrassed the prudish Bao Luong. She was full of resentment; it seemed to her that knowing how to write was another source of pain. She would bend over the paper for an hour, listening to Binh laboriously produce each word. By the time the letter was finished, Bao Luong's back ached. Then came Chin Xich, Muoi Thinh, and Sau Xim with their own requests that she act as their scribe; Nga and others from the next cell also asked her to write for them. Bao Luong tired of the clichés she had to write down day after day. In other respects she had to endure much, but her mind was free. Writing letters, however, involved listening to the women, trying to organize their words into sentences, then writing them down on pieces of crumpled paper or cigarette wrappers, often at night. It prevented her from being free to think her own thoughts.

"Hey, political prisoner! Do you know how to embroider? Can you embroider things for Chinese Mother?" And so Bao Luong acquired another chore to perform. She had to peer in the gloom of the cell to embroider handkerchiefs for the enforcers so that they could throw them down into the men's cells. The enforcers also offered the handkerchiefs to the macaques and to Mr. Kiem, who was in charge of purchases for the prison. He furtively bought embroidery threads and gave them to the enforcers to buy protection for his lover, a woman who was in jail for having stolen diamonds. Bao Luong knew that if she stopped writing letters or doing embroidery, there would be major trouble; she did not dare to stop then because her situation was not yet clear. She had just received a note telling her to present herself at the police station the next day.

· · ·

Bao Luong was given ordinary clothes to wear for her trip to the police station. When she got there and walked up the spiral staircase, she saw Ngoc Anh and Ngoc Tho, the daughters of Headman Hoai, seated next to Inspector Bertin.

"You lured these two women to engage in revolutionary activities, right?" Bertin demanded of her. "What say you?"

"Oh, no," said Bao Luong. "I don't know anything."

"They've already confessed; they've confessed everything," Bertin told her.

Bao Luong looked at Ngoc Anh and Ngoc Tho and smiled: "I did study with them, but I acted toward them as with all my other friends. We did not talk about revolution." Ngoc Anh and Ngoc Tho frowned and pretended to finally remember that they knew Bao Luong, telling Bertin, "She did study with us; we are slightly acquainted with her."

"Why did you say earlier that she lured you into revolutionary activities?" Bertin asked. "Go downstairs—you'll see what happens."

As Bao Luong watched her two friends descend the staircase, her heart was filled with joy. They were clever! It would be all right.

"Lie down," Bertin commanded. "I'm going to beat you until you spit out blood."

Bao Luong lay down, thinking about death. It would be a good thing, though not easy to achieve. Biting her tongue was the easiest thing to do. Her teeth were sharp, but was her courage as sharp as her will? Silently, she called out, "Ngoc Anh and Ngoc Tho, beloved friends, farewell." She put her head down on her hands, waiting for the tempest of strokes and kicks. But Bertin merely ordered, "Get up." She sat up, bewildered.

"You really do not know Headman Hoai and you did not lead his daughters into misdeeds?" he asked.

"I have never led these two women into mischief."

"So who suggested you go there?"

"If there are teachers, there must be students. No one introduced me to him; it's not like being a trader."

"So why did they say what they did?"

"You must have heard wrong. Ninety percent of what we talked about did not involve anything outside the topic of studies."

"Then lie down. You really want to receive a caning! They've confessed everything already," Bertin replied.

Bao Luong lay down again. Her heart beating furiously, she waited for Bertin and the other Frenchmen to try to turn her into a witness against her friends. Bertin suddenly said, "Get up, miss. You really did not plot anything with these two girls?"

"I don't understand what this 'anything' means, so how can I confess?"

"All right," Bertin said, "go back to the cell. Tomorrow we'll have all the evidence we need."

Ton the gofer and Sergeants Qui and Thinh saw Bao Luong as she walked past their room; they smiled but did not dare speak. Bao Luong was taken to a cell that turned out to contain Ngoc Anh and Ngoc Tho, as well as a girl she did not know. They just looked at one another without greeting. Each went to a separate corner. Someone was constantly looking into the door opening. The strange girl asked, "You're here because of the Barbier Street murder, right?"

"Yes."

"But I heard you knew these two very well."

Ngoc Anh, Ngoc Tho, and Bao Luong pretended indifference; eventually Ngoc Anh said, "When we were students, I hated you more than devils or ghosts. I did not care to exchange confidences with you. When I came here, the inspector claimed that someone had said I'd been lured into crime. But did anyone lure me into doing anything?" Bao Luong knew all too well that Ngoc Anh was taking precautions in case there was a hidden recorder, and because the strange girl was probably a stool pigeon. "I did not know their father," Bao Luong explained to the girl. "I had only heard that he was teaching martial arts; as for them, they were just fellow students whom I met only a few times. Mr. Tu [the Chinese teacher] explained to me the meaning of the name of the school. Is it true that it's a Chinese Hakka establishment?" Ngoc Tho burst out laughing. "Idiot! No wonder no one wanted to befriend you."

The sky darkened. Bao Luong opened the window a crack and saw that the place was deserted. Ngoc Anh noticed that the strange girl had fallen asleep, so she crawled to where Bao Luong sat, squeezed her arm, and whispered, "Not to worry; we'll be fine."

"You liked to play chess," Bao Luong said. "Let's play." When gofer Ton walked by their cell, Bao Luong asked him for a chessboard. He gave them one but said: "If the inspector comes, you'll have to hide it, and if you can't, just say that you found it. Don't say that I lent it to you or I'll be in trouble." Ngoc Anh, Ngoc Tho, and Bao Luong set out the chessboard. "What do we do for a forfeit?" "Let's just play for fun." The door opened. Inspector Bertin came in and observed, "Playing chess? Great! You used to play a lot?" "She plays badly," said Ngoc Anh. Inspector Bertin came back twice. The friends acted as if they were totally engrossed in their playing, without cares or secrets.

Suddenly, they could hear someone rapping on a chair. Ngoc Anh ran to the door. "Look, do you know any of these people?" Bao Luong looked and saw Ton Duc Thang, Tran Truong, Dang van Sam, and Bui van Them tied together.

Truong looked at Ngoc Anh and said to Bao Luong. "Who are they?"

"Ninth and Tenth sisters," Bao Luong replied, using their birth order. "They're okay. How about you?"

"Interrogated again," he answered. "Not to worry."

Bao Luong was taken back to the prison the next day. Ngoc Anh, Ngoc Tho, and she continued to pretend indifference and did not even say good-bye. They could not run the risk that the strange girl might be a spy. But once outside the station her heart broke. How was her sister Hue Minh? And her other friends? Did the work of mobilization continue or had it been suspended? Where was her father, how was her family? So many worries chased one another in her head, slowing her steps. She saw that the policy of clearing the field had not spared anyone. As Do Dinh Tho had said, ordinary human feelings could not survive on the stony field of struggle where the strong prevailed and the weak were destroyed. Love and friendship were illusions. This was reinforced by the loneliness of prison life, especially after Dzung was released one month after Bao Luong arrived.

[Bao Luong had reason to worry about her father. According to her sister Han Xuan, "My mother told Mr. (Phan van) Gia that my father was on hunger strike and was demanding to be put on trial because he had been imprisoned for a long time without knowing of what he was being accused. Mr. Gia said, 'He is not guilty of anything. The Sûreté wants him to tell Bao Luong and Vien Dai not to follow the revolution, to return to an ordinary life like everyone else. I don't know what he told the Sûreté, but he was held back. I will take care of his defense.'

"Afraid that its prisoner would die, the Sûreté let it be known that a number of prisoners would be released on the occasion of Lunar Year (January 30 in 1930) and among them would be my father; he needed to resume eating to recover his health."]

Autumn had arrived. The rain blew through the tamarind trees with a crackling sound, and leaves fell everywhere. Bao Luong lost track of time. It had been summer when she was arrested, but it felt as if she had been in Central Prison for decades. Those involved in the Barbier Street affair had been told that their case would not be tried until the following year.

10

The Verdict

[*By the time the Barbier Street case was tried, the political landscape had changed again. In January 1930 the Vietnamese Nationalist Party staged an uprising that led to thousands of arrests and deportations. In February the Indochinese Communist Party was formed after a year of argument among various factions and numerous exchanges with Moscow. In April and May mass protests erupted, first in the provinces of Nghe An and Ha Tinh and later in other regions throughout Vietnam. The Nghe-Tinh Soviets, as this first wave of mass protests became known, unleashed another wave of repression with thousands of arrests.*]

Bao Luong had been in cell 18 for a year. One morning she went to the office to meet her lawyer; her case was about to be brought before the court. Lawyer Giaccobbi held her hand: "Remember, deny everything. Don't admit to anything!" Phan van Gia smiled and added: "Deny what you can. Don't worry about what the lawyers will say. The day after tomorrow you'll appear before the tribunal. The three judges in red robes were brought in from France. Prepare your speech so that it is smooth and logically organized." Two days later, on July 15, 1930, one year after police had arrested their suspects, the Barbier Street case was brought to the tribunal in Saigon.

Outside the prison Bao Luong was surprised to see Nguyen Dinh Kien, the head of the Tan Viet Revolutionary Party, and the journalist Tran Huy Lieu. There were many other men she did not know, perhaps forty or fifty men in all; she was the only woman.

As they walked from the prison to the courthouse, Dang van Sam observed to Bao Luong, "You're pretty well dressed. How did you manage?"

"The clothes I wore when I entered the prison were put into a wooden box," she said. "When they were taken out, they'd become so mildewed that they'd turned white. So I had to wash and dry them. Then I took a jug of water and boiled it and passed the jug over my clothes before folding them under my mat overnight."

"I knew women were clothes conscious," Sam teased.

Along the way to the courthouse, relatives of the prisoners lined up to give baskets of goods to their sons or fathers. No familiar face greeted Bao Luong on the way to the courthouse, but after they got there she saw her father as she was making her way between rows of people who had come to see the show. He was dressed in a long gauze tunic, and she was relieved to see that he looked healthy despite the hunger strike. She nodded to him as she walked past him; he smiled back without saying a word. Sitting next to him were her friends Ngoc Anh and Ngoc Tho. Ngoc Anh was sobbing unrestrainedly. Kim Lang sat next to her father, Councillor Ton, who had been arrested because someone had accused him of giving money to Nguyen An Ninh. Kim Lang called out to Bao Luong, using one of her aliases, "Sister Nam, Sister Nam!" then burst out crying. Nguyen van Ba, the editor-in-chief of the newspaper *Than Chung*, sat on the right side of the aisle with his wife, Thu Cuu, who called out, "Nguyet, my dear niece!"

The group was told where to sit on the bench reserved for defendants. Ton Duc Thang sat at the end; next to him were Tran Truong, Nguyen van Thinh, Ngo Thiem, and then Bao Luong. Then came Bui van Them and Dang van Sam. This was the Barbier Street group. Vien Dai, who had been arrested at the same time, was sitting elsewhere. Members of the Tan Viet Revolutionary Party sat on the other side of the aisle with Nguyen Kim Cuong and Pham van Dong (the teachers who were friends of Lang's); Dinh, the treasurer of the Ben Tre cell; and Hoai Nghia. On the right side of the room sat reporters, including the interpreter Phan van Gia in his other role as the journalist Van Trinh.

Van Trinh threw a packet to Tran Truong. When a police officer yelled at him, he threw packets to Bao Luong and to Dang van Sam. The officer came over and grabbed her arm to pull her up; she yanked her arm out of his grip. Her packet was full of sweets: candied orange, chocolate, chewing gum. Disregarding the officer, Van Trinh threw more packets to the defendants. Lawyer Giaccobbi came over to Bao Luong and urged her, through Ton Duc Thang, to eat the sweets. Bao Luong blurted out, "Aren't you French?"

The reading of the indictments lasted the whole morning. The same thing happened in the afternoon. An increasingly sleepy Bao Luong whispered to Nguyen van Thinh, "Why is this taking so long? When do you think they'll pronounce sentence?" Thinh commented, "Reading the files of forty people could last a whole month!" "It will probably take just a few days," someone said. Bao Luong glanced at her father; she wanted to tell him to go home and rest. He had a weak constitution, and even when in good health he tired easily. She stopped listening to the indictments. The reporters were looking at the accused as if they had become cameras and were trying to fix their images. Suddenly, from the back of the room came the voices of Dang van Sam's mother and wife: "Oh, son! Oh, husband!" Sam looked in their direction, stricken.

When the reading of the indictments was finished, the judges called each of the accused to the bar. There were three French judges in red robes flanked by Vietnamese judges who sat silently throughout the proceedings. Ton Duc Thang went first. He was told, "You have been to France, answer in French." Ton Duc Thang replied that he preferred to speak in Vietnamese. He declared that he had not been directly involved in the Barbier Street murder; he'd joined the Communist Party but had not yet become active. Then it was Tran Truong's turn. He repeated what he had already admitted during the investigation. When the judges asked him, "Why did you kill?" Tran Truong replied, "Because Lang undermined the good name of the revolutionary party."

"You lured someone into wrongdoing and he refused, so you killed him?" one judge asked.

"Expelling invaders is not wrongdoing," Tran Truong replied. "Anyone who undermines this enterprise must be eliminated."

"Do you repent?"

"I have nothing to repent. As long as I live, I will fight the French."

The judge sitting in the middle slapped his hand on the desk angrily, told Truong to return to his seat, and called Ngo Thiem: "You need to fold your arms when addressing the bench!"

Thiem glared at him and retorted, "I don't know how!"

"Then put your hands on the bar," the judge instructed. "You may not wave your arms and point."

"That's my habit."

"Return to your seat!"

Then it was Nguyen van Thinh's turn. Thinh admitted that he had been involved in the murder and had done so to serve the cause. He spoke calmly; the red-robed judges nodded and let him speak. After he had spoken for a while, a judge asked, "Do you repent?" "I feel sad only. I am not used to spilling blood, but I had a duty to perform," Thinh said.

Bao Luong came next. When she stood up, Lawyer Giaccobbi gave her some water, nodded, and smiled to remind her of his advice. Bao Luong had seen him shake his head when her cousin Truong was speaking, but she had changed her mind about what she wanted to say. She would not deny nor would she pass off the murder as a crime of passion. Still, she was nervous and flustered; her arms felt like unnecessary baggage. After Ngo Thiem's experience, she did not want to fold them or to clasp her hands; she did not want to put them on the bar, either. The reporters bent forward, staring at her avidly. People were standing up. Others were shouting, "Sit down so we can see!" She looked back at her father. In front of her the lawyers were pacing. Lawyer Giaccobbi was staring at her. She heard an interpreter say:

"Raise your hand like the previous accused and swear to speak the whole truth."
She obeyed, thinking: "What idiots! Would anyone who has lost his country tell the
whole truth to those who stole it?" After her name and occupation were recorded,
the questions began: "Who organized your trip to China and who trained you? What
did you do upon your return? How many people did you recruit? Who are they?"

"No one enticed me," she said. "I don't know the names of the people who provided the training. I was arrested soon after my return, so I did not have much of
a chance to carry out work."

"Why did you plot to overthrow the French?" one judge asked. "Has anyone oppressed you? If you want something, why don't you petition the authorities? Why
did you feel the need to go to China to train as a revolutionary?"

"Is that how you see it?" Bao Luong answered. "What I have been seeing is a group
of people who asked the authorities to reform the land tenure system; they did not
get their rights. Instead they were thrown into jail." (She probably was referring to
the Ninh Thanh Loi case of 1928, involving peasants near Phuoc Long who tried
for twenty years to obtain title to land they had cleared but were stymied by collu-
sion between local authorities and speculators.)

"They're different. Let's stick to your case. The Revolutionary Youth League is a
bunch of scoundrels," a judge said. "If people don't follow you, you kill them."

Bao Luong's ears burned at the insults and the discourteous tone of the judges.
She had thought that, since they were newly arrived from France, perhaps the taste
of civilization had not yet left them and they still held the ideal of liberty when they
went to the colonies to represent the country that had proclaimed "the Rights of
Man." How naive she felt!

"We have eyes and ears," she declared. "We see and we hear things, and we have
concluded that we must make revolution to free ourselves from slavery and recover
our independence and liberty. We cannot ask it of France because when we ask, we
are executed or sent to prison. There is no reason to prevent us from working to recover the rights we have lost, such as freedom of thought, of speech, of writing, and
doing what is right. Let me ask: Why do we not have the right to behave as human
beings? Who is standing in the way of our progress? We will get rid of those who
do so. Why do you slander us and call this the behavior of scoundrels?"

The judges were as angry as she was. They demanded, "What are you deprived
of? What made you so angry that you followed uneducated men into anticolonial
activities? As a woman, you don't have to pay taxes or perform compulsory labor
or military service. Doesn't this show that you were tricked into wrongdoing?"

"We women are the worst off," she declared. "We are not allowed to go to
school—"

"That's your family's fault!" a judge interrupted.

"The government collects taxes but does not build schools," she retorted. "What
could my parents do? I cannot list all the things that are needed but which the French

neglect. And let me say that I have never heard the word *scoundrels* applied to a revolutionary party, especially from the mouth of a learned judge."

Lawyer Giaccobbi was glaring at her as if to remind her of his advice, but, as Bao Luong wrote, she was young and reckless: "I know you want to discredit the revolution so that women won't take part in it, but it's useless. Oppressed people will not be taken in by the smears of oppressors. They will join the ranks of revolutionaries in ever greater numbers to oppose the cruel government of France. The truth is here."

"They're not waging revolution!" one judge declared. "They protested some minor problem in their village, but they created public disorder; that's why they were arrested."

"Coming from civilized people, this is unmannerly language!" Bao Luong reprimanded the judges.

"What did you say?"

"Impolite Frenchmen!"

The judge in the middle waved her back to her seat, his face furious, his mouth working rapidly.

Dang van Sam and Bui van Them were next. Sam's mother and wife were sobbing softly. Perhaps that was why the two men looked anxious and answered questions briefly, not trying to proselytize. When he was called, Nguyen Kim Cuong answered in French. Whatever he said caused the judges to nod and sometimes even smile. After members of the Youth League had been called, it was the turn of members of the Tan Viet Revolutionary Party. Nguyen Dinh Kien, its leader, was used to appearing in court; he knew that he needed to use measured tones so that he would be allowed to speak and to analyze the issue at length. In a calm, clear voice he spoke about the conflicting interests of the French and the Vietnamese in Vietnam. Then came the journalist Tran Huy Lieu, tiny in his gauze tunic. He too spoke at length and fluently, watched attentively by his colleagues.

For three days Bao Luong and others went from prison to courthouse and back. Each was called back to the bar several times. But the judges had figured out the prisoners' intention to use those occasions to harangue the French about their treatment of the Vietnamese, so after the first day the judges did not allow prisoners to make speeches. After the prisoners' depositions had been taken, the lawyers were allowed to present their defense. One after the other they showed off their rhetorical and acting skills. Some banged on tables and shouted, others pleaded in low voices. It was like a piece of theater. But it was all empty playacting. The verdicts had already been decided. Perhaps the pleadings might have some effect at the margins, but there was no way that they could materially affect the judgments. Bao Luong caught whiffs of conversations: "It's going to be severe sentences. I feel so bored looking at the lawyers. There's no hope." "Hiring them is such a waste of money. Why retain Frenchmen to defend enemies of the French?" "So that everything that could be done was done."

[An account of the trial that appeared in the newspaper L'Indochine on October 5, 1930, gives a hint of the sensationalism with which the murder was reported. Bao Luong was described as "Nguyen Trung Nguyet, 21, cousin of Sau Truong. Pretty, timid and reserved, she runs a tailoring shop in Phu Nhuan. She is a mystic who went to Guangzhou to be 'educated,' she claims. She is a feminist and a communist." The newspaper further stated that Ton Duc Thang's jealousy had led to the slaying of Lang. Ton Duc Thang had fallen in love with Lê Oanh, although she had become Lang's mistress, and Thang had taken up the role of defender of the party's ideals and discipline. Lê Oanh had been a sister, and Lang had committed a grave infraction in turning her into his mistress. Tran Truong, Nguyen van Thinh, Ngo Thiem, and Bao Luong were charged with executing Lang, by giving him poison.

"The four executioners fix the date of his death as December 8. Bao Luong is responsible for keeping Lang at home. She does her job so well that Lang, whose habit is to go out in the evenings, is at home at 8 P.M. on that day.

"At 8 P.M. he is visited by Nguyen van Thinh and Ngo Thiem. The latter goes to a coffee shop and buys three cups of coffee; he puts a narcotic in Lang's cup. Tired from his afternoon with Bao Luong, Lang soon falls asleep."

The article concluded: "The impression that this affair leaves is similar to one involving gang members. A crime without redeeming features and that inspires only disgust and in which neither assassins nor victim presents the least interest. What kind of patriots are these who have no ideals? Who sacrifice their party for a pretty girl to satisfy their grudges and their vanity? Who are these men who love justice yet condemn, then execute, one of their members without allowing him to defend himself? And what about this ostentation, these theatrical gestures before the tribunal? There was nary a heartfelt accent, none of the simplicity and sincerity that come from noble feelings. Patriots? Come on! Pleasure seekers, vainglorious ruffians."]

By the afternoon of July 18, 1930, the lawyers had finished. They went over to those who had retained their services and comforted them, saying, "It will be all right." Giaccobbi had pleaded fiercely, but after he completed his speech, his face became sad. He went over to Tran Truong and Bao Luong and shook his head. "You were too fierce, I could not help you," he said. "I think you'll even receive an additional sentence." Ton Duc Thang translated for Bao Luong, who was still suspicious of the lawyer and asked him, "You are French, why don't you want us to go to prison?"

"I am a French lawyer, not a judge. France too has patriotic women," Giaccobi replied.

"Vietnam also has many patriotic women. Loving one's country is not a crime," Bao Luong said.

"Yes," agreed Giaccobbi. "Loving one's country indeed is not a crime."

Everyone was tense. Reporters, spectators, accused—everyone sat down, only to get up. The atmosphere was heavy. The court had recessed twice, and yet no verdict had been returned. Familiar-looking prison wardens stood next to police. Suddenly, a voice called out: "Anyone want to appeal?" On the way back to the prison the previous day, Bao Luong's comrades had agreed that when the sentences were read, they would all call out "Down! Down!" Now they immediately stood up and shouted: "Appeal to whom? The French have stolen our country and murdered revolutionaries. Vietnamese must stand up and overthrow the French!" Tran Truong and Ngo Thiem kept yelling until police came over and held them by the throats. "Anyone who causes trouble will immediately be returned to his cell and will not be allowed to listen to the verdict," one of the judges said. "He can go down to the netherworld to wage revolution there."

The noise had begun to abate when the first verdicts came out: "Tran van Hoai [Headman Hoai] and Nguyen van Dai, acquitted." Bao Luong felt a load slide off her back. Her parents would be relieved that their only son was going to be released. Listening to the verdicts was a tense, anxious experience. Only two men had been acquitted. Then came the list of people who were condemned to one or two years in prison. The wardens brought those whose sentence had been read to the front of the courthouse. When death sentences were pronounced against Tran Truong, Nguyen van Thinh, and Ngo Thiem, everyone, regardless of party affiliation, stood up and yelled, "Down with French colonialism!" They repeated the chant until their throats became dry, while Truong, Thiem, and Thinh were taken out of the courtroom. No one was listening to the rest of the verdicts.

By the time the police managed to restore order, the reading of sentences had also stopped. Calls to heaven, cries, sobs, sighs, and commentaries mingled with shouts from the police and the clang of manacles. The courtroom was like the nine circles of hell. Police and prison wardens with faces as brutal as those of horses and buffaloes were manhandling prisoners, while the three condemned men kept on shouting, "Down with French colonialism!" until a warden stepped forward, put manacles on their wrists, and took them away. Bao Luong ran after them crying, "Brothers!" The three men said, "Farewell to all. Bao Luong, be well. We put our trust and our hope in you, young ones. Continue the revolutionary work. Don't worry. We look upon death as a return home. We will be smiling as we walk up to the scaffold. Even though we will die, we will die happy."

Dang van Sam and Bui van Them held Tran Truong's arm tightly until a police officer pushed them so hard that they fell down. Pham van Dong and Nguyen van Thinh were embracing Ngo Thiem and Hoai Nghia. They too were pushed away and manacled into a long line. It was nine in the evening when they finally left the courthouse. On the way back to the prison, Bao Luong asked Ton Duc Thang, "How many years did you get?"

"Twenty." (According to the story in *L'Indochine* on October 5, 1930, the prosecutor had sought the death penalty for Ton Duc Thang.)

"And I?"

"Didn't you hear?"

"It was too noisy, I could not hear."

"Ah, yours was eight years of hard labor and ten years of house arrest."

Bao Luong's original sentence had been set at five years of prison, but her performance in court had caused the judges to give her three additional years.

"And Hoai Nghia?"

"He got seven years, and so did Dong and Dang van Sam. Bui van Them got ten! His wife will die of missing him. Bao Luong, stay well in prison. When you are sad, write poetry to distract yourself. It will be a very long time until we can meet again."

"Don't worry about me, Nghia and Thang," she replied. "I will be all right."

They were walking back to the prison under strict guard, with police on either side of the prisoners like fences. Bao Luong had thought that the prisoners whose sentences had been read first would already be inside their cells, but they were all outside. Vien Dai called, "Older sister! You got eight years? Don't be sad." He then walked over to his cousin Truong to bid him farewell. The three men going off to the condemned men's cell tried to smile to reassure their friends. Bao Luong recalled, "The men looked back at me, as if pitying their young sister for having been given such a heavy sentence. They said, 'Bao Luong, have courage!'"

It turned out that this was not quite the end. They all had to go back to the courthouse twice over the next few months to appeal their sentences. Hoai Nghia and Bao Luong walked close to the three condemned men. Truong said to his cousin, "That's it for us three. We face death without regret, but we do worry about you."

"Why just me?" Bao Luong wanted to know.

"Because you are a girl and weak, we're afraid that you won't be able to endure the harsh regime."

Nguyen van Thinh added, "We knew beforehand that we would die. We're just concerned about you. I've told my wife that after my death, she should take care of you." Bao Luong was taken aback: "Please don't tell her that. She needs to care for your children. I can take care of myself. I can tell you, lots of female protesters have come into the prison, it's quite lively!"

"It's the same on our side," said Thinh. "There are plenty of new prisoners. But they are keeping to themselves because they consider that they belong to different political parties, as if social revolution belonged exclusively to them. We don't mind and don't argue; in fact, we rejoice. That's the way it should be. A political party comes to an end, another emerges; failure yields experience. The next time the results of action will be more favorable, and one day we will expel the invaders. On that day we will celebrate in the netherworld. Bao Luong, our beloved, beloved comrade!"

Nghia said, "Please think up a few lines to commemorate this scene. I want to cry, to shout, to break something—"

"Didn't you just tell me I must be brave?" said Bao Luong, seizing his arm affectionately. "Will we ever meet again?"

After they had signed their appeal petitions, Tran Truong said, "We will meet only once more. If the verdict is left to stand, we will appeal to France. It's of no real use, actually, but it's a pretext to meet again."

"If the verdict stands, when will you die?" Bao Luong asked.

"We'll choose a month that is holy so that we can spread blessings onto our friends. And if they answer our appeals, it will probably be next month before we have another chance to shout 'Down with colonialism' again."

"I'll shout 'Long live Vietnam' and smoke a cigarette on the scaffold," Thiem promised.

"I'm older than you, Thiem, so I get to die before you," Tran Truong said.

How melancholy it was listening to the three vie to be the first to die!

. . .

Dzung had long since left the prison. Among the common criminals who shared a cell with Bao Luong was a new inmate, a woman of about sixty who was serving a four-year sentence for debt. One day she asked Bao Luong, "I've heard that you are a Communist. What does that mean?" Bao Luong replied, "Communism means that if you owe money, you will not have to go to jail. Those who will are the ones charging high interest." The old woman was so pleased with this explanation that she made herself Bao Luong's "foster mother." Since the trial began, the foster mother had been crying, afraid that Bao Luong would be sad; she redoubled her efforts to care for the young woman and even enlisted other inmates in that effort. Bao Luong told her, "Foster mother, don't worry. You are old and have another two years of prison to serve. I am young. I am not afraid of serving eight."

Bao Luong refused to surrender to despair. In her opinion the whole trial had been a sham, designed only to punish those who had dared to oppose colonial rule. The most risible aspect of the spectacle had been Vietnamese judges sitting silently like stooges beside the French judges. The whole thing was a travesty. Such a display of naked power surely meant that the days of French colonial rule were numbered. Bao Luong comforted herself with the thought that she had survived one year of prison even though she had never before eaten moldy rice and rotting fish or lived in filthy, crowded quarters or been deprived of everything. Although she had often been harassed, she had managed to keep her head up. She would get used to it, and eventually she would go home. She only had seven more years to go. She had no reason to give in to self-pity.

11

Life and Death

Tran Truong, Ngo Thiem, and Nguyen van Thinh were executed on May 21, 1931, nearly a year after their trial and two years after their arrests.

A mystery hangs over the fate of Do Dinh Tho and Lê Oanh. They are listed as having fled, yet their mug shots are part of the Barbier Street case file. Had they been arrested and turned informants in exchange for their freedom?

Soon after his release from prison, Bao Luong's brother Vien Dai joined the Indochinese Communist Party. On May 3, 1930, Uncle Trieu's wife took part in a demonstration in Cao Lanh. She was badly beaten and miscarried; she died of her wounds the following month. In 1931 Bao Luong's sister Hue Minh met a student who had been expelled from school in 1926 and had gone to France, where he had become a Trotskyist. After her marriage Hue Minh's activities on behalf of the revolution became largely subordinated to her husband's. Headman Hoai's daughter, Ngoc Anh, continued to be heavily involved in anticolonial activities. She often came to visit the family of her old friend, staying for days or weeks at a time. During one such visit in 1932 Ngoc Anh fell gravely ill and died. She was buried behind Bao Luong's house.

Interpreter and reporter Phan van Gia made good on his promise to help Bao Luong's family by taking in one of her sisters, thirteen-year-old Han Xuan, and sending her to the Young Ladies' School. He was on hand to welcome Bao Luong on the day she was released from prison in July 1937.

Ton Duc Thang (1888–1980) did not serve the full twenty years of his sentence. After the August Revolution of 1945, he made his way back to the South. The following year he left for northern Vietnam, where he was lionized as a true proletarian but given positions that were more honorific than truly authoritative, even after he succeeded Ho Chi Minh as president of the Democratic Republic of Vietnam in 1969. Bao Luong and he never met again, although he kept in touch with some of her Tran relatives.

The house at 13 Wenming Street in Guangzhou has become a historic site that is much visited by Vietnamese. In the kitchen is a list of members of the Vietnam Revolutionary Youth League who lived there for a time. On the list appears the name of Nguyen Trung Nguyet. As for the men and women whom she met in that house, it turned out that Lam Duc Thu, the big man who had been elected to head the Youth League just before she began classes in China, had long been an informer, reporting to his French masters as "Agent Pinot." Ly Phuong Duc divorced Hong Son in 1929 so that she could marry another league founder, Le Quang Dat. Duc's sister Ly Ung Thuan followed her own lover, Ho Tung Mau, to Hong Kong. When he was arrested and deported to Vietnam in 1931, she remained in China as a member of the Chinese Communist Party. Their adoptive brother Ly Tu Trong did return to Vietnam. In February 1931 he was attending a demonstration in Saigon when he saw a French police detective attempt to arrest the speaker. Trong shot the detective and was arrested. He was executed on November 21, 1931, in front of Central Prison. At seventeen he was the youngest revolutionary to suffer that fate.

Saigon's Central Prison was razed in the 1950s after the end of French colonial rule. In its place stands the General Sciences Library. The street is now called Ly Tu Trong Street. As for the headquarters of the French Sûreté, it served as the Ministry of the Interior for the Republic of Vietnam between 1955 and 1975. It is now the site of the Office of Culture, Sports and Tourism of Ho Chi Minh City. Near the entrance, where the old wing meets a newer addition, is a plaque that recalls its past as the infamous "bot Catinat."

Rue Barbier became Nguyen Phi Khanh Street. By coincidence, it is right around the corner from the house into which Hue Minh and her family moved one year after Bao Luong came to live in Saigon in 1967. By then the geography of the city and all the names of its streets had changed so much since the 1920s that she may not have recognized Nguyen Phi Khanh Street as the site of the tragedy in which she had once been involved. Since her death the city has expanded even farther. In 2005 a small street in one of the newer outlying districts of greater Ho Chi Minh City was named after Nguyen Trung Nguyet.

. . .

While Bao Luong was incarcerated in Central Prison, a young male nurse named Nguyen van Thom was assigned to tend to ill prisoners. His name does not appear in her memoir because he began working at Central Prison after her trial, but Van Trang describes how he became part of her sister's life: "The hardened criminals had nothing to lose and had become brutal and exploitative. And yet they left alone the young woman whose body still bore the scars of torture and who coughed blood every once in a while. . . . The *caplans* not only left her alone but appeared to hold her in awe. They did not dare to confiscate the goods she received, as they did with other inmates. She would spread the contents of the basket she had received from her mother out on her mat, then distribute them to other inmates but never to the *caplans*. If some of them held out their hand, she would merely say: 'Let me give it to the mothers. If the children have milk to drink, they will be less likely to cry.' "

Days and years passed. Nguyen van Thom realized he was falling for the young woman. In that hellhole no one could disguise one's true self. One day he decided to declare his love—an extraordinary love blooming in a strange place. It was not a place where two people could stand apart even for five seconds to have a private conversation when one could say "I love you" to the other. After much thought he had an idea. The previous week she had coughed up a lot of blood; everybody had seen that it was dark red. Perhaps he could assign an extra can of milk to her, even though she had used up her milk ration for the month. When he gave her the can of milk, his hand was shaking. He had unstuck a corner of the label and had written on its back in tiny letters, "I will wait for the end of your sentence."

According to Van Trang, "A few days before Bao Luong's release, the prison director called in nurse Thom and said, 'If you marry her, you won't be able to go on working here.' Thom left without answering. A month after Bao Luong returned home, Thom used an intermediary to ask her parents for her hand in marriage."

Because Bao Luong was under house arrest, she could not follow him to his native place in Vinh Long. Instead, they made their home in O Mon, where her family had moved during her incarceration. Thom devoted the early months of their marriage to helping her recover her health. Her first child was born the following year.

Bao Luong retained her faith in the revolutionary cause to the end. But, as she had once predicted, having a family restricted her choices. After 1954 she received an invitation (from Ho Chi Minh, according to her daughter) to go to Hanoi. But her mother-in-law depended on her and her husband, and Bao Luong's youngest child was only four. She could not go. Later she would mention this invitation to her children to explain her refusal to marry Nguyen Bao Toan back in 1927. When she was eighteen and single, she had chosen the path to revolution; once she married, family obligations held her back. And so, she was content to live in obscurity as the wife of a village nurse.

After her death in October 1976, her husband asked his children to hang out her *ao dai* so that he could sit gazing at them for hours on end. When he died three years later, he asked that the *ao dai* be buried with him; this was the closest he could be to his beloved wife.

FIGURE 11. Nguyen Trung Nguyet in the early
1970s. Photograph courtesy of Nguyen Minh Tri.

• • •

"The Barbier Street murder unfolded just as the newspapers described it, 'like a romantic novel, both tragic and thrilling,'" Bao Luong wrote. "But what was the truth?"

I was preparing to leave Vietnam when the telephone rang. It was my aunt Han
Xuan. At ninety-one she was in full possession of her mental faculties. She urged
me to come see her as she had something to tell me that she did not feel she could
say over the telephone or in a letter. When I arrived at her house, she gave me a
photograph of herself standing below the street sign that bore the name Nguyen
Trung Nguyet; a copy of her own memoir, which she had completed in 2003; and
a booklet of poems that Bao Luong had written throughout her life, including many
that she had composed while in prison. Han Xuan then gave me her version of what
had happened. She claimed she had had it straight from her sister after her release
from prison, but what Han Xuan told me was embellished with a great deal of editorializing. It was not clear to me whose editorializing I was hearing—Han Xuan's,
right there in 2008, or Bao Luong's of seventy years earlier:

> You know that after she was released from prison, she was placed under house arrest
> for another ten years? We were living in O Mon then. That's when she told me what
> had happened.

Well, what happened was the result of policy. In those days there were strict ex-pectations regarding women's behavior. Men and women were not supposed to mix. Elite families were unwilling to let their unmarried daughters leave home and strike out on their own. Too many of them came back, still unmarried, with their round bel-lies before them proclaiming their shame and the shame of their families for all to see. It had happened to several families we knew. But the revolution needed both men and women from the elite to lead it; peasants were not used to positions of responsibility and leadership. So patriotic families had to be willing to let their daughters become involved in revolutionary work.

To avoid problems arising from so many young men and women working along-side one another, Ton Duc Thang made a rule that there should be no romantic in-volvement among members of the Revolutionary Youth League. He was the head of the Regional Committee. Trung Nguyet was living at his house. But there was this man who had fallen in love with your aunt. And he kept pressuring her to marry him. Trung Nguyet was not interested in getting married, and she was conscientious about following party discipline. As she resisted his advances, he threatened to reveal all the secrets of the Youth League, the names of all its members, all the secret meeting places. That could not be allowed. So he had to die; there was no alternative. It was enor-mously painful when she had to write the letter that brought him to the place where he was to be killed. She had to do it, but she was anguished about her betrayal. She did not return his feelings, but how could she not be moved by his love? He'd even written poems to her. She atoned for what she had done by letting her reputation be besmirched during the trial, by allowing herself to be described as a woman of loose morals.

Han Xuan seemed to have recalled a garbled version of events and combined two sets of narratives, one involving Lang and the other Nguyen Bao Toan. Ton Duc Thang had made no such policy against romantic attachments. In fact, Bao Luong had been urged time and again to "settle her status" so as to avoid creating conflicts among the young and mostly unmarried men alongside whom she worked closely. Lê Oanh might not have become the target of Lang's amorous advances had she been married. But both had valued their freedom to choose whom and when to marry; they had been drawn into revolutionary activities as much by the promise of gender equality and women's emancipation as by the hope of national indepen-dence. Perhaps Nguyen van Thinh and Ngo Thiem, not really aware of the personal lives of their colleagues outside the Youth League, had been too eager to "settle things" at the expense of their female colleague, just as stowaways had disposed of inconvenient women by throwing them overboard.

Bao Luong had written a love letter to make it appear that Lang had been the victim of a crime of passion, substituting it for the forged "suicide letter" that could no longer be used when things went awry. But her letter had not lured Lang to his death. Another, far more fateful letter, the one to the Sûreté, had sent members of the Youth League to their death or to long imprisonment, and it had nothing to do with illicit passion. There seems little doubt that it was written by Nguyen Bao Toan. Two stories, two men, two letters. One, penned by Bao Luong, pretending to be about a lover betrayed; the other, by Bao Toan, betraying those he loved. It was not clear to me whether it was Han Xuan or Bao Luong who had confused the different story lines. Whose memory had been playing tricks?

Bao Luong's greatest loyalty was to the cause of independence, her love to her friends. But she had considered Nguyen Bao Toan a good friend and had relied on him. His betrayal must have hurt. And yet Bao Luong's daughter never heard of his role in the demise of her mother's beloved Revolutionary Youth League. Bao Luong accepted that waging revolution would include sacrifices and pain. Nguyen Bao Toan, for his part, had loved her. Like her, however, he put the revolutionary cause above everything and everyone. He had been willing to sacrifice all his friends and the woman he professed to love in order to prepare the stage for a new party. Both had been pure of purpose and ruthless in its execution.

Thirty years passed between the time Bao Luong had set off for Guangzhou full of revolutionary fervor and the time when she set pen to paper and tried to recollect the young woman she had been before she became the Second Aunt I knew, with her embroidery threads and her lectures about decorum. In writing her memoir, had Bao Luong looked back on her younger self and thought about the rights and wrongs of what she and others had done? It was not a question she was willing to ponder publicly or even with her children in the privacy of her home. Bao Luong died in September 1976, just a couple of months before the two halves of the country were united into the new Socialist Republic of Vietnam with Ton Duc Thang as its president. The woman who had endured torture so as not to betray her comrades kept her counsel and took to her grave whatever regrets and remorse she might have felt.

NOTES

INTRODUCTION

1. *Kach menh* is a less frequently used variation of *cach mang*.
2. Tran Hong Thuan, interview by the author, February 26, 2008.

1. THE GIRL FROM THE SOUTH

1. Nguyen Chanh Sat, *Dieu Co Ha Kim* (Eulogies for the Past, Praise for the Present) (Saigon: n.p., 1915).
2. For a study of Phan Boi Chau and Cuong De, see David Marr, *Vietnamese Anti-Colonialism, 1885–1925* (Berkeley: University of California Press, 1971).
3. Han Xuan, unpublished memoir (2003), p. 11, in the author's files.
4. Hoang Hoa Tham, also known as De Tham, was captured and beheaded in 1913 after leading an anticolonial movement for more than two decades. See Marr, *Vietnamese Anti-colonialism*, pp. 73–75 and 194.
5. Han Xuan, unpublished memoir, p. 16.
6. Ibid., p. 12.
7. Ibid., p. 25.
8. Ibid., p. 15.
9. For a description of the strikes, see Hue-Tam Ho Tai, *Radicalism and the Origins of the Vietnamese Revolution* (Cambridge, Mass.: Harvard University Press, 1992), pp. 146–70.
10. Han Xuan, unpublished memoir, p. 33.

2. FROM FAITHFUL MOON TO PRECIOUS HONESTY

1. GGI65535: Interrogation of Ton Duc Thang, July 30, 1929.
2. See Christoph Giebel, *Imagined Ancestries of Vietnamese Communism: Ton Duc Thang*

and the Politics of History and Memory (Seattle: University of Washington Press, 2004), for a discussion of Ton Duc Thang's supposed participation in the Black Sea Mutiny.

3. Contemporaries of parents were often addressed as "Aunt" or "Uncle."

4. In Bao Luong's memoir, Ngo Thiem's name is rendered as Ngo Them. In both Bao Luong's memoir and official documents, he is also often referred to by his alias Hue.

5. Interrogation of Ton Duc Thang, July 30, 1929.

6. He appears in French Sûreté accounts as Tran Su Chinh or Bang Thong. In China, Bao Luong also knew Nguyen Bao Toan as Lê and sometimes called him Fifth Brother (Anh Nam).

7. A photograph taken on June 19, 1927, about a week before Truong returned to Saigon, shows Tran Truong at the revolutionary oath-taking ceremony in front of the tomb of Pham Hong Thai, a revolutionary who committed suicide in 1924 after a failed attempt to assassinate the governor-general of French Indochina. See chapter 3.

8. Bao Luong did not include this date in her memoir; it appears in her police file GGI 65535: Interrogation of Nguyen Trung Nguyet, July 28, 1929.

9. It was the *Telemachus* (GGI 65535: Crime de la rue Barbier, Bill of Indictment, March 1930, p. 123). An exchange between Nguyen Trung Nguyet and Ngo Thiem suggests that the Youth League bribed crew members to let trainees travel as stowaways.

10. The names by which they introduced themselves were aliases. Van Thong was Nguyen Hanh Thong, from Phuoc Long. Hoai Nghia was a member of the Youth League whose real name was Nguyen van Ngoc; he was probably thirty-one or thirty-two in 1927. The identities of Truong Phong, Kim Huong, and Thanh Huyen have not been ascertained.

3. APPRENTICE REVOLUTIONARIES

1. The Aid-the-King Movement (Can vuong) was launched in 1885 to restore the Vietnamese monarchy after the French extended their rule over northern and central Vietnam. After the death of its leader, Phan Dinh Phung, in 1895, many of its participants fled to Siam. For more on the Aid-the-King Movement, see David Marr, *Vietnamese Anticolonialism, 1885–1925* (Berkeley: University of California Press, 1971). For more on the remnants of the Aid-the-King Movement in Siam, see Christopher Goscha, *Thailand and the Southeast Asian Networks of the Vietnamese Revolution, 1885–1954* (Richmond, Surrey, U.K.: Curzon, 1999).

2. In her account to the police, Bao Luong changed the gender of A Tac: "Finally, we found a Vietnamese man with short hair who, I believe, came from Hue. He asked what we wanted, and we told him we wanted to study. He then led us to a house where I separated myself from the rest of the group" (GGI65535: Interrogation of Nguyen Trung Nguyet, July 28, 1929).

3. Bao Luong uses Tran and Le Hong Phong interchangeably in her memoir but does not reveal how she learned Tran's real name. However, Le Hong Phong, one of the most important leaders of the Youth League, was in Moscow in 1927, so she must have been mistaken. I will use Tran for consistency since his actual identity is not clear.

4. Hong Son's real name was Le van Phan. He also went by Vu Tam Anh and Le Tan Anh. See Quang Hung and Quoc Anh, "Le Hong Son: Nguoi chien si xuat sac thuoc the he nhung nguoi cong san dau tien o Viet Nam" (Le Hong Son: A Brilliant Fighter of the Generation of Early Communists), *Nghien Cuu Lich su* (Historical Research) 184 (January–February 1979): 11–26. See also profiles in Sophie Quinn-Judge, *Ho Chi Minh: The Missing Years* (Berkeley:

University of California Press, 2002), pp. 320–21, and R. B. Smith, "The Foundation of the Indochinese Communist Party, 1929–1930," *Modern Asian Studies* 32, no. 4 (October 1998): 769–805.

5. At the time Ho Chi Minh was known variously as Nguyen Ai Quoc, Ly Thuy, and Vuong Son Nhi, among other aliases.

6. Interrogation of Nguyen Trung Nguyet, July 28, 1929.

7. Archives Nationales SLOTFOM III-129: Repressive measures against members of the revolutionary association, "Viet Nam Cach Mang Thanh Nien," March 30, 1930.

8. Two years after this conversation, Duc divorced Hong Son and married Le Quang Dat, another founder of the Revolutionary Youth League (Quinn-Judge, *Ho Chi Minh*, pp. 318–20).

9. In fact, Tang Tuyet Minh never reunited with her husband despite attempts by both to get in touch.

10. Archives Nationales SLOTFOM III-129: Report regarding repression measures against members of the revolutionary association, "Viet Nam Cach Mang Thanh Nien," Hue, March 10, 1930.

11. GGI65535: Bill of Indictment, March 8, 1930.

12. Interrogation of Nguyen Trung Nguyet, July 28, 1929. The margin notes state: "Tran Ngoc Que, aka Danh; also in the company of Nguyen Si Sach, Tran van Cong aka Que [Nguyen van Thinh] and of Dinh who could well be Bui van Them."

4. VIGNETTES FROM THE REVOLUTION

1. Tran van Hoai was about fifty-six in 1927; his daughters appear in Sûreté reports as Tran thi Chin(h) and Tran thi Muoi, names that reflect their birth order, ninth and tenth, respectively (GGI65535: Bill of Indictment, March 1930, p. 111).

2. The annual festival of the Trung sisters is held on the sixth day of the second month of the lunar calendar. This would have been in March 1928.

3. Aunt Trieu's real name was Nguyen thi Danh. The Dong Nu Ban troupe was shut down in 1929 for anti-French activities.

4. Gouvernement Général de l'Indochine, *Contribution à l'histoire des mouvements politiques de l'Indochine française* (Hanoi, 1934), 4:20.

5. PRELUDE TO A MURDER

1. Gouvernement Général de l'Indochine, *Contribution à l'histoire des mouvements politiques de l'Indochine française* (Hanoi, 1934), 4:20.

2. Ibid.

3. Ibid.

4. Both his wife and mother claimed to have seen him in January 1929, even after the investigators pointed out that he had been murdered the month before (GGI65535: "Travel to My Thanh and My Nhon to Identify Victim," November 30, 1929).

5. GGI65535: Interrogation of Ton Duc Thang, November 23, 1929.

6. GGI65535: Interrogation of Tran Truong (Sau Truong), November 24, 1929.

7. Ibid. "Luong" was Ho Tung Mau, one of the founders of the Youth League; "Truong" was Lam Duc Thu, an original leader of the league. The identity of "Hoang" has not been ascertained.

8. The photograph is contained in the police file "Affaire Tran Truong et consorts," used in the interrogation of Tran Truong on January 3, 1929.

9. GGI65535: Interrogation of Ngo Thiem (Hue), November 27, 1929.

10. GGI65535: "Affaire Tran Truong," p. 127.

11. GGI65535: Interrogation of Nguyen Trung Ninh [sic] aka Hai, aka Bao Luong, November 24, 1929.

12. "Friends across the Southern Sea" might be a reference to A Tac, Duc, Thuan, Little Thong, and Trong in Guangzhou.

13. Bui van Them, who was twenty-three in 1928, was also known as Muoi Them and Chau; Dang van Sam, of the same age, was also known as Hai Sam and Nhuan. The police files often use these aliases to refer to them. They had gone to Guangzhou with Tran Truong.

14. Lê Oanh's real name was Tran Thu Thuy; she also went by the nickname "Nhut." A Sûreté report, which referred to her as Thi Sau, gave her age in 1928 as twenty-one, though Bao Luong says she was eighteen. Nhu figures only in Bao Luong's memoir; she is not mentioned in any of the Sûreté documents regarding the Barbier Street murder.

15. Thanh Huyen was the recruit who had favored monarchism during their training in Guangzhou.

16. Huynh Nhuan's real name was Nguyen van Hai.

17. GGI65535: Interrogation of Nguyen Trung Nguyet, July 28, 1929.

18. Han Xuan, unpublished memoir, 2003, p. 35.

19. GGI65535: Interrogation of Ton Duc Thang, July 30, 1929.

20. GGI65535: Interrogation of Nguyen Trung Nguyet, July 28, 1929.

21. This is the only reference to Pham van Dong's presence at a meeting before the murder. He was twenty-two in 1928.

22. It is not clear from Bao Luong's memoir who was to do the investigating and reprimanding.

23. This is the only time that Pham van Dong, who was in charge of investigating the murder and later became prime minister of the Democratic Republic of Vietnam, is said to belong to the same cell as Bao Luong.

24. GGI65535: Interrogation of Tran Truong, July 30, 1929.

25. GGI65535: Interrogation of Dang van Sam, July 29, 1929.

26. GGI65535: Interrogation of Nguyen Trung Nguyet, July 28, 1929.

27. GGI65535: Interrogation of Ton Duc Thang, July 30, 1929.

28. GGI65535: Interrogation of Dang van Sam, July 29, 1929.

29. GGI65535: Interrogation of Nguyen van Thinh (aka Tran van Cong, aka Que aka Phong), August 12, 1929.

30. GGI65535: Bill of Indictment, March 30, 1929.

31. I relied on this single report to suggest that Ton Duc Thang was vying with Lang for the affections of Le Oanh in my book *Radicalism and the Origins of the Vietnamese Revolution,* p. 216. Bao Luong's memoir renders this interpretation implausible.

32. GGI65535: Interrogation of Nguyen van Thinh, August 12, 1929.

33. GGI65535: Interrogation of Tran Truong, July 30, 1929.

6. THE CRIME ON BARBIER STREET

1. GGI65535: Interrogation of Ngo Thiem, Sept. 20, 1929.

2. *L'Indochine*, Dec. 5, 1930.

7. THE END OF THE REVOLUTIONARY YOUTH LEAGUE

1. Gouvernement Général de l'Indochine, *Contribution à l'histoire des mouvements politiques de l'Indochine française* (Hanoi, 1934), 4:22–23. This volume contains a photograph on p. 25 of Nguyen Bao Toan (using his aliases of Bang Thong and Tran Su Chinh) that is too blurred to allow its reproduction.

2. GGI65535: Interrogation of Luu van Phung, July 27, 1929.

8. THE ROAD TO HELL

1. For more on Phan Xich Long, alias Tu Mat, see Hue-Tam Ho Tai, *Millenarianism and Peasant Politics in Vietnam* (Cambridge, Mass.: Harvard University Press, 1983), pp. 69–80.

2. GGI65535: Interrogation of Tran Truong, August 6, 1929.

3. According to *Than Chung*, November 15, 1929, Headman Hoai had been arrested "recently" in Go Cong.

4. GGI 65535: Bill of Indictment, March 1930, p. 123.

5. The *caplans* were inmates who were used as overseers in their cells. See Peter Zinoman, *The Colonial Bastille: A History of Imprisonment in Colonial Vietnam, 1862–1940* (Berkeley: University of California Press, 2001), p. 112.

9. DOWN AMONG WOMEN

1. My thanks to Peter Zinoman for checking the French term.

2. For a discussion of the role of enforcers, see Peter Zinoman, *The Colonial Bastille* (Berkeley: University of California Press, 2001).

3. "Behaving like a grandmother" is a Vietnamese expression used to refer to someone who is treating someone else as an inferior.

4. Phan van Gia had been arrested soon after returning from France and had spent two months at Central Prison.

5. Trung Trac was the older of the two sisters who led a rebellion against Chinese occupation in 39 C.E. and were the subjects of a commemorative ceremony in which Bao Luong took part in 1928.

GLOSSARY

Anh chị
Anh Năm
Aó dài

Bà Chiểu
Ba Sơn
Bà Vạt
Bạc Liêu
Bàn Cờ
Bảy
Bến Lức
Bến Ngự
Bến Tre
Bình
Bình Đại
Bình Lợi Bridge
Bộ Tòng (real name
 Nguyễn văn Dưỡng)
Bối rôn

Cà Mau
Cải lương
Cần Thơ
Cao Lãnh
Chín Xích

Chợ Gạo
Chợ Ông Văn
Côn Sơn
Công
Cường Để

Dân Chủ Mới
Đào Duy Chung
 (grandfather)
Đào Duy Từ (ancestor)
Đỗ thị Ngự
Đỗ văn Cẩm
Đồng Hới
Đồng Nữ Ban
Đường Kách Mệnh
Đường vào Cách Mạng
Dzung

Giồng Trôm
Gò Đen

Hà Tĩnh
Hóc Môn
Hoài Nghĩa (real name
 Nguyễn văn Ngọc)

Hội An
Hồ Chí Minh aka
 Nguyễn Aí Quốc aka
 Lý Thụy aka Vương
 Sơn Nhị
Hồ Tùng Mậu aka Old
 Lương
Hội Khai Trí Tiến Đức
Hoàng
Hoàng Đôn Dzân
Hoàng Hoa Thám
Hồng Sơn aka Lê văn Phan
 aka Lê Tán Anh aka
 Vũ Tam Anh
Hủ nho
Hương trưởng
Huỳnh Khương Ninh
Huỳnh Nhuận

Khánh Hội
Kiên Giang
Kim Hương
Kim Lang
Kiệu Bridge
Kỳ bộ

Lạc
Lâm Đức Thụ aka Trương
   mập
Lê Hồng Phong
Lê Quang Đạt
Lê văn Duyệt
Lương Huệ Quân
Lời Bạn Gái
Long Bình
Long Xuyên
Lục Vân Tiên
Lưu Hữu Phụng
Lý Phương Đức
Lý Thường Kiệt
Lý Tri Thông aka Little
   Thông
Lý Tự Trọng
Lý Ưng Thuận

Mai Bạch Ngọc
Mai Huỳnh Hoa
Mẫu
Mỹ Chánh
Mỹ Nhơn
Mỹ Tho
Mỏ Cày
Mười Thinh

Nam
Nam Kỳ Công Hội
Nga
Nghệ An
Nghệ Tĩnh
Ngô Gia Tự
Ngọc An
Ngồi tù Khám Lớn
Người con gái Nam Bộ
Nguyễn An Ninh
Nguyễn Đình Kiên
Nguyễn Huệ Minh
Nguyễn Hoài Xuân aka
   Hàn Xuân
Nguyễn Kim Cương
Nguyễn Mộng Trung
Nguyễn Phi Khanh

Nguyễn thị Trang aka
   Vân Trang
Nguyễn văn Thơm
Nguyễn văn Bá
Nguyễn văn Triệu
Nguyễn văn Tuấn aka
   Kim Tôn
Nguyễn văn Út
Nhỏ
Nhu
Ninh Thạnh Lợi

Ô Môn

Phạm Hồng Thái
Phạm văn Đồng
Phan Bội Châu
Phan Chu Trinh
Phan văn Gia aka Vân
   Trình
Phan văn Hùm
Phan Xích Long
Phong kiến
Phú Nhuận
Phục hương lễ
Phước Long

Quảng
Quí
Quới

Rạch Gía

Sáu Xịm

Tâm Tâm Xã
Tân Định
Tân Việt
Tăng Tuyết Minh aka Sister
   Vương
Thần Chung
Thành chung
Thanh Huyền
Thanh Niên
Thinh

Thủ Thiêm
Tôn
Trà Vinh
Trần Hoè
Trần Hưng Đạo
Trần Huy Liệu
Trần Ngọc Anh
Trần Ngọc Quế
Trần Ngọc Viện
Trần Nhân Tông
Trần Sum
Trần thị Bân
Trần Thủ Cựu
Trần Trọng An
Trần văn Đôn
Trần văn Cung Quốc Anh
Trần văn Hoài (Headman
   Hoài)
Trần văn Triều
Trưng sisters
Trưng Trắc
Trường Áo Tím
Trương Quang Ngô
Trường Phong
Tú
Tự Đức
Tư Thanh

Văn Thông (real name
   Nguyễn Hạnh Thông)
Việt Nam Thanh Niên
   Cách Mạng Đồng Chí
   Hội
Vĩnh Kim
Vĩnh Long
Vĩnh Phú
Võ Công Tồn (Councilor
   Tồn)
Vọng cổ
Vũng Tàu

Xuân Diệu
Xuyến

BIBLIOGRAPHY

PRIMARY SOURCES

Archives nationales d'Outre-mer (ANOM)—Gouvernement-général de l'Indochine (GGI) GGI 65535: "Affaire Tran Truong et Consorts."

Archives nationales—Service de liaison des originaires des territoires français d'outre-mer (SLOTFOM), III-129: "Le Thanh Nien Cach Mang Dong Chi Hoi" (The Revolutionary Youth League).

Bao Luong Nguyen Trung Nguyet. Unpublished memoir. In the author's files.

Bao Luong Nguyen Trung Nguyet and Van Trang. *Nguoi con Gai Nam Bo* (The Girl from the South). Hanoi: Phu Nu, 1996; 2d ed., Ho Chi Minh City: Hoi Nha Van, 2004.

Han Xuan. Unpublished memoir, 2003. In the author's files.

L'Indochine, October 5, 1930.

Than Chung, 1929–31.

Van Trang. Unpublished memoir, 2004. In the author's files.

SECONDARY SOURCES

Brocheux, Pierre. *Ho Chi Minh: Du révolutionnaire à l'icône*. Paris: Biographie Payot, 2003.

Giebel, Christoph. *Imagined Ancestries of Vietnamese Communism: Ton Duc Thang and the Politics of History and Memory*. Seattle: University of Washington Press, 2004.

Goscha, Christopher. *Thailand and the Southeast Asian Networks of the Vietnamese Revolution, 1885–1954*. Richmond, Surrey, U.K.: Curzon, 1999.

Gouvernement Général de l'Indochine. *Contribution à l'histoire des mouvements politiques de l'Indochine française*, vol. 4. Hanoi, 1934.

Marr, David. *Vietnamese Anticolonialism, 1885–1925*. Berkeley: University of California Press, 1971.

Quang Hung and Quoc Anh. "Le Hong Son: Nguoi chien si xuat sac thuoc the he nhung nguoi cong san dau tien o Viet Nam" (Le Hong Son: A Brilliant Fighter of the Generation of Early Communists), *Nghien Cuu Lich su* (Historical Research) 184 (January–February 1979): 11–26.

Quinn-Judge, Sophie. *Ho Chi Minh: The Missing Years*. Berkeley: University of California Press, 2002.

Smith, R. B. "The Foundation of the Indochinese Communist Party, 1929–1930," *Modern Asian Studies* 32, no. 4 (October 1998): 769–805.

Tai, Hue-Tam Ho. *Millenarianism and Peasant Politics in Vietnam*. Cambridge, Mass.: Harvard University Press, 1983.

———. *Radicalism and the Origins of the Vietnamese Revolution*. Cambridge, Mass.: Harvard University Press, 1992.

Zinoman, Peter. *The Colonial Bastille*. Berkeley: University of California Press, 2001.

INDEX

TEXT
10/13 Sabon

DISPLAY
Sabon

COMPOSITOR
Integrated Composition Systems

CARTOGRAPHER
Bill Nelson

PRINTER
Maple-Vail Book Manufacturing Group